The Many Faces of NEHRU

Dr Tapan Chattopadhyay, PhD, DLitt, is the author of *The Story of Lalbazar—Its Origin and Growth* (Kolkata, 1982), *Lepchas and Their Heritage* (New Delhi, 1990), *The INA's Secret Service in Southeast Asia—Its Background, Infrastructure, Resources and Activities during World War II* (Kolkata, 2011), *Kolkata and Its Police—A History of City Police from Charnock's to Present Day* (Kolkata, 2013), *The Horizon of Hope* (San Bernadino, 2017), and *Rivalry that Cost India—Jawaharlal Nehru, Subhas Bose, and Congress Politics 1921–1941* (London, 2023).

He has also contributed articles on Indian prehistory and written poems, novels, and short stories in Bengali. After a brief stint in teaching and research, Dr Chattopadhyay joined the IPS in 1970 and had a peripatetic career in five organizations and seven states, undergoing training in England and the USA and visiting a number of Asian and European countries before he retired in the rank of Director General.

After superannuation, he was appointed Member of the West Bengal Public Service Commission. He is presently engaged in academic work.

The Many Faces of NEHRU
An Untrammelled Political Biography

Tapan Chattopadhyay

Published by
Rupa Publications India Pvt. Ltd 2024
7/16, Ansari Road, Daryaganj
New Delhi 110002

Sales centres:
Prayagraj Bengaluru Chennai
Hyderabad Jaipur Kathmandu
Kolkata Mumbai

Copyright © Tapan Chattopadhyay 2024

The views and opinions expressed in this book are the author's own and the facts are as reported by him which have been verified to the extent possible, and the publishers are not in any way liable for the same.

All rights reserved.
No part of this publication may be reproduced, transmitted, or stored in a retrieval system, in any form or by any means, electronic, mechanical, photocopying, recording or otherwise, without the prior permission of the publisher.

P-ISBN: 978-93-6156-049–1
E-ISBN: 978-93-6156-230-3

First impression 2024

10 9 8 7 6 5 4 3 2 1

The moral right of the author has been asserted.

This book is sold subject to the condition that it shall not, by way of trade or otherwise, be lent, resold, hired out, or otherwise circulated, without the publisher's prior consent, in any form of binding or cover other than that in which it is published.

In memory of
Swami Sumedhananda (Sujit Maharaj).
Humanist, educator, and friend

CONTENTS

Prologue	ix
1. The Rise of the Nehrus	1
2. Boyhood Days	12
3. A Passage to England	20
4. Tryst with Politics	28
5. Father, Son, and the Holy Ghost	37
6. Presidency for Jawaharlal	60
7. A Fellow Traveller	79
8. Consolidation and Compromise	94
9. Jinnah and Congress Politics	119
10. The Politics of Partition	133
11. The Kashmir Imbroglio	172
12. The Orphan of Politics: Tibet	207
13. The Chinese Episode	224
14. The Making of a Dynast	236
Epilogue	250
Acknowledgements	254
End Notes	256
Index	295

PROLOGUE

When Jawaharlal Nehru entered politics in 1916, he had no clear aim in life. But in about three years, he developed such great clout in the Congress Party and grew so close to Mohandas Karamchand Gandhi, who was then fast becoming the party supremo, that he could have his say in the selection of his father, Motilal Nehru, as the party president in 1919.

The year before that, he had proposed Bal Gangadhar Tilak's name for the post, but the veteran leader had declined. By now, he had earned the confidence of Chittaranjan Das, the charismatic leader from Bengal who had become a go-between for him and Gandhi. Even his father sought his help, then and later, whenever he had any problem with Gandhi. A certain narrative about Jawaharlal thus began to unfold in the party circle quite early on. He had learned the immense value of such a mystique from his mentor.

In 1936, when he was a little over forty-six, Jawaharlal Nehru could finally establish his own identity in the West as a sensitive, well-meaning and intellectual politician following the publication of his autobiography in London. Few men have used the written word with such facility as he did in this book. It helped him tell his story as he wanted it to be told, and his narrative prevailed. Here, we discover a delightfully troubled soul, a veritable bundle of contradictions—a queer mixture of the East and the West, out of place everywhere, at home nowhere. He can admit his shortcomings freely, earn the reader's empathy and even his indulgence for his weaknesses, and keep committing the same acts again and again.

Constraints from his family and his career did not allow Jawaharlal to pursue his militant political ideals, although he continued to admire Irish militants all his life. Nevertheless, he deprecated the sacrifices of Indian militant nationalists as undesirable and harmful adventurism. His criticism of the 'growing fascism' in Bengal in the 1930s was, from all indications, a veiled apprehension about the rising popularity of Subhas Chandra Bose, his rival in national politics, the courage of whose convictions he admired but often avoided following in his own life.

Again, despite his socialist beliefs, he liked to be considered an aristocrat. But at the same time, he had unbridled animosity towards Indian princes and aristocrats. His overwhelming dislike of Maharaja Hari Singh, which dismayed Vallabhbhai Patel and Lord Mountbatten, led to the crisis in Kashmir whose legacy India still bears today. Similarly, his animus against the charismatic and professionally successful Muhammad Ali Jinnah, and his biased assessment of the latter's political importance contributed significantly to his party's inability to accommodate the Muslim point of view.

Jawaharlal took to mass politics seriously after his fortuitous involvement with the peasant movement in Pratapgarh in the United Provinces. Half a decade later, he became a socialist and began to take part in labour politics under the guidance of Virendranath Chattopadhyaya, aka Chatto, a covert Soviet agent. In 1934, the Congress Socialists took inspiration from him to form a group within the Congress. Still, instead of leading them from the front, he kept away from them and engaged in gradualist politics under Gandhi. However, he continued to criticize the party's bourgeois-nationalist ideology and apparatus.

Jawaharlal Nehru's extraordinary success as a politician did not, however, come from his 'irresistible' luck as is commonly believed, but from careful planning and circumspection. His mental make-up was such that he could be a Gandhian, a socialist, and an 'Englishman at heart' without feeling any sense of contradiction. His mobile, majestically handsome face and dark thoughtful eyes could successfully hide his fecund, razor-sharp mind that was capable of coming up with ten good reasons for doing something and ten equally good reasons for not doing it at the same time. This trait helped him make friends in both radical and conservative circles and simultaneously remain close to Gandhi.

During his secret parlays with Mountbatten over the Partition, Jawaharlal Nehru kept his mentor out of the picture out of necessity. By this time, he had taken control of the situation and made common cause with Vallabhbhai Patel, as he had done on innumerable occasions in the past. As prime minister, he similarly acquired the trappings of the leaders of the Second International, which he had openly criticized earlier. Nonetheless, his liberal, non-sectarian and democratic approach helped heal the wounds of the Partition to a great extent. It also helped the democratic and secular institutions of India grow after Independence. This was no mean feat in a communally torn country released from a long and painful colonial bondage.

Jawaharlal Nehru's popularity took a dip just before his death; in the last couple of decades, he had come under serious scrutiny for various reasons. But the story of his life, which is also the story of the most significant phase of the Indian freedom movement, continues to remain as important as ever. The present book is a re-examination of Jawaharlal Nehru's life and the important developments taking place around him where he was both a participant and a spectator. It brings to light lesser-known facts, assiduously researched for over a decade. It should be useful to the reader as an unbiased view of the man and his times.

1
THE RISE OF THE NEHRUS

THE BEGINNING OF A JOURNEY

For someone who is universally considered high-born, which was also a notion he actively encouraged,[1] Jawaharlal Nehru's origins were rather humble. His father, Motilal Nehru (1861–1931), literally rose from rags to riches. In fact, he mentioned this in a letter to his son: 'I can without vanity say that I am the founder of the fortunes of the Nehru family.'[2] Motilal was a fiercely proud man and he bequeathed his pride, wealth and good looks to his descendants, which, in many ways, helped them build their political careers in the future.

Years later, his daughter, Vijaya Lakshmi Pandit (1900–1990), reminisced:

> My father's pride in his family was tremendous, a feeling he passed on to each of us. The Nehrus, he seemed to convey without actually saying so, were better than other people... We were different because the family was more progressive than others and our way of living was foreign-oriented.[3]

Motilal's fortune and influence aided Jawaharlal's political activities till the very end. This, however, did not lead him to become defensive about his family's wealth and privileges; quite the contrary. Allahabad's laidback social milieu generated many legends about the wealth and luxuries possessed by the Nehrus, most of which had no factual basis.[4] Mohandas Karamchand Gandhi (1869–1948), who took the Indian political stage by storm in the 1920s, was fascinated by the Nehru family. As such, he significantly contributed to the growth of the family's success and fame all over India through both his writings and his memorable utterances.

Motilal's success as a lawyer allowed him to make many close friends in British circles. Even some provincial governors were on friendly terms with him. One of them, Sir Harcourt Butler, was referred to as 'Uncle Harcourt' by Vijaya Lakshmi when he visited their home.[5] In those days, British officials often made connections among influential Indians to counteract the burgeoning militancy in various parts of the country and the Nehrus were considered an ally. Even when Motilal took to serious politics and his son became a follower of Gandhi, the government could count on them for their temperance and good sense.[6]

The family became so famous by 1931 that Jawaharlal proudly wrote to his sister, Vijaya Lakshmi, from Bardoli in Gujarat, while returning from a month-long holiday in Ceylon:

> Everywhere the crowds and the welcomes were overwhelming, and everywhere the welcome was not so much to me as to the Nehru family. Our family captured the imagination of the millions in this country and 'Nehru' has become a magic word with which you can conjure. It is a great honour and a great responsibility. I feel frightened and overwhelmed by my own popularity. It is a great burden to shoulder.[7]

Such public adulation would have gone to a lesser man's head, but Jawaharlal knew how to keep things on an even keel. This trait made him valuable to Gandhi as a political asset and endeared him to the West as a valuable ally. When Jawaharlal joined the Congress Party in 1916 under the shadow of his father, there were many luminaries in Indian politics, and he had nothing to show for himself. However, he had an active mind, a capacity for reading and hard work, and a knack for penning English prose with great facility; his self-discovery was slow but steady.

Besides, unlike Motilal, he had understood the value of Gandhi quite early on. By 1918, he had established himself as his trusted aide. Starting in 1923, he functioned as the Congress Party's general secretary for nearly two decades. His tenure was hardly ever interrupted. Under Gandhi's tutelage, he learned the finer points of organizational work, the nitty-gritty of backroom politics, and the art of drafting political resolutions. No other Indian leader had this privilege at that time. At the end of the day, his prescience and perseverance helped him emerge as the winner in the political arena at that time.

KASHMIR TO ALLAHABAD

Nothing is known for certain about the ancestry of the Nehru family. According to one source, Jawaharlal's original family name was Kaula, a word used in medieval Kashmiri texts to refer to a devotee of Shakti, the goddess of power and energy.[8] His ancestor Raj Kaula, a scholar of Persian and Sanskrit, came from Brij Bihara, a small village in the Kashmir Valley, to Shahjahanabad during the reign of Mughal Emperor Farrukhsiyar in 1716. He was allotted a small *jagir* (plot of land) near one of Delhi's canals, also called *nehr* in Farsi. Here, he built a house and took the family name Nehr-Kaul.[9]

Raj Kaula had a son, Viswanath Kaula, who was born in Delhi around 1725. After Viswanath completed his studies in Persian, Raj Kaula procured a job for him at the Mughal Court. Viswanath had three sons: Sahib Ram, Mansa Ram, and Tika Ram. Sahib Ram was born in Delhi around 1755 and he studied Persian near where Ajmeri Gate stands today. He had a son, Ram Narayan, who migrated to Ambala for better job opportunities. Some of his descendants still live in Ambala, Meerut, Dehradun and Lucknow.[10] Sahib Ram's younger brother, Mansa Ram, was born ten years later in Delhi. His son, Lakshmi Narayan, became a *vakil* (lawyer) for the East India Company at the Mughal Court. Unfortunately, nothing is known about Tika Ram, the youngest brother, who was born around 1767, or his descendants.

Lakshmi Narayan's son, Ganga Dhar (1827–1861), learned Persian, but he was more of an outdoorsman—stout, brave and given to riding and fencing. His imperious wife, Indrani, who was popularly known as Jiomaji, knew Persian and frequently quoted Persian poets.[11] Her granddaughter once said that she gave one the impression of possessing greater knowledge than she actually possessed—a streak of character she said she might have inherited from her![12] Their youngest son, Motilal, adopted 'Nehru' as his surname.[13]

Jawaharlal, by and large, offered the same narrative in his autobiography, skipping only some details about the names of the places his ancestors had migrated from and where they settled down later.[14] In his long autobiography, he only mentioned Raj Kaula, Sahib Ram, Mansa Ram, Lakshmi Narayan and Ganga Dhar among his ancestors. This is probably because he had to depend on his memory when he wrote the book in prison. Also, whatever he knew about them came from his father, who did not like to talk about them.[15]

The jagir granted by Emperor Farukhsiyar to Raj Kaula dwindled to nominal rights in the lifetime of his grandsons, Mansa Ram and Sahib Ram. Mansa Ram's son, Lakshmi Narayan, Jawaharlal's great-grandfather, did well for himself as the first *vakil* of the British East India Company at the court of the Emperor of Delhi,[16] although this claim has not been corroborated independently. The veracity of the story of the 'Nehru' name's provenance, which Jawaharlal had inherited from his father, has not been ascertained either. This is because there were a few more Nehrus in the Kashmir Valley at that time.[17]

In his autobiography, Jawaharlal has misleadingly portrayed Ganga Dhar as an aristocrat and the *kotwal* (police chief) of Delhi sometime before the Revolt of 1857. His sister, Vijaya Lakshmi, has also done the same in her memoir.[18] In reality, Qazi Faizulla was the kotwal of Delhi[19] and Mirza Abdulla was his deputy[20] when the city fell to the rebels on 11 May 1857. Faizulla failed to control the pandemonium that lasted a couple of weeks, so he was replaced by Mainodin (Muinuddin) Hassan Khan by a royal order.

Earlier, in 1848, Mainodin had been appointed to the Delhi Police by Sir Thomas Theophilus Metcalfe, an agent of the Governor-General of India at the imperial court of Emperor Bahadur Shah Zafar. Mainodin was, at heart, a supporter of the British, but he joined the rebels during the uprising to save himself from danger and managed to become the city's chief kotwal and a colonel in the rebel army. However, he was soon replaced by Syed Mubarak Shah owing to his inability to handle the situation and bring the chaos under control.[21] Khuda Bakhsh Khan was Mubarak's outstanding deputy during the uprising.[22] Mubarak functioned as the police chief of Delhi till the end of the uprising and handled the situation with such rare efficiency that on 31 May 1857, the *Delhi Urdu Akhbar* praised him effusively for bringing the tumultuous city under control.[23] At no point of time before, during, or after the uprising did the city have a Hindu police chief.

It would, therefore, be fair to conjecture that Ganga Dhar was a junior functionary (perhaps a *chaprasi* or attendant, as Ram Manohar Lohia once said in Parliament[24]) at the Mughal Court. Nehru's old family papers and documents were avowedly destroyed during the holocaust of 1857.[25] In that case, it remains unclear why his grandfather, Ganga Dhar, who was around thirty years old at that point, had to flee Delhi, given that he had nothing to fear from the British.

Ganga Dhar's other kith and kin—Sahib Ram's family, for example—did not leave the city when the rebels took over. Yet, Ganga Dhar fled Delhi in a huff. With him went his wife, one teenage daughter, two teenage sons (Motilal had not been born yet), and a very fair-skinned girl child. The British soldiers in the outskirts of the city mistook the child for an English infant and hauled the family up for interrogation. Ganga Dhar's sons, Bansi Dhar and Nand Lal, who knew some English, were somehow able to explain the mistake to them and save themselves from being hanged on the nearest tree.[26]

At that time, quite a few insiders at the Mughal Court, including Emperor Bahadur Shah Zafar's favourite queen Zinat Mahal, were secretly in communication with the British and some of them were even spying for them. The Emperor's overactive premier, Hakim Ahsanullah Khan, contacted the British himself through an intermediary.[27] Zinat Mahal clandestinely sought British help to promote her son, Mirza Jawan Bakht, as heir to the throne.[28] It was quite possible that Ganga Dhar had played some part in the court intrigues of the time and had come to the notice of his detractors to his own detriment.

From Jawaharlal Nehru's pen picture of his great-grandfather, as well as the one miniature painting that exists of him, one can see that he looks a lot like a Mughal officer. Nehru writes, 'In a little painting that we have of my grandfather, he wears the Moghal court dress with a covered sword in his hand, and might well be taken for a Moghal nobleman, although his features are distinctly Kashmiri.'[29] In the painting, Ganga Dhar is portrayed as a fair-skinned, red-bearded man with reflective blue eyes and can easily be mistaken for a tough Muslim official rather than a Kashmiri Brahmin with delicate features. Even Motilal's features were markedly Mughal, though he was not tall. Jawaharlal acquired his delicate looks and his relatively short stature from his mother.

In Agra, Ganga Dhar's family maintained a low profile. His sons, Bansi Dhar (1842–1913) and Nand Lal (1845–1887), were both industrious and meritorious. When he died in 1861, he was only thirty-four; Motilal was born three months later. Jawaharlal has treated his ancestors rather summarily in the slender first chapter of his autobiographical tome.

Soon after coming to Agra, Bansi Dhar entered the judiciary and was partly cut off from the rest of the family because of his postings to various far-flung places. He was a learned man with an eccentric mind—strikingly handsome with grey-blue eyes and a fine flowing beard. He was an astrologer of some repute and after retirement he settled in Solan, a Himalayan resort where he devoted himself to the comparative study of various religions.[30]

Ganga Dhar's younger son, Nand Lal, became the diwan of the princely state of Khetri in Rajputana and remained so for a decade; after ten years of service, he took charge of the household. Subsequently, he settled down as a practising lawyer at the Agra High Court. Later, he came to live with the family in Allahabad when the High Court was shifted there. The young Motilal was brought up by Nand Lal and was greatly attached to him.

77 MIRGANJ CHOWK

Motilal followed in the footsteps of his brother and became a lawyer. His education had been somewhat haphazard. He first attended a madrasa (Muslim school), then a Christian mission school and later Muir Central College in Allahabad, which he left without accepting his bachelor's degree. Subsequently, he appeared at the vakils' examination in Kanpur in 1883, topped the list of successful candidates and started practising in the district court. For the first time ever, he began to take things seriously and did very well in his professional and social life. In 1886, he came to Allahabad to practise law as a vakil[31] at the High Court under his brother's tutelage.

But as ill luck would have it, Nand Lal died the next year. Though Motilal was yet to find his feet in the unknown city, he dealt with the situation with his usual courage and determination. He took care of Nand Lal's family and survived, living with his newly married second wife (his first wife had died at childbirth in Kanpur), in a rented house at 77 Mirganj Chowk,[32] waiting for better days. Mirganj was, and still is, in a squalid and congested part of the city, primarily inhabited by grocers and jewellers, pimps and prostitutes. Jawaharlal was born in this rented house in Mirganj on 14 November 1889. He spent his infancy and a part of his childhood in this infamous area.

The squalor of Mirganj tormented Motilal as if it were a physical affliction. He was worried about the kind of upbringing Jawahar would receive in such a sordid atmosphere. He had always yearned for a son and now that his second wife Swarup Rani (her family name was Thussu) had fulfilled his desire six years after their marriage, he felt miserable for being unable to give him a proper environment to grow up in. His friend and associate Munshi Mubarak Ali stood by him and his family during these days of hardship. He was like a second father to Jawahar.[33]

RISE TO THE TOP

One significant aspect of Motilal's personality was that he was a cheerful extrovert, full of the confidence and inner balance that come from self-made success. His mind was cast in an aristocratic mould. People took him for an aristocrat even in his early days when he was yet to acquire the trappings of one. His handsome and dignified mien, fair complexion common to the Kashmiris, and refined behaviour helped him enormously in his profession and politics.

Motilal's success as a combative lawyer secured him a large clientele of rich land-owning families; he became wealthy beyond measure within a decade. Money and respectability (and later, power and influence for his son) were the main motivating factors in his life.[34] In 1896, he became one of the four to receive the status and privilege of 'Advocates of the Allahabad High Court'. People remembered the occasions when he would go to Lucknow on a case for one of the big *taluqdar*s (estate owners). The retinue that travelled with him was second to no prince's.[35] Munshi Mubarak Ali helped him in his job and made deals for him, which were not always above board. He became a sort of majordomo of the household.[36]

Nehru has mentioned Ali as a subordinate of his father.[37] But he was Motilal's friend and benefactor rather than a subordinate and wielded considerable authority in the household, independent of Motilal. He had a particularly soft corner in his heart for Jawaharlal. Long afterwards, when Jawaharlal's daughter Indira was born, she was taken to the old, ailing Ali's residence and presented to him for his blessings.[38] Jawaharlal wrote later that his memory '...remains with me as a dear and precious possession.'[39]

Before the turn of the century, Motilal Nehru shifted his family to a rented house at 9 Elgin Road in the Civil Lines, inhabited by British bureaucrats and businessmen.[40] A few years later, in 1900, he would possess a sprawling forty-two-room bungalow at 1 Church Road in the upscale area of the city and name it Anand Bhavan ('House of Joy'). He was the second Indian to own a house in this locality.

The property originally belonged to Shaikh Fayyaz Ali of Allahabad. He had built the bungalow in a rent-free plot of land allotted to him by the British government in 1861, in compensation for losses he had sustained during the 1857 uprising.[41] When he died in 1873, he left behind his minor children, and the property was administered by the Court of Wards. In 1888, at his heirs' request, the Court of Wards authorized the district collector to sell the property, which was then purchased by Syed Mahmud, a justice of the Allahabad High Court and the son of Syed Ahmad Khan of Aligarh Muslim University fame, for INR 9,000. Mahmud made some alterations and additions to the property, as the sale deed indicates. Six years later, he sold the property to his close friend Raja Jaikishen Das for INR 13,250, which Motilal purchased in 1900 for INR 20,000.[42]

Motilal renovated the bungalow tastefully. He also added a tennis court, a swimming pool (which was the first of its kind in an Indian house), well-manicured lawns, outhouses, expensive furniture and other luxurious appurtenances. The eleven-year-old Jawaharlal enjoyed seeing the labourers at work when the bungalow was being renovated.[43] Motilal organized elegant parties and get-togethers for Englishmen and Indians in his house, which were quite fun. His lusty laughter on such occasions was famous in the city. He was among the first to buy a motor car in Allahabad. Legends about his taste and fondness for luxury thus proliferated.

This was indeed a fairytale in the making. As Motilal relocated his family to the luxurious new bungalow, he swept his past under the carpet and encouraged the rest of the family to do the same. Swarup Rani (1868–1938) had a profound understanding of her husband's ways. She followed suit, as did the other members of the household, and they all collectively buried their shabby past. Mubarak Ali remained Motilal's only link to this past and he continued to be a well-wisher of the family right till the end.

Motilal Nehru's professional success helped him become a leader of the Congress Party in Allahabad when he found it expedient to do so. In 1910, he became a member of the constituent assembly of the Central Provinces. Having sent his son to Harrow in 1905, he now had time to look around for other pursuits. He began to attend Congress meetings off and on, cautiously, without taking any real interest in its work initially.[44] He had no wish to join any movement or organization where he would have to play second fiddle to someone else.[45] He felt only contempt for Indian politicians who, he thought, talked endlessly without doing anything concrete.[46] Also, there was the thought, born out of his pride in his own professional success, that many—though certainly not all—of those who took up politics had been failures in the other spheres of their lives.[47]

This was the time when militant nationalism was sending shockwaves through Bengal, Maharashtra, the United Provinces and the Punjab. A section of Indians had started resenting imperial attitudes towards Indians, typically structured by insult and exclusion—the 'subject races' label, the 'Ganga Din' image, and the all-pervasive presence of white supremacy, so secure in its omnipotence that it did not even need the prop of an official policy of apartheid. Railway carriages, station retiring rooms, clubs, and park benches reserved 'For Europeans Only' were a blatant manifestation of this outlook. Indians wanted freedom from the British and supported the militants who resorted to violent activities to drive away the foreign rulers. A sizeable section of the Congress Party—known as the Extremists—was in sympathy with them. On the other hand, the Moderates in the party—lawyers, professors, landowners and entrepreneurs—opposed militant nationalism and believed that they could bring out the best in the British through well-reasoned petitions to attain self-government and equal status with the White Dominions. Motilal Nehru endorsed their views and activities.

Motilal's attitude towards Indian politics and politicians changed during the course of the decade, as he shrewdly realised that British rule in India was in a state of decay. He now began to take an interest in politics more actively and, in 1907, he presided over a provincial conference of the Indian National Congress in Allahabad, saying at the conference that British rule was not so bad after all. Jawaharlal welcomed his active participation in Congress politics. He was confident that Motilal was bound to succeed in his new role as a political leader. He was in England then and could observe the winds of change and the possibilities that lay ahead more clearly, although he thought that his father's overcautious approach to politics was still 'too immoderately moderate.'[48]

2
BOYHOOD DAYS

LONELY LITTLE PARADISE

Jawaharlal spent over three years of his infancy at Mirganj, in a house owned by Jagmohan Lal Gurtu before his father shifted his family to a rented bungalow at 9 Elgin Road, now Lal Bahadur Shastri Marg, close to the historical Alfred Park, now Chandrashekhar Azad Park.[1] The Elgin Road bungalow no longer exists, while Mirganj remains busy as ever. The two-storey house where the Nehrus lived in Mirganj was demolished by the Allahabad Municipality in 1931 to broaden the road in the locality.[2]

The Nehrus and their biographers have maintained silence on this part of their history in Mirganj. There is only a passing mention by Frank Moraes that it was '…a house standing in a lane in one of Allahabad's more congested localities. The entrance to the lane was said to be haunted.'[3] People living in the locality now only have a vague idea that Motilal Nehru and his family had once lived here. According to local gossip, Mubarak Ali, a lean and aristocratic gentleman, used to visit this house in a fashionable horse-driven carriage.[4] Hemvati Nandan Bahuguna (1919–89), the chief minister of Uttar Pradesh, attempted to build a memorial here in 1975. However, he was soon removed from his office by Indira Gandhi (1917–1984), the then prime minister of India. The bungalow at 9 Elgin Road, where the family lived till 1900, was also demolished after Independence.

Jawaharlal did not like to discuss his family's past beyond his boyhood days at Anand Bhavan. He fondly recalled myths and gossip that grew around the family's wealth and luxury, but he conveniently glossed over his father's hard work that made these possible. These legends helped his political career a great deal, especially in a country like India where the nobility is practically worshipped like gods. He wrote:

> I found that one of the most persistent legends about my father or myself was to the effect that we used to send our linen weekly from India to a Paris laundry. We have repeatedly contradicted this, but the legend persists... Another equally persistent legend, often repeated in spite of denial, is that I was at school with the Prince of Wales. The story goes on to say that when the Prince came to India in 1921 he asked for me; I was then in gaol. As a matter of fact, I was not only not at school with him, but I have never had the advantage of meeting him or speaking to him.[5]

Motilal's ever-increasing income brought many changes in the family's lifestyle, which grew more and more extravagant and Westernized over the years. Jawaharlal moved about in the sheltered milieu of Anand Bhavan in the company of his older cousins, his father's other dependants and many servants. But he did not mention any of them individually in his memoir. Presumably, therefore, they had a negligible role to play in his life while he was growing up.

The household was divided into Indian and Western sections. The reception, the dining rooms and Motilal's offices were at the front of the house, overlooking the garden. The Western-style parties were held here. The other part of the house was Swarup Rani's domain. It was, in effect, run by her elder sister, known as Bibima to Jawahar and others, and had a Brahmin cook and upper-caste Hindu servants.[6] Miss Smith, the Anglo-Indian housekeeper, looked after the Western side of the house with Christian, Muslim and low-caste servants.[7] There was no quarrel between the two worlds. Swarup Rani often joined her husband and the children at the dining table. Except for Motilal, whose meals were adjusted to his working hours and eaten in the Western dining room, the other members of the large family ate whenever and wherever it suited them.[8]

The house had many visitors in the morning till Motilal left for the court. After his departure, there would be a lull in activity. Again, when he got back in the evening, there would be people, parties and get-togethers, and the place would light up with peals of laughter, passionate debates and desultory banter.[9] In spite of growing up in this bustling house, Jawahar did not have anyone of his own age group to spend time with. He was chaperoned by his English governesses and the servants. His adoring mother and his saintly aunt, Nandrani, were too busy with household chores to have enough time for him. So, their *jawahar* ('precious stone' in Arabic) learned to live alone, for and within his own self.

This habit of loneliness helped Jawahar during his days at Harrow when he was getting used to his supercilious English schoolmates, and even later in his life, when he found himself in prison. Prison life suited him so well that he sometimes welcomed it as a relief from his irksome political engagements,[10] albeit he was always kept in the better prisons, in cooler regions where he did not have to face hardships or health hazards like other political prisoners.[11] He thought that this preferential treatment was due to his English public school background, for which Englishmen considered him to be one of their own. Indeed, he wrote all his serious works in prison.

LIKE FATHER, LIKE SON

Motilal was a dictator in the house. However, he was considerate by nature and intervened only when something went very wrong.[12] He allowed the women of his family to continue their traditional religious practices without taking part in them himself. Jawaharlal's cousins and other menfolk followed his example. As for Jawaharlal, he really enjoyed the religious activities of his mother and his aunt. Sometimes, he accompanied his mother to take a holy dip in the Ganges. However, at the same time, he also tried to imitate the casual attitude of the adult men of the family.[13] He eagerly listened to the grown-up conversations of his cousins without understanding all of it. He would get excited when they talked about British atrocities against Indians and would be glad when he heard of instances of Indians hitting back. But he ultimately admired the English as a race.[14] Right from his childhood, then, Jawaharlal knew how to balance opposing emotions and accommodate ideological contradictions.

At this time, the Nehrus did not subscribe to any particular notion of patriotism or nationalism. They felt they were different from their neighbours and had a sense of their own superiority, much like most other Kashmiri families living in Allahabad at that time. They felt this because of their fair complexion, their capacity for upward social mobility, the absence of extreme restrictions on the women, and their complex cuisine and eating habits.[15] Much later, in his conversations and writings, an older Nehru sometimes ended up revealing his notions about exclusivity and superiority that he acquired from his 'culturally elevated and liberated' family, living in a big house far from the madding crowd.[16]

His sense of being one-of-the-elect was accentuated by his education at Harrow and Trinity College, Cambridge. His rather elite educational background stuck with him when he went on to become a political leader. It prevented him from relating to the Indian situation like other, more grounded political leaders of his time. It also conditioned him to position everything within a global context like an outsider. He could think of India's independence only in relation to global socio-economic privations, the general lack of socio-political justice, and capitalist-imperialist exploitations in other Third World countries. In this he was influenced, no doubt, by the socialist interface from the late 1920s.

One thing that affected Jawaharlal's emotional growth as a child was his father's violent temper. Motilal even went so far as to beat his servants up with his own hands when he got angry, even in front of company.[17] Even as an adult, Jawaharlal found it difficult to protest against his father's behaviour. During his childhood, Motilal once beat him up so severely for stealing a pen that the wounds on his body took several days to heal.[18]

Jawaharlal rationalized his father's behaviour the same way he would later rationalize and even justify many of Gandhi's actions which he did not believe in. Moreover, he also inherited his father's temper and arrogance later in life.[19] Although he did not physically assault his servants like his father, he threw files at his secretaries and misbehaved with his office staff.[20] Often enough, he would lose his temper with his party workers if they dared oppose his views.[21] He slapped members of the crowd[22] and even trampled over them if he got angry or nervous.[23] Also, he would get petulant when criticized, and in spite of being a believer in democratic norms, he tended to be secretive and autocratic in his manner of functioning. He would mistrust his co-workers, and refuse to delegate any responsibility to them.[24]

Fear constituted a significant part of his feelings towards his father when he was a boy, although the love and the admiration that he felt for him were almost equally powerful.[25] It was not the same with his mother. He could turn to her for emotional sustenance whenever he wanted, and he confided in her without reservations, often sharing his innermost thoughts with her. He appreciated her beauty and admired her amazingly small and beautiful hands and feet. Because of her unconditional love for him, he would even browbeat her from time to time and exploit her weakness for him to achieve his own ends.[26]

Munshi Mubarak Ali was his other confidant. He would snuggle up to him and listen, wide-eyed, to his innumerable stories by the hour—old tales of magic and mystery from the *Arabian Nights* and other books, and the accounts of the uprisings of 1857–58. On the two days of Eid, he would visit his house and consume sweet vermicelli and other dainties.[27]

Sometimes when his father entertained guests in his house, Jawaharlal would peep at him and his friends from behind a curtain and try to make out what they were saying. If he was caught in the act, his father would drag him out of his hiding place and make him sit on his knee for a while.[28] Once, while peeping in during one of his father's parties, he thought the red-coloured claret was blood and immediately ran to the Indian part of the house to deliver the horrendous tidings to his mother, that his father and his friends were drinking blood.[29] He also loved playing pranks on people. He would find it funny to push people who did not know how to swim into the swimming pool at Anand Bhavan. Dr Tej Bahadur Sapru (1875–1949), who was a young lawyer at the Allahabad Bar at that time, was often the subject of his pranks.[30]

CAREER, BOOKS, AND DREAMS

When his son was ten or eleven years old, Motilal Nehru encouraged him to study hard so that he could be a part of the 'heaven-born' ranks of the Indian Civil Service (ICS) and bring honour to the family. Only when Jawaharlal continued to fare badly at both Harrow and Cambridge did he change his mind and settle for a career in law for his son. On 8 August 1905, when his mind was still set on the ICS for Jawaharlal, he wrote to him at Harrow, 'It would be a proud day for me when I shall have the satisfaction of seeing you a full blown ICS and Kishen an IMS [Indian Medical Servant].'[31] He spared neither pains nor money to help his son prepare for achieving this goal.

In 1900, when Jawaharlal was a little over ten, his father engaged two English governesses at Anand Bhavan to teach him English and European etiquette. Jawaharlal was also sent to a local convent school for a few months. This phase of his academic journey proved to be somewhat desultory, so Motilal decided that he would receive private instruction at home with the help of qualified teachers. Though the emphasis was on English, he engaged a Sanskrit scholar, Pandit Ganganath Jha, to teach him Sanskrit and Hindi. As Jawaharlal showed no aptitude or inclination for studies,[32] Motilal appointed a young Irish-Belgian theosophist thinker, Ferdinand T. Brooks (1873–1916), as his home tutor on the recommendation of Annie Besant (1847–1933), a socialist leader and friend of George Bernard Shaw. Brooks would coin the term 'neo-theosophy' in his book *Neo-Theosophy Exposed* (1912). Brooks remained in charge of Jawaharlal's education from 1901 to 1904 and gave his pupil wide latitude in what he read and how he thought. Motilal was not happy with his method of teaching and wanted him to lay down a strict study regime for his son.[33] For him, the goal of education was to ensure good living and material success. He was, however, unable to influence Brooks. Still, he continued the arrangement as he could not find a better alternative.

By the time Jawaharlal was twelve, Brooks developed in him, albeit in a haphazard manner,[34] a taste for reading.[35] Among his favourite books were Lewis Carroll's fantasies, Rudyard Kipling's *The Jungle Book* and *Kim*, Gustave Doré's illustrations for *Don Quixote* by Miguel de Cervantes, and Fridtjof Nansen's *Farthest North*, apart from the novels of Walter Scott, Charles Dickens and William Makepeace Thackeray, the thrilling adventure stories by H.G. Wells and Mark Twain, and the Sherlock Holmes stories. He was thrilled by Anthony Hope's *The Prisoner of Zenda*. For him, Jerome K. Jerome's *Three Men in a Boat* was the last word in humour. Two other books he recalled later were George du Maurier's *Trilby* and *Peter Ibbetson*.[36] Apart from these prose texts, Brooks developed in him a lifelong love for English poetry that would later lead him to appreciate poems in Indian languages and make him an admirer of Rabindranath Tagore. Painting did not attract him much, but he later developed an ear for music; he was also taught to appreciate and patronize art and artists of various kinds as he grew up.[37]

Brooks moreover acquainted his pupil with his surroundings. Japan's military prowess excited him as a boy and he mused on the prospect of freedom for India, and even Asia. He dreamed of doing great deeds.[38] When he was fourteen, there were a few changes around the house. His older cousins had all become professional men by then, so they left the family home and set up their own households. Fresh thoughts and vague fancies began to form in his mind at this time. He also took a little more interest in the opposite sex, although he still preferred the company of boys and thought it a little beneath his dignity to associate with groups of girls. But sometimes at the Kashmiri parties, where there was no dearth of pretty girls, a furtive glance here or a surreptitious touch there did not fail to thrill him.[39]

This was the time when Jawaharlal started dreaming of astral bodies and imagining that he was flying across vast distances high up in the air, while the countryside lay underneath him in a vast panorama. This was a recurrent dream that came and went throughout his life.[40] He wondered how Sigmund Freud and others would interpret his dream.[41] Indeed, according to Freud, a sense of euphoria and freedom is usually associated with flying in a dream, signifying that the dreamer has freed himself or herself from a sticky situation or has achieved a goal recently. In case of men, flying may also signify coarse sensuality and sexual thoughts.[42] According to Dr Paul Federn, a great many flying dreams are actually erection dreams.[43]

Alternately, flying can be a manifestation of wish fulfilment, making up for a lack of freedom in one's waking life, as in Jawaharlal's case. It can also be an expression of a yearning to transcend existing reality. Looking downwards may indicate that the dreamer feels negatively about something or someone, perhaps himself or herself. The recurrence of the dream in his later life could signify that Jawaharlal suffered from a guilty conscience and self-pity.

3

A PASSAGE TO ENGLAND

HARROWING HARROW

In May 1905, the Nehrus—father, mother, son and the baby daughter, Vijaya Lakshmi—set sail for England to get Jawaharlal enrolled at the famous Harrow School, founded in 1572 under a Royal Charter of Queen Elizabeth I. Long before their journey, news of their impending trip to Europe had made the rounds in Allahabad.[1] At that time, Motilal was suffering from nervous prostration, the natural consequence of years of hard work. He planned to move straight to London from Marseilles with his family and consult a few specialists about his wife's ailment after putting Jawaharlal in school.[2] In matters of his own health, he relied on Indian doctors.[3]

It was the heyday of the luxurious Edwardian era in England in 1905. A Liberal administration headed by Sir Henry Campbell-Bannerman took office in December that year. Germany had already kicked off an arms race with England; World War I was nine years away. This was also the time when a sturdy campaign for women's franchise began in England. On the other hand, there was this new toy, the motor car, travelling at twenty miles an hour and bringing in its wake 'these fast, forward and frantic days'.[4] Edwardian England had ushered in a decade of prosperous and opulent living, in contrast to the class-based morality, economic conservatism and reformist zeal of the Victorian era. A variety of vehicles such as steam buses, hansoms and four-wheeled cabs plied London's streets now.

The young Jawaharlal Nehru liked what he saw, but homesickness overtook him after his family left England. His father tried to console him in a letter from Marseilles on his way back home: 'You must bear in mind that in you we are leaving the dearest treasure we have in this world and perhaps in other worlds to come... It is not a question of providing for you as I can do that perhaps in one single year's income.'[5] Motilal told Jawaharlal that it would be selfish and even sinful to keep him in India with a fortune in gold, but with little or no education. He wrote:

> I think I can say without vanity that I am the founder of the fortunes of the Nehru family. I look upon you, my dear son, as the man who will build upon the foundation I have laid and have the satisfaction of seeing a noble structure of renown rearing up its head to the skies... It seems to me that the one ambition of my life is to see you successful.[6]

For Motilal, success meant doing well in the material world. He advised his son to practise shooting in order to get along with his English schoolmates. For him, shooting was 'one of the most necessary qualifications of a well-educated man.'[7] He also advised him to have a rifle of his own.[8] Worried about Jawaharlal's lack of expertise in games, he wrote from SS *Macedonia*: 'Cricket and football cannot be learnt in a day. It was my mistake that I did not give you some practice in both. I think it will be well if you can arrange to have some practice during your vacation.'[9]

Jawaharlal was slightly older than the average age for admission into Harrow and had to try hard to catch up with his schoolmates. Brooks had developed in him a kind of stoicism and an aptitude for reading which came to his aid now. After his father left for India, he sought succour in school curricula and even sports. On the eve of his departure from London, Motilal had written to his son, 'I am going back to India with the firm conviction that I have sown the seed of your future greatness and I have not a shadow of doubt that you have a great career before you. We have seen enough of you at Harrow to be satisfied that you will be quite happy there.'[10] Motilal believed that rhetorical flourishes were the best way to inspire people.

Thanks to his father's influence, Jawaharlal began to live in the Headmaster's House at Harrow. The housemaster, Rev. (Dr) Joseph Wood, was a genial and sympathetic man. Motilal wrote to his son from Villa Branicka in Homburg, Germany: 'It is very good of Dr Wood to interest himself so far in you as to be concerned with the qualifications of your private tutor and show his solicitude for the progress you are making.'[11] In spite of his father's good rapport with the headmaster, Jawaharlal considered it prudent to keep a low profile before his supercilious schoolmates.

Among the four or five Indian boys who were at Harrow then, one was the son of an Indian prince, from the Gaekwad family of Baroda. He was a popular cricketer and Jawaharlal's senior by many years. Although he lived in the same House, he left the school soon after Jawaharlal's arrival. After his departure came Paramjit Singh, the eldest son of the Maharaja of Kapurthala. He was a 'complete misfit' and an object of ridicule for his English schoolmates. Jawaharlal's sympathies, however, did not lie with him. Rather, he went with the flow and impishly enjoyed Paramjit's reaction to the torments hurled at him by his British schoolmates.[12] He resented the way Paramjit treated him as if he were a plebeian. He quite possibly developed his lifelong antipathy towards the Indian nobility at Harrow.

Soon after his father departed for home, his interest in his studies lessened. A worried Motilal wrote from Allahabad on 4 December 1905:

> I find that the Science column is left blank in the Report. Perhaps you will take it up next term. As you know I want you specifically to develop a taste for Science and Mathematics. You are no doubt doing all that can be done and nothing will please me more than to have you in the first Senior Wrangler of your year. The I.C.S. will then be child's play for you.[13]

His encouragement had little effect on Jawaharlal. In October 1906, he pleaded with him to take him back to India and enrol him at 'the Hindu Ideal' school. Motilal was flabbergasted at his request and sternly informed his son that it was absolutely necessary for him to remain at Harrow for at least one year. He tried to convince Jawaharlal that he had no time to lose since the age limit for the ICS was between twenty-one and twenty-four years, with only three chances for entry.

Simultaneously, he prevailed upon Dr Wood to let his ward appear for Part I of the previous examination in March and for Part II in June 1907 so that he could get into Trinity College, Cambridge, in time.[14] Dr Wood consented to this against his better judgement. In those days, it was mandatory to graduate from either Oxford or Cambridge to appear for the ICS examination. With the headmaster's help, Motilal arranged special coaching sessions for his son to help him cope with his studies.

Soon, Motilal had second thoughts about this arrangement. He was afraid that his son would not be able to clear the Part I examination in March. So, he asked him to consult his cousin Brijlal to determine whether he should take on the extra pressure. This was because even if he started at Cambridge in October, he would still have over two years to prepare for the special subjects for the ICS examination after completing the three-year course at Cambridge. He told Jawaharlal that he was not in favour of rushing things if they could be managed more easily and quietly.[15] Meanwhile, he suggested, Jawaharlal should practise riding[16] since one had to pass the riding test for being accepted into the ICS.

Jawaharlal, or 'Joe,' as he was known to his English classmates, completed his studies at Harrow in 1907 without a hitch but with no distinction either. No one in the school took any serious notice of him.[17] Motilal was constantly goading him to make friends among the English boys. He was glad when Jawaharlal informed him that one of them had invited him to lunch in London. But when he said that his English friend lived a 'swell' life, Motilal wrote back, 'I am glad to hear you have at least one Harrow friend in London who cared sufficiently for him to ask you to lunch. The fact that he is swell does not matter as you are not likely to envy his way of living.'[18] Motilal was much too rooted in his national and cultural identity to encourage his son to admire his British friend's wealth uncritically.

Jawaharlal was duly accepted into Trinity College, Cambridge, in October 1907. He was happy to leave Harrow, but he cried at the time of leaving the school because the Harrow tradition demanded that a student be sad at the time of leaving his alma mater.[19]

LIBERATED AT CAMBRIDGE

At Cambridge, Jawaharlal chose the Natural Sciences Tripos comprising chemistry, geology and botany. He disregarded his father's desire for him to take up mathematics and physics instead of geology and botany. Motilal was disappointed, but he did not make an issue out of it. His confidence in his son's abilities had dwindled considerably by this time.

In the summer of 1910, Jawaharlal spent a few weeks in Ireland and was impressed by the Sinn Fein movement.[20] In a bout of youthful bravado, he even regretted that he had missed the riots in Belfast and bemoaned the fact that Dublin was just quiet and ordinary during his stay. The Irish freedom movement could be seen as an apt parallel to the militant nationalist movements that originated in Bengal and Maharashtra and were rapidly spreading to other provinces of India. Jawaharlal's new extremist sympathies made him decry his father's moderate attitude towards politics. He later regretted that he had not dismissed the idea of joining the ICS at that time and becoming a cog in the British administrative machinery.[21]

Jawaharlal continued to vouch for these extremist views well after he returned to India, until Gandhi's influence and his own practical sense transformed his outlook. Thereafter, he would oppose Indian nationalist extremists and call them 'fascists,' while still retaining a lot of admiration for the Sinn Fein movement in Ireland. He would underplay and even justify the colonial government's repressive action against Indian nationalist extremists, calling it a confrontation between nationalist fascism and imperialist fascism exemplified by Europeans, Anglo-Indians and some upper-class Indians.[22] In this, he was no different from Sir Charles Tegart, IP (Indian Police), who was an Irishman but played an active role in repressing the Irish nationalist movement.[23] The only difference between the two was that it was Tegart's job to uphold British imperialism, while it was Nehru's job to oppose it.

The three years that Jawaharlal spent at Cambridge passed slowly, much like the sluggish Cam. He read a wide range of books and discussed them with the people he met.[24] He cultivated a ragged image modelled after the legendary J. Alfred Prufrock from the poem by T.S. Eliot, which was fashionable at Cambridge at that time. This usually struck a sympathetic chord with the people he met, both in his college days and beyond. Later, even Gandhi was deeply touched by his 'loneliness' and considered it a sign of his spiritual purity.[25]

Jawaharlal wrote about this phase of his life:

> My real conflict lay within me, a conflict of ideas, desires and loyalties, of subconscious depths struggling with outer circumstances, of an inner hunger unsatisfied. I became a battleground, where various forces struggled for mastery. I sought an escape from this; I tried to find harmony and equilibrium, and in this attempt I rushed into action. That gave me some peace; outer conflict relieved the train of the inner struggle.[26]

While studying at Cambridge, his interest in sex grew, but he did not have the courage to pursue it.[27] He attended the Indian Majlis, a socio-political forum of local Indians,[28] and joined the college debating society, Magpie and Stump, but he did not actively participate in their programmes.[29] Though '...not particularly attracted to a soft life...' he became admittedly superficial and a little hedonistic, occasionally indulging in drinking, gambling and a few other vices. In short, he was completely confused and lacked a goal in life. His '...general attitude to life was a vague kind of cyrenaicism...'[30], which was a belief that people were motivated purely by self-interest.

In 1910, Jawaharlal left Cambridge with a measly second-class honours degree in the Natural Science Tripos. Motilal had him enlist his name at London's Inner Temple even before he took the examination. By this time, he was thoroughly disenchanted with the idea of the ICS. His hardworking nephew, Brijlal, could not get into ICS proper and had joined the Indian Audit and Accounts Service. His other nephew, Shridhar, in whom he had a great deal of confidence, also failed to clear the examination in his first attempt. Motilal developed a suspicion that the examiners were biased against Indian candidates.[31]

Jawaharlal wanted to spend some more time in England and study further at Oxford. But Motilal was in no mood to spend any more money or time on his education. Later in his life, Jawaharlal gave the impression that he was too young for the ICS examination after completing his Tripos and did not want to stay in England any longer.[32] A little over twenty now, Jawaharlal could dress, speak, gamble, toast, and swear like any highbred English student. He liked to describe himself as 'a torn being,' not mentally but emotionally and psychologically,[33] and cultivated a sort of fashionable Janus-like look that he continued to sport till much later in his life, with some variations.

Around this time, his parents chose a bride for him. With his new-found freedom, he argued with them that he must select his life partner. Motilal gave him several other reasons why he must not do any such thing. He told his son firmly that he did not believe in love at first sight[34] and warned him against marrying an Englishwoman since marriage outside one's community or culture could not bring one any happiness in life.[35]

When Jawaharlal joined the Inner Temple, Motilal believed that his son had finally found his calling. But Jawaharlal had no enthusiasm for the legal profession. For the next two years, he enjoyed London life to the fullest and became known as a man of fashion and intellect and as a connoisseur of fine wines at fashionable restaurants. He appeared to be supremely careless about mundane matters like money and material success and was often in debt. He even had to pawn his watch and chain, and sometimes did not have any money for his bus and tube fares.[36] Alarmed by his behaviour, Motilal gave him supplementary grants to support himself.[37]

After living in England for seven years, Jawaharlal barely managed to pass the Bar examination and returned home in 1912, admittedly a 'prig' with 'mongrel,' or at least mixed, education.'[38] He brought back with him his lifelong attachment to England and the values that he considered English. All his life, he traced a feeling of kinship with England on a very personal level. By his own admission, his attitude towards British rule in India resembled that of an average Englishman, without, possibly, the blatantly imperialist edge.[39]

4

TRYST WITH POLITICS

RETURN TO ALLAHABAD

In the autumn of 1912, Jawaharlal had no clear idea of what his future had in store for him. When he was at Cambridge, Motilal had painted a rather rosy picture of the prospect of being a barrister for him and had promised to take care of his career.[1] But at heart, he was deeply disappointed in his son's performance. He did not go to England with his family to fetch his son as planned. Neither did he paint the house for his homecoming. In the end, he did not even go to Bombay to receive Jawaharlal and had him picked up and put on a train to Allahabad by one of his cousins.[2] In Allahabad, Jawaharlal took a tonga (a one-horse cart) to reach home.

His work at the High Court interested Jawaharlal for a while, but soon, the dullness of his daily routine began to affect him. The atmosphere at home was fairly congenial, yet the overall atmosphere of the place was intellectually stifling.[3] To his great annoyance, the young British officials of the city showed no interest in befriending him.[4] He could not join the kind of militant politics that was close to his heart either, because of familial and professional constraints.[5] He took part in some recreational activities, such as hunting and taking trips to the jungle, to interrupt the monotony, but he was not a good shot and soon acquired the reputation of being a bloodless hunter. He did some trekking and climbing, both of which became his lifelong passion.

Out of sheer boredom, he occasionally began to attend the meetings of the Congress Party in Allahabad.[6] In December 1912, he was impressed by the Moderate leader from Maharashtra, Gopal Krishna Gokhale (1866–1915), CIE, at the party's annual session in Bankipur in Bihar.[7] He knew about and admired Gokhale's Servants of India Society, founded in Poona (now Pune) in 1905, and modelled on the Society of Jesus, for its dedication to public service.[8] But the organization was too moderate for his tastes, and he did not join it. Besides, he had no intention of giving up his profession.[9]

During this period, Jawaharlal had no clear notion of what he wanted to do in life. For a time, he was keen on joining the newly formed Indian Defence Force and sent an enrolment application, knowing that this force was treated as subordinate to the regular European army.[10] He became a member of a committee formed by his father, Tej Bahadur Sapru and C.Y. Chintamani (1880–1941) to encourage Indians to join the army during war. But the scheme was abandoned in protest against Annie Besant's arrest in June 1917.[11]

Besant was a British citizen and a diehard social activist and theosophist. She helped Madan Mohan Malaviya (1861–1946) found the Banaras Hindu University in 1916. The same year, with Bal Gangadhar Tilak, she launched the All India Home Rule League, which declared India's complete independence from British rule as its goal. This was the first time that such a declaration was made. Jawaharlal joined the League and attended a few meetings,[12] but he was too terrified of public speaking to become a politician at this point.[13] He could hardly contain his elation when he was granted an opportunity to speak very briefly and in English at a protest meeting sometime in 1915 against a new act passed by the government muzzling the press. Tej Bahadur Sapru was so happy about his first political speech that he embraced him and kissed him at the dais.[14] Jawaharlal was lucky to have such powerful props throughout his relatively smooth public career.

In February 1916, he married Kamala, aged seventeen, and there was some excitement in his life for a while. She was the eldest daughter of Rajpati and Jawaharmal Mull Atal-Kaul, who belonged to a middle-class Brahmin family. Her father ran a small flour mill in Delhi. There was, however, one snag: Kamala did not know English, and in Motilal's household, English was spoken more often than Hindustani. Motilal had made arrangements for Kamala to be taught English and European etiquette at her natal house in Delhi soon after finalising the match. A few months before marriage, she was brought to Allahabad to stay with her aunt and attend Nehru family functions at Anand Bhavan. Kamala had also taken lessons from the English governess who catered to Jawaharlal's sisters.[15]

Jawaharlal's two sisters did not like Kamala's intrusion in their lives. Vijaya Lakshmi was the same age as Kamala and she slighted her at every opportunity, invoking her lack of sophistication, inability to converse in English, and low social status as a mill-owner's daughter. If Kamala suggested a menu to the butler, it was liable to be shot down on the grounds that the newcomer did not know her brother's tastes. If tickets were to be obtained for an English movie, Kamala would be left out as she would not follow the language. It was unlikely that Jawaharlal was unaware of her meanness towards his wife, but he kept quiet about it. The torment continued till their daughter, Indira, was old enough to protest.[16]

BAPTISM IN POLITICS

Shortly after the wedding, two things happened in Jawaharlal's life that defined his future: the beginning of his political apprenticeship to Gandhi shortly after the Lucknow session of the Congress in 1916 and his close association with Chittaranjan Das, popularly known as C.R. Das, during the Jallianwala Bagh probe in 1919. Mohandas Karamchand Gandhi was still a largely unknown political entity in 1916. A year ago, he had failed to be elected to a committee at the Bombay session of the Congress[17] and had only been nominated as a member courtesy of Sir Satyendra Prasanna Sinha (1863–1928), KCIE, who was the resident of the party.[18]

Bal Gangadhar Tilak (1856–1920) and Muhammad Ali Jinnah (1876–1948) dominated the session, which brought the Moderates and the Extremists in the Congress on the same platform after a decade. Also, for the first time, the Muslim League under Jinnah's leadership and the Congress Party took a few significant resolutions together on Hindu-Muslim unity. Jinnah was also a member of the Congress Party, which was an umbrella organization then. The resolutions, drafted at Anand Bhavan,[19] included one-third representation for Muslims in the central government, separate electorates for all communities unless a community demanded a joint electorate, and a system of 'weightage' for the representation of minority communities. The resolutions stimulated Muslim aspirations in the future, but that was more due to political mismanagement by the Congress leadership.

Jawaharlal observed the whole process keenly, ran errands for the leaders, and made useful contacts. Subsequently, when Annie Besant was arrested in June 1917, he joined the agitations demanding her release, which were launched by the combined leadership of the Congress and the Muslim League. But what brought him some prominence was his relief work in Amritsar after the Jallianwala Bagh massacre on 13 April 1919—this he did under C.R. Das's encouragement. At that point, Das, along with Tilak, had the most powerful hold over the Indian public.[20] And he mainly conducted the probe into the incident instituted by the Congress Party. Motilal managed to have his son assist C.R. Das during the probe. Gandhi was also consulted in the matter because by this time, he had become the main arbiter within the party.

The government, however, believed that Jawaharlal's relief work was more political in nature than it was humanitarian.[21] Jawaharlal collected over one lakh rupees through the Allahabad Seva Samiti, a relief organization, and gathered a group of volunteers to do this work.[22] One result of his enterprise was that he earned Gandhi's accolade for the first time.

In May 1920, Jawaharlal had his first brush with the authorities while staying at the Savoy Hotel in Mussoorie with his mother and his wife, who had gone there to spend a period of convalescence. At that time, Motilal was away from Allahabad representing the government in an important case. While fighting this case, as the defendant's barrister, he was pitted against C.R. Das; to his chagrin, he lost the case.[23] Since an Afghan delegation was also staying at the hotel, Jawaharlal was asked by the district authorities to give an undertaking of safe conduct that he would not meet them or have anything to do with them.

Jawaharlal found it insulting to give such an undertaking, although he had no desire to contact the Afghans. He met the district magistrate in Dehradun, and agreed during their conversation to leave Mussoorie without giving the undertaking. However, back at the hotel, he felt like rebelling against the idea of meekly submitting to the pressure and wrote to the district magistrate, asking him to issue a formal order.[24] The order was duly issued, and he was asked to leave the district within twenty-four hours. Accordingly, he returned to Allahabad, leaving his mother and his wife behind at the hotel.[25]

When Motilal came to know of the incident, he remonstrated against the order of externment in a polite but firm letter that he sent to his friend Sir Harcourt Butler, Lieutenant Governor, on 19 May.[26] Equally politely, Sir Harcourt declined to intervene in a letter dated 26 May. At this, Motilal sent him a formal appeal on 2 June to rescind the order and followed it up with a polite threat on 8 June, which stated that if the order was not withdrawn, Jawaharlal would violate it and the government would have to face the consequences.[27] The threat worked and the ban was lifted by the Lieutenant Governor on 15 June. Around two weeks later, father and son visited Mussoorie and found that the Afghan families had become quite friendly with Swarup Rani and Kamala, and were actually looking after them in his absence.

THE PRATAPGARH EXPERIENCE

Before his second visit to Mussoorie, a momentous incident took place in Jawaharlal's life. It happened in the course of the two weeks when he was staying alone in Allahabad, as his father was away from town. In early June, the peasant leader Baba Ram Chandra (1864–1950) came to the city from a village near Allahabad, called Pratapgarh, in search of senior leaders of the Congress who could help the peasants in their fight against their landowners' misdeeds. He approached Jawaharlal in the absence of any such leader and requested him to visit their village and look into the situation.[28] Initially reluctant to accept the request, Jawaharlal was persuaded to visit the village after a couple of days. This visit had a cathartic effect on him, as for the first time in his entire life he was exposed to a world of poverty, mud and slush that characterized rural India.

The unscrupulous landowners of the Awadh region were forcing poor peasants to offer free labour, arbitrary cesses, and such others. As the peasants had no tenancy rights, they were liable to be evicted at any time, without any notice. The UP Kisan Sabha, which had come into existence in February 1918, was ineffective, as its office-bearers were mostly from the influential sections of society and some of them were landlords themselves.[29]

The condition of Pratapgarh, which was inhabited by proud Kurmis, was particularly precarious because it had less land compared to the neighbouring districts of Allahabad and Jaunpur in the Agra division. Besides, the tillers of Jaunpur and Allahabad could enjoy occupancy rights after cultivating the land for twelve years at a stretch. This provided them some security. The Kurmis of Pratapgarh also had to pay a higher rent than upper-caste tenants.[30] Their economic condition was such that villagers from other districts of the province chose not to marry into their community.

In this scenario, they rallied around their saffron-clad leader, Baba Ram Chandra, a Brahmin man from Maharashtra who was married to a low-caste Kurmi woman. His real name was Shridhar Balwant Jodhpurkar and he had earlier been an indentured worker in Fiji for thirteen years under the assumed name Ram Chandra Rao. There, he fought for the rights of his fellow labourers. He had instructed the peasants of Pratapgarh to stand up for their rights and pay the rent that they owed to the landowners, but not the illegal cesses.³¹ As a result, they had been served notices of eviction a month earlier. Hoping that Gandhi might help, Baba Ram Chandra had led his five hundred followers to Allahabad on foot. Although they came to meet Gandhi, they settled for Motilal Nehru's son instead when they found that neither he nor any other senior leader was available.³²

Jawaharlal was moved by the misery of the villagers. But more than that, he was impressed by the firmness and courage he saw in these men. Soon, peasant agitations spread to Raebareli, Faizabad, Jaunpur and other places in the United Provinces. Jawaharlal concentrated his attention on Pratapgarh and Raebareli districts and not on Allahabad, where there were many Muslim landlords.³³ He did not want to antagonize them at the height of the Khilafat movement in which Gandhi had a big stake.³⁴

Jawaharlal wanted to link the peasants' agitations in the United Provinces to nationalist politics, imitating what C.R. Das was doing in Bengal. But he had no clear idea how to go about this.³⁵ Since he was not seriously moved by the economic wretchedness of these peasants and saw them only as brave men demonstrating exemplary resilience who could be used by the party,³⁶ he could not provide a revolutionary dimension to the movement that could bring about any real change in their condition.³⁷ He was only happy that he was dealing with a situation that was authentically and completely Indian.³⁸ In their turn, the peasants did not rely on the Congress or their own power. But they ultimately appealed to the British government for enacting measures to improve their condition.³⁹

Now, for the first time, Jawaharlal could speak to the common people without his usual inhibition. He was absolutely overwhelmed by their adulation.⁴⁰ This experience was new to him and it perennially bound him to the masses.⁴¹ After this, he tried to hijack the movement from Ram Chandra and went out of the way to belittle him in the eyes of the people. He sought Gauri Shankar Misra's (1888–1955) help in all his endeavours. He was the secretary of the UP Kisan Sabha in addition to being an experienced organizer. Gandhi visited the place in December 1920. Around the same time, the Kisan Congress held a meeting in nearby Faizabad. In spite of drawing people from only a few neighbouring districts, it ended up being a much bigger congregation than the Nagpur Congress held in December 1920.

Jawaharlal and Gauri Shankar Misra asked the peasants to avoid violence of any kind in their agitations and not to seek confrontation with the landlords or the administration. Instead, they suggested that the peasants organize themselves into village *kisan sabha*s (assemblies) and formulate their demands regarding restrictions on eviction and forced labour, fourteen-year leases, the right to pay cesses at customary rates, and the cessation of fines, among others. They could then present these for the consideration of the landlords.[42] Neither Jawaharlal nor the Congress thought of getting the law changed to protect the peasants' interests. But the situation did change partially in favour of the peasants after the Awadh Rent (Amendment) Act was passed in 1921 owing largely to the efforts of Baba Ram Chandra.[43]

The district authorities had expected a tough positioning from Jawaharlal and were surprised at his accommodating stance. When a serious riot broke out at the time of Ram Chandra's arrest in February 1921, Jawaharlal urged the peasants to obey Gandhi, who was in Banaras (now Varanasi) at that time, and asked them to allow the peasant leader to be arrested peacefully.[44] The British officials in the district were so impressed with his approach that they were now keen to see to it that the leadership of the movement remain with Gandhi and Jawaharlal, and not with Ram Chandra and his followers.[45]

Motilal Nehru had joined him in the meantime. He and Jawaharlal now tried to consolidate their influence among the peasants in the area. In a leaflet, Motilal urged them to join the Congress, take up spinning, settle disputes with the help of panchayats instead of the law courts, subscribe to the Swaraj Fund, and promote caste and communal harmony. The leaflet did not mention rent, eviction or any other serious issue. Rather, it instructed the protesting peasants to avoid gathering in districts where public meetings were prohibited.[46] In spite of being rather harmless, the leaflet was proscribed and six young men were jailed for six months for distributing it. No action was, however, taken against the author of the leaflet or against Jawaharlal, who distributed it inside the courtroom. This act of leniency on the part of the government deeply embarrassed Jawaharlal, who was eager to court his first political arrest.[47]

Nonetheless, the agitations helped him build his political image, albeit rather out of proportion, and brought him instant fame. Also, he learned a good deal about ground-level politics: for instance, how to outdo and malign a political competitor with finesse and ruthlessness, even if he were a benefactor to him like Ram Chandra, and how to downplay the contributions of a dedicated companion and resource person like Gauri Shankar Misra. Most significantly, he got rid of his inhibitions around public speaking.[48] Finally, Jawaharlal also realized that he liked to be the centre of attention and was tremendously roused by the adulation of the masses, which acted like a revitalizing tonic for him.[49] Pratapgarh taught him the value of a political image as well as a dedicated following.

5
FATHER, SON, AND THE HOLY GHOST

MEETING THE MAHATMA

Jawaharlal met Mohandas Karamchand Gandhi for the first time during the Lucknow Congress in December 1916,[1] which was presided over by Ambica Charan Mazumdar (1851–1922) from Faridpur, East Bengal (now Bangladesh). Prior to the session, Gandhi's heroic but unsuccessful struggle for the civic rights of immigrant Indians in South Africa[2] had been brought to the public's notice by Gokhale, C.F. Andrews and W.W. Pearson. But when Jawaharlal met Gandhi, he found him to be very different—he seemed distant and, in some ways, even non-political.[3]

He was not alone in misjudging Gandhi at first sight. Most of the delegates did not take any notice of him during the session.[4] Mohandas did not show any interest in Jawaharlal either, even though he was meticulous about his contacts, and Jawaharlal, as Motilal Nehru's son, should have been important to him. One reason could be that Gandhi did not think that this young man with European manners and a clipped British accent could be of any use to him at that time. By his own admission, Jawaharlal had little to recommend him.[5] Even when Jawaharlal was already his favourite in the 1920s, Gandhi did not mention their first meeting in his memoir published serially in *Navjivan* from 1925.

Prior to the Congress session in Lucknow, there were serious efforts to bring the Congress Party and the Muslim League on a common platform to sort out their differences and finalize a scheme of reforms acceptable to both parties so that they could take a united stand on the issue before the government. Annie Besant, Tej Bahadur Sapru, Jinnah and Syed Wajir Hasan (1874–1947) played a major role in the efforts to bring them together to prepare the scheme.[6] Motilal assisted them in every possible way and opened his home to them. Tilak and his dissident group's support was crucial for the success of the scheme. He played his part well and even persuaded the Hindu revivalist leader Madan Mohan Malaviya (1861–1946) to agree to the arrangement.[7] Together with Tilak, Jinnah was hailed as the 'Ambassador of Hindu-Muslim Unity'.[8]

The issue of unity between Hindus and Muslims had been hanging fire since 1888 when Sir Syed Ahmad Khan (1817–1898) had founded the United Indian Patriotic Association, aiming to combat the influence of the Congress.[9] He had propounded a 'two-nation theory' to propose and define the outlines of the idea of a separate Muslim nationhood in the Indian context. He wanted Muslims to side with the British and educate themselves in English to compete with Hindus. His fear was that the pressure of Hindu nationalism would compel the British to create democratic institutions which would lead to a situation where the Muslim minority would be completely dominated by the Hindu majority.[10]

The activities of Swami Dayananda Saraswati (1824–83) and other religious leaders, as well as the founding of the Cow Protection Society in 1882, had distinctly anti-Muslim overtones.[11] These had all fanned Syed Ahmad Khan's fears, although in his early life he had been a staunch supporter of Hindu-Muslim unity. The most significant wedge between the two communities was, however, driven by the intellectual viceroy George Nathaniel Curzon (1859–1925) in October 1905, when he partitioned Bengal. He hated Bengali Hindus and even the fact that the province was quite large, almost the size of France. In spite of his pious pretences, this act was intended to subdue Bengali nationalism.[12] Muslim aspirations and their demand for reservations and a separate electorate in Bengal and other provinces all arose as a natural corollary to these processes. In December 1906, the All

India Muslim League was formed in Dhaka to spearhead Muslim political activity.

Tilak's political outlook had undergone a marked change since 1908. He had realized that a broad-based unity between the two religious communities was essential for achieving *swaraj*, or independence.[13] Jinnah held the same view as well, but swaraj to him was home rule on the Canadian model and not complete independence. He opposed the reservation of seats or a separate electorate for Muslims and advocated a joint national political platform. In 1918, he told the Joint Parliamentary Committee on Constitutional Reforms that Hindus and Muslims should stop thinking of politics in terms of religion and become one political entity.[14]

When Gandhi took control of the Congress and started deciding its political voice, he began to use religion for political purposes. Jinnah opposed his opportunism and had to leave the party, which he had joined long before Gandhi in 1906. Subsequent events proved that it was a mistake not to give him due recognition and grant him his proper place in the national political stage.

Meanwhile, Gandhi kept a low profile at the Lucknow session and confined himself to the South African question. However, he quietly exhibited his own distinctiveness from the other delegates by donning a Gujarati peasant's clothing and moving resolutions in broken Hindustani (he was yet to learn the language well) and not in English as was customary, despite repeated requests from the organizers to do so. His position in the Congress was still tentative. On Gokhale's advice, he had kept away from active politics till February 1916[15] and used the time touring the country, studying the political situation and making connections on a grassroots level. Indeed, he succeeded in making an impact at the session as a politician with a difference.

In February 1916, ten months before the Lucknow Congress, Gandhi made his political debut at the foundation ceremony of the Banaras Hindu University. Madan Mohan Malaviya had invited him to attend the ceremony where Lord Hardinge, the viceroy of India, was to lay the foundation stone. After the viceroy's departure, the Raja of Darbhanga, who presided over the ceremony, requested Gandhi to speak. To Malaviya's utter dismay, he berated the Raja and the other dignitaries for wallowing in luxury and neglecting the poor. He asked them to strip themselves of their resplendent jewellery and hold it in trust for the poor.[16] The Raja and the other guests, including Annie Besant, were aghast at his conduct and left the meeting,[17] but Gandhi's speech was heartily received by the audience.

Indeed, Gandhi had tried to use Rabindranath Tagore's name for launching his political career in India, just as he had used Tolstoy's name in South Africa. For this purpose, he had corresponded with C.F. Andrews and W.W. Pearson, Tagore's close associates from South Africa, about establishing a camp at Santiniketan, a town in Bengal where Tagore had established his ashram and an experimental school, without the poet's full knowledge.[18] Following his plan, his Phoenix family set up camp at Santiniketan in March 1915. He visited the place shortly afterwards and stayed for a week,[19] hoping to make the place his future headquarters. He also tried to change the pattern of work, the sanitary arrangements, and the dietary habits of the members of Tagore's ashram, and the poet indulged him benignly.[20] However, within two months, he faced serious opposition from the ashramites and had to shift his headquarters to Ahmedabad.[21]

Gandhi soon began to have reservations about Bengal, although he wanted to infuse Bengal's pre-1910 political fervour into the Congress's politics. Bengal, together with Maharashtra, used to dominate Indian politics at that time. Gandhi's genius gradually led to a shift in the political balance and North India, particularly Gujarat and the United Provinces, became the new centres of importance. For this purpose, he brought the Nehrus into prominence as the foremost family in India in terms of their dedication, talent and willingness to sacrifice their own interests for the nationalist cause. He made them the symbol of India's struggle for freedom. In those days, it was said that Gandhi could make heroes out of clay. He did so with Jawaharlal in less than a decade.

OF TWO MINDS

Motilal could see that Gandhi was emerging as a major force in Indian politics, but he was in two minds about him till the latter part of 1920, when he decided to throw in his lot with him. Even then, he found it difficult to accept Gandhi's obscurantist ideas that contradicted his long-held progressive beliefs. He was averse to Gandhi's religion-based politics and his idiosyncrasies, eccentric food habits and lifestyle choices. He was unhappy that his son had left his own way of life to follow him. During this period, he often had arguments with Jawaharlal over Gandhi's politics and his way of life, and lost his temper with him and other members of the household on the flimsiest of grounds.[22]

Meanwhile, Gandhi's well-directed Champaran campaign, so very different from the speech-making and petitioning witnessed so far, had deeply impressed Jawaharlal. The core idea was not new; Sikh gurus had used this method against the Mughals in the past and it was recently used with a few variations during the partition of Bengal. But the neo-moral and neo-ethical packaging of Gandhi's movement, which robbed opponents of their legal-moralist justification for counteraction, was indeed a new experiment.

Jawaharlal was ideologically confused during this period. He still entertained his vague extremist inclinations that he had acquired at Cambridge.[23] Simultaneously, he was drawn to Bertrand Russell's humanist ideas.[24] Russell was among the few intellectuals who were not ensnared by the communist ideology that was animating Russia at that time. His influence kept Jawaharlal's thoughts in equilibrium.[25] On the one hand, he was profoundly impressed by Sarojini Naidu's moderate-nationalist speeches,[26] and on the other, the 'wonderful speech' delivered by the militant Irish nationalist Roger David Casement at his trial in 1916 fascinated him.[27] While Casement's speech '...seemed to point out exactly how a member of the subject nation should feel...[28], he remained unmoved by the same sentiments when they were expressed by Indian revolutionaries.

Politics seemed to him to be an '...all-absorbing aggressive nationalist activity against foreign rule...' which '...gave no scope for anything else in life...'[29]; he was uncertain whether he should give up his career in law and embrace the uncertainties of a life in politics. He found it shocking that the older politician Srinivasa Sastri (1869–1946) should advise the audience at a students' gathering in Allahabad that they must always be respectful and obedient to their teachers and observe all the rules and regulations made by the authorities.[30] Be that as it may, Jawaharlal did not clarify what his own advice to the students was. He did not join Gokhale's Servants of India Society because he found its politics 'too moderate',[31] but he did not explain what type of politics he supported. His off-the-cuff innuendos became something of a mannerism for him and they often befuddled the people who had to depend on him for various reasons.[32]

As his restless energy was trying to find some sort of release during this period, he found Gandhi's political ideas to be the most suitable for him to embrace. By 1918, both he and Kamala became Gandhi's disciples. A life of sacrifice and renunciation appealed more particularly to Kamala, who inspired her husband to take it seriously.[33] They put on khadi, took up frugal food habits and led an austere life, though they ignored the prohibition of conjugal sex. Jawaharlal had no faith in this particular taboo and it was never imposed upon the couple.

Motilal found it hard to reconcile to this change in his son. He was particularly sad that Kamala had to suffer because of Jawaharlal's foibles, and that too at such a young age. The change also disturbed the equilibrium that the Nehru household was famous for. Swarup Rani was miserable that the person she loved the most, her son, was deeply disturbed by these newfangled ideas and that serious trouble seemed to be developing between her husband and her son.[34] As it often happens with mothers-in-law, she blamed Kamala for not exerting proper influence on Jawaharlal.[35] In her simplicity, Swarup Rani also failed to understand why the 'Mahatma', whose business was to look after people's spiritual lives, should meddle in politics and family affairs.[36] She considered it ridiculous to fight a powerful government by getting oneself locked up in jail or dying in the struggle.[37] However, when the nineteen-year-old Vijaya Lakshmi eloped with Syud Hossain (1888–1949), Motilal's journalist aide and the editor of *The Independent*, and married him according to Muslim customs, Gandhi intervened and had them terminate their relationship amicably and settle the issue. After this, her attitude towards him changed.

As far as Gandhi was concerned, Motilal was still not sure if Jawaharlal was betting on the right horse. Besides, the colonial state was still powerful. Even Gandhi kowtowed to the English in his own fashion. Motilal was worried that his son's impetuosity would land him in jail and even take him to the gallows.[38] But Jawaharlal was not to be daunted anymore by his father's anger or his solicitude, for he had chosen a path for himself for the first time in his life, and he had done it without his father's help. Kamala had helped him know his own mind and follow his own inclinations, even though he continued to be more comfortable with books and ideas than he was with people.[39]

At this time, Gandhi was looking for some effective means of organizing an all-India movement. In February 1919, the repressive Anarchical and Revolutionary Crimes Bill, popularly known as the Rowlatt Bill, allowed him to do just that. At his instance and under his leadership, five public figures from Gujarat took the 'satyagraha' pledge on 24 February and asked the government to withdraw the Bill in a telegram, failing which '...satyagraha would enforce the dictates of conscience.'[40] Jawaharlal joined the Satyagraha Sabha and became one of the signatories of the Satyagraha vow, formulated by Gandhi, pledging to disobey certain laws passed by the government. He took part in organizing meetings and processions in and around Allahabad and wrote articles against the Bill in *The Independent*, his father's newspaper.[41]

Gandhi was in Madras (now Chennai) when the Bill became an Act on 10 March 1919; he immediately called for a countrywide *hartal* or moral strike on the issue on 30 March (the date was later changed to 6 April). This idea had come to him in a dream.[42] A week afterwards, on 13 April, the Jallianwala Bagh incident in Amritsar—the massacre of innocent and unarmed men, women and children by the military—fundamentally transformed the country's political climate. Gandhi used this situation to emerge as the chief arbiter of the Congress.

He had already acquired Malaviya's support by then and formed a nucleus of strength in the party consisting of Rajendra Prasad (1884–1963), J.B. Kripalani (1888–1982), Chakravarti Rajagopalachari (1878–1972), Vallabhbhai Patel (1875–1950), Ganesh Vasudev Mavalankar (1888–1956), Vinoba Bhave (1895–1982) and Dattatreya Balkrishna Kalelkar (1885–1981), etc. Soon, he established a permanent bridgehead among liberals like Srinivasa Sastri, Tej Bahadur Sapru and Thakkar Bapa (1869–1951). Among his favourite disciples was Jawaharlal, his young Galahad, immensely more urbane, intellectual, articulate, and charming than the rest.

GANDHI AND MOTILAL NEHRU

From the very beginning, Gandhi had his eyes on Motilal Nehru, who was eight years older than him. In December 1919, he made him the president of the Amritsar Congress on Jawaharlal's suggestion. He had gained Gandhi's confidence by now and was in his inner circle. A year earlier, Motilal had found a place on the dais with several big shots of the party at the Bombay Special Congress due to his son's influence. By then, Jawaharlal was actively associated with the UP Congress affairs.[43]

After Amritsar, Gandhi's next plan was to get his noncooperation programme approved at the party's special session in Calcutta in September 1920. For this, he did his homework meticulously and undertook the task of drafting a constitution for the Congress Party with the help of Tilak and C.R. Das, the two stalwarts he wanted to please. He included one representative on the recommendation of each of the two—N.C. Kelkar and I.B. Sen respectively—in the drafting committee. Das and Tilak were to be consulted through correspondence.[44] The party's constitution that was subsequently adopted in Nagpur was practically Gandhi's own draft.[45] This was an important step for him. In his own words, 'With the assumption of this responsibility I may be said to have made my real entrance into the Congress politics.'[46]

Having thus built up his credibility, Gandhi proceeded with the next step. He knew that 'an imposing phalanx of veteran warriors' comprising the likes of Annie Besant, Lala Lajpat Rai, Madan Mohan Malaviya, T. Vijayaraghavacharya, Motilal Nehru, and C.R. Das would be waiting to challenge him in Calcutta.[47] He was also aware that his programme would not be passed if it was not endorsed by Das.[48] He had noticed that Bal Gangadhar Tilak had implicit trust in Das's opinion and often looked up to him for guidance.[49] He therefore used Jawaharlal to win over Motilal Nehru in order to obtain his friend's support for his programme.

According to Chaudhry Khaliquzzaman, Motilal was not easily persuaded and often had heated arguments with his son on the issue. Motilal was '...full of doubts and misgivings...' and Jawaharlal full of '...youthful enthusiasm for fireworks, meetings, processions, hartals and other things associated with Gandhi's movements...' Khaliquzzaman, who was close to both, did his bit to 'soften' Motilal's opposition to Gandhi's programme.[50] Even after Jawaharlal persuaded his father to endorse it, it still hit some rough weather in the form of opposition from C.R. Das, Madan Mohan Malaviya and Annie Besant, all of whom had support from influential people from many provinces.[51]

Gandhi could finally persuade Das to endorse his programme at the Nagpur session in December 1920. In his words:

> Motilalji was the first to join the movement. I still remember the sweet discussion that I had with him on the [non-cooperation] resolution [at Calcutta]. He suggested changes

in the phraseology which I adopted. He undertook to win the Deshbandhu [C.R. Das] for the movement. The Deshbandhu's heart was inclined towards it, but he felt sceptical as to the capacity of the people to carry out the programme. It was only at the Nagpur Congress that he and Lalaji accepted it wholeheartedly.[52]

The Nagpur session was momentous for two other reasons. It saw the rise of Mohandas Karamchand Gandhi and his policy of flexible and religion-based politics that would later pervade India's political, social and economic life and the exit, in humiliation and in tears, of the secular and principled Muhammad Ali Jinnah, who took politics to be a constructive way to improve the condition of the people and whose political goal was for India to attain dominion status, on a par with Canada, Australia and New Zealand.

C.R. Das had doubts whether ordinary people could afford to quit their jobs to participate in the movement which was a major requirement of noncooperation. Personally, he had no hesitation to do so and made an example of himself, as did Motilal Nehru and many others. Gandhi declared happily: '...although law courts may not be completely boycotted, by the sacrifice of Messrs. Nehru and Das...we have successfully demolished the prestige of these institutions.'[53]

Before the beginning of the movement, Gandhi played his cards with a lot of care. The draft instructions were signed by Motilal first, followed by himself, and then by another one of C.R. Das's close friends, Vithalbhai Patel, although he did not like Vithalbhai personally.[54] Likewise, the circular of the programme that was issued to the Home Rule League branches around the same time in September carried his own signature as president as well as the signatures of Jawaharlal and Rajagopalachari as general secretaries. All of this was done in such a way that Motilal, Jawaharlal and Rajagopalachari came to be identified as his closest lieutenants in the public imagination.[55]

ALL FOR ONE, ONE FOR ALL

Gandhi's idea of cooperative functioning and nonviolent resistance came from Leo Tolstoy's writings and correspondence. After the King of Italy was assassinated by an anarchist in 1900, Leo Tolstoy (1828–1910) wrote an open letter to the anarchists. There, he denounced violence stating that it was morally wrong and politically of little use. On the contrary, the proper method to paralyze an oppressive government was to refuse taxes, resign from all services, and boycott institutions supporting the government.

Gandhi came to know about Tolstoy's idea in London in 1909 from the latter's 413-page manuscript, *Letter to a Hindu*, sent to the Indian revolutionary, Taraknath Das (1884–1958), in the USA in response to his appeal to publicize British tyranny in India.[56] Gandhi was so taken with Tolstoy's idea of passive resistance that he had the manuscript printed forthwith with the help of a friend and publicized it. He wrote to Tolstoy praising his ideas and a correspondence ensued between them. Later, in South Africa, he named his headquarters 'Tolstoy Farm' after the great author.

In January 1915, while returning to India from South Africa, Gandhi stayed in London for some time and pledged his services to the British government in the ongoing war. His action dismayed his followers and he received a strong statement of protest from Henry Polak, his foremost disciple in South Africa, via cable.[57] This was not new. Gandhi had also supported the British government during the Boer and the Zulu Wars, where African indigenous people fought the colonial government for their rights. He had subsequently tried to justify his action in both cases by saying that he wanted to '...acquire the capacity and fitness for resisting the violence of war.'[58] Indeed, he avoided speaking of India's freedom till he was pressured by younger leaders like Subhas Chandra Bose and Jawaharlal to do so in 1923. Like Hitler, Gandhi had an innate affinity for the English.

The period from 1919 to 1926 constituted a formative stage in Jawaharlal's political career. He came to know from Bertrand

Russell's *Roads to Freedom* about the disturbing influence of money, militarism, and bureaucracy in Western democracies, but in his incomplete review of the book, he also recognized the following:

> ...orthodox socialism does not give us much hope. The war has shown that an all-powerful state is no lover of individual liberty. It is the breeding ground for the bureaucrat, who, in the West as in the East, is most intolerant of criticism and is seldom enamoured of progress. Life under Socialism would be a joyless and soulless thing, regulated to the minutest detail by rules and orders framed by the all-powerful Cortes.[59]

He would modify his views as his career progressed.

In 1920, Jawaharlal deputized for his father in the Working Committee when he was occupied. Motilal was the president and often busy with professional commitments. He assisted him again in 1921–22 when Motilal was the general secretary. Gandhi extolled Motilal's performance during both the tenures, which was, in effect, an expression of appreciation for Jawaharlal's performance. When both of them were arrested in December 1921 during the noncooperation movement, Gandhi highlighted their arrest and that of two of Jawaharlal's cousins in *Young India*,[60] ignoring a host of others who suffered a much worse fate for the same cause. He published the full text of the message that Jawaharlal issued soon after his arrest. Drafted on the model of Roger Casement's speech prior to his arrest, it became a manifesto of a sort for the educated youth of India.[61]

Jawaharlal's position within the party improved further between 1922 and 1925. He now began to assume a posture of independence and kept a discreet distance from Rajagopalachari, Vallabhbhai Patel and Rajendra Prasad, whom he considered backward. He used this to project a progressive image of himself. His growing maturity as a politician became evident when he refrained from exhibiting his disappointment openly when Gandhi abruptly suspended the noncooperation movement in February

1922. Both Jawaharlal and Motilal were in prison then. Unlike Jawaharlal, Motilal wrote a strongly worded letter of protest to Gandhi,[62] but Jawaharlal discussed the issue with him at Sabarmati Central Jail in private soon after his release and earned both his affection and his goodwill.

Subsequently, he kept his cool during a period of infighting within the party that started on the issue of entering the councils. C.R. Das, Motilal Nehru, Hakim Ajmal Khan and a few others were in favour of taking part in the elections to prevent the Moderates from capturing too many seats and to obstruct the functioning of the councils from the inside. They were aiming to pressure the British to grant India dominion status. In December 1921, they had lost a chance to get dominion status owing to Gandhi's obduracy and dilatoriness. At that point, Viceroy Reading had expressed his readiness to Madan Mohan Malaviya—and through him to C.R. Das—to discuss the issue at a Round Table Conference if the Congress agreed to call off its proposed boycott of an impending visit of the Prince of Wales.[63]

Gandhi was not prepared for electoral politics yet. So, he opposed Das's move for council entry, as did his Khilafat partners who were also not sure of their electoral might in Bengal and other provinces. Therefore, he took a stand that their entry into the council would compromise the principle of noncooperation and negatively impact this more honest approach to politics. Personally, Jawaharlal was not averse to Das's idea, for this method had been successfully practised by the Sinn Fein in Ireland. In fact, he had discussed the idea with his mentor in the summer of 1920. Gandhi had then avoided the issue on the grounds that the Indian masses would not understand it as much as they would a direct call for boycotting the polls. It would seem that at that time Gandhi was trying to find ways to take his own political career forward and thus did not want to rock the boat.

To Jawaharlal, it was really immaterial what others thought, as ultimately Gandhi's view was bound to prevail. So, he stood by his mentor; he made himself useful to the party as much as he could and maintained a low profile vis-à-vis both the 'Pro-Changers' led by Das and his father and the 'No-Changers', i.e., those who, like Rajagopalachari, Rajendra Prasad and Vallabhbhai Patel, were dogmatic in their stand against participation in the electoral process. It was like walking on a tightrope for him, but he performed well.

In December 1922, both groups fought over the future of Congress policies at the Gaya session held under C.R. Das's presidency. On one side there were C.R. Das, Motilal, Vithalbhai Patel, Hakim Ajmal Khan, N.C. Kelkar, M. R. Jayakar and other bigwigs, while on the other side, there were staunch Gandhians led by Rajagopalachari as well as Khilafat Muslims. Gandhi was imprisoned in Poona then. While the first group with all its formidable names was confident about its success, the second group took care to covertly consolidate their vote bank among the six thousand delegates. Therefore, upsetting all prognoses, the No-Changers' viewpoint prevailed at the session.

C.R. Das tendered his resignation after the Gaya Congress but was persuaded to withdraw it. Consequently, he and his associates met separately in Gaya and decided to launch a new parliamentary party within the Congress called the Congress Khilafat Swarajya Party, or simply the Swaraj Party, with C.R. Das as president and Motilal Nehru as secretary. The party was formally launched in January 1923. Das visited Bombay and Poona to broaden its base. Jinnah supported the move actively, as did many others.

Soon, the Swaraj Party eclipsed the Congress in terms of both its profile and its various activities. Das had learned his lesson from the debacle in Gaya and was now careful about electoral success. The Swaraj Party won the council elections and occupied all important administrative positions. As Jawaharlal mentioned in his autobiography, people were led to believe that this was the real Congress and that Gandhi was no longer in the driver's seat.[64] To many like Swami Sahajanand Saraswati (1889–1950), a radical peasant leader, 'It had become clear that peace in the Congress was contingent on the victory of one party and that had to be the party of C.R. Das.'[65] A special session of the Congress was held in Delhi on 15–16 September 1923 to settle the issue of council entry. Maulana Azad, who was presiding over the session, supported the proposal for council entry. At this point, Gandhi came up with his formula for a compromise. It was decided that Congressmen would participate in the elections and enter the council in the name of the Swaraj Party but not under the banner of the Congress.[66]

However, intra-party differences did not end there. Sahajanand has written about an incident that took place at the All India Congress Committee (AICC) meeting held in Ahmedabad in June 1924. The meeting was on the Gopinath Saha issue. He wrote:

> I was a member of the AICC [from Ghazipur] and attended that meeting. The scene I witnessed there is unforgettable. Shri Gopinath Saha, a prominent young revolutionary of Bengal, had recently been hanged. In the face of Gandhiji's strong views on violence, Das Sahab introduced a resolution praising not Gopinath's violence but his noble goal. The issue aroused a heated debate and, in the end, when the voting took place, the resolution failed. Maulana Muhammad [Mohammad] Ali was presiding at the session. The vote led to Deshbandhu, Pandit Motilal Nehru and a large number of their supporters to walk out of the Committee proceedings.
> At this Gandhiji became nervous and asked for a count of those who had staged the walk out and those who had remained and it was found that the numbers were almost even. Indeed, the difference between the two groups was very small. On seeing this Gandhiji called Das Sahab and the others back, offered to have the resolution placed before the Committee a second time, but this time it was adopted! At this Gandhiji was deeply offended.[67]

This was a period of euphoria for the Swaraj Party. Then, Evelyn Roy, a communist and M.N. Roy's wife, sounded the death knell for Gandhian politics in India in her article captioned

'Politics in Gaya', published in the *Communist International*. Its imminent demise, she said, had symbolically begun at a place where Hindus offered *pinda* or ceremonial balls of rice to the spirits of their dead ancestors. She averred that the Left represented by C.R. Das and the liberal intellectuals had joined forces with the rightists within the Congress, to create a state of 'responsible cooperation' that was going to dominate Indian politics from then.[68] M.N. Roy, the Comintern leader, also welcomed the development.

Many of Gandhi's adherents, including Jawaharlal, enjoyed the fruits of the elections and occupied positions of power. In Jawaharlal's words:

> It so happened that year [1923] that leading Congressmen all over the country became presidents of municipalities. Mr. C.R. Das became the first Mayor of Calcutta, Mr. Vithalbhai Patel the President of Bombay Corporation, Sardar Vallabhbhai Patel of Ahmedabad. In the United Provinces most of the big municipalities had Congressmen for their chairman. Municipal work in all its varied forms began to interest me. Some of its problems fascinated me. I studied the subject and developed ambitious notions of municipal reform.[69]

In 1925, he became chairman of Allahabad Municipality.

However, he found very soon that the job was difficult, tedious and unattractive.[70] He spent the summer in the cool hills of Dalhousie and Chamba in the Himalayas, with his father and the rest of his family. It was here that they received a telegram that gave them the news of C.R. Das's death.[71] Jawaharlal discovered that he preferred political work to administrative work[72] and he left his municipal responsibilities in early 1927 to visit Europe to attend to his ailing wife and meet his political friends.

Meanwhile, his career graph in the Congress secretariat continued to rise. In early 1923, Dr Mukhtar Ahmed Ansari (1880–1936), whom Jawaharlal knew from his London days, became the acting president following Das's resignation. Jawaharlal was chosen as one of the secretaries.[73] Shortly afterwards, in December 1923, the Khilafat leader Maulana Mohammad Ali, a close family friend, was elected the president at the Coconada (now Kakinada) session. He made Jawaharlal the party's all-India general secretary.[74] Jawaharlal retained this position when Ali left the party the same month and Maulana Abul Kalam Azad (1888–1958) took over as the youngest president in the history of the Congress. He was chosen again as the working general secretary when Gandhi assumed the mantle at Belgaum in December 1924. This practice continued intermittently for the next two decades. This way, he and the party came to be inextricably bonded with one another.[75]

From the very beginning, many party stalwarts resented Gandhi's intimacy with the Nehrus. Some of them, like Madan Mohan Malaviya, N.C. Kelkar, Chakravarti Rajagopalachari, Rajendra Prasad and even M.R. Jayakar, who were offended by Motilal's haughty behaviour, did not conceal their disappointment in this. Pattabhi Sitaramayya (1880–1959), one of those wronged, asked Gandhi sarcastically in a letter whether he had '...emerged out of his seclusion after three years because of his lingering love for Motilal.' Not to be outdone, Gandhi replied that it was not only his 'lingering love' but his 'burning love' for him that prompted him to stand by Motilal.[76]

To the conservative elements in the party, Jawaharlal's 'leftism' and radical utterances were detrimental to Gandhism. Gandhi was, however, impervious to their criticism. In humorous despair, Srinivasa Iyenger (1874–1941), who disliked Motilal's arrogance and Jawaharlal's egotism, called the trio 'the father, the son and the holy ghost.'[77] The sobriquet stuck with the party's hierarchy.[78]

In July 1924, a newspaper clipping from *The Leader* was brought to Gandhi's notice. It contained a juicy account of Motilal having 'rich wines' at a dinner party in Simla (now Shimla) hosted by Tulsi Charan Goswami (1898–1957), a wealthy Swaraj Party leader from Bengal. The dinner was attended, among others, by M.R. Jayakar who had also partaken of the drink. Motilal suspected that Vithalbhai Patel had this 'sensational' story leaked to the press by one of his cronies. The proprietor of the newspaper published from Allahabad was C.Y. Chintamani, once Motilal's close liberal associate and now his staunch adversary.[79]

As expected, Gandhi vehemently reacted to Motilal's 'return to wine drinking' and wrote to him on 3 July: '...I cannot but be grieved that you, who lead the anti-liquor campaign, should publicly drink it and, what is worse, chaff at teetotalism.'[80] Motilal was not a person to keep quiet when his dignity was hurt. He took C.R. Das and M.R. Jayakar into confidence and sent off a strong reply to Gandhi. Admitting that he had drunk wine at the dinner party, he stated that he differed from him ideologically on several counts. He wrote:

> .....I have made clear to you from time to time, that my agreement with you on several items of your programme is not based on the identical grounds upon which you rely and, if I have come to the same conclusions, as you have, it is purely on political or economic and sometimes also moral grounds, having no reference whatever to the religious beliefs of any section of the Congress... I have so far never taken any active part in the anti-drink campaign, but when it was begun by others in right earnest at your bidding, I felt it was only right for me who was in the general movement to give up even the harmless stimulant I had allowed myself after the day's hard work for years past.[81]

To men like M.R. Jayakar, the matter was trivial, but not so for Gandhi, to whom abstinence from drinking was an article of faith and a question of ethics. The matter was made worse by Gandhi's envious inner circle. Later, M.R. Jayakar wrote in his memoir that Motilal was very upset about this vindictive behaviour on the part of his colleagues and made it an issue at Coconada where he said that he had chanced upon a party of 'No-Changers' (he did not mention names) drinking in private. However, he was not going to drink and admit to having double standards. Instead he might not like to observe strict abstinence in future and be weighed in such stoic scales. He sent the newspaper clipping containing his remarks to Gandhi and wrote: 'I would have the world judge me as I am and not as others would wish me to appear.'[82] Gandhi did not pursue the matter further.

At this time, two other issues caused friction between the two leaders, one of which had to do with a very personal family matter, namely Jawaharlal's daughter Indira's education. Motilal was of the opinion that his granddaughter should be sent to a school and not taught by private tutors at home because she should have company of children of her own age at school. His own experience with his son's schooling probably influenced his judgement. He had a reputed convent school in Allahabad in mind. Jawaharlal did not agree with his father in his choice of a school for his daughter, but Motilal overrode his objection. Someone reported this to Gandhi and he took umbrage at Motilal's 'autocratic' mindset and his preference for 'government-sponsored' education. The matter ended there for the time being, but Motilal had a hard time disabusing Gandhi's mind of this impression.

The second issue was more serious and fell in the public domain. Motilal often joked with his friends that Gandhi's extreme attitude was quite likely to drive him and many others to discard khadi despite their faith in it as a political programme. He took care not to say this in Jawaharlal's presence, but their detractors blew it out of proportion before Gandhi. Motilal had to write a long letter to pacify him.[83] This time too, Jawaharlal brought them close together, for he knew the value of both the men for his own political career.

CONTROLLING THE POLITICS OF SWARAJ

In the years 1926–29, Motilal Nehru relentlessly pursued the goal of having his son at the helm of the Congress. C.R. Das's premature death in June 1925 had made him the boss of the Swaraj Party. No two people could be more apart in ideology, temperament and demeanour as were Motilal Nehru and C.R. Das, yet there was a deep and abiding bond between them.[84] Das was a revolutionary visionary, a poet and an affectionate leader,[85] whereas Motilal was a no-holds-barred achiever and an overridingly doting parent. In the absence of Das's restraining influence on him, he became a freewheeler in politics.

Soon after Das's death, many of his pet projects, like the Hindu-Muslim Pact in Bengal, council obstruction and the escalation of the movement to achieve dominion status, were discarded.[86] In February 1926, the Swaraj Party modified its stance from strict obstruction of council activity to responsive cooperation with the government. Motilal felt that this would help them get concessions, like the revision of the Government of India Act of 1919 and getting the colonial government to hold a Round Table Conference with a view to framing a scheme for the rights and interests of the minorities and for securing the enactment of a statute in Parliament on this basis. He argued that the Swarajists had, after all, been striving to get these very concessions in the past. The demand for swaraj was put on the backburner.

Motilal's direction was welcomed in some quarters, but the government's attitude remained lukewarm. The bulk of the party leaders were happy, as this might entitle them to government perks.[87] This change in the party's policy orientation allowed Motilal to maintain cordial relations with Indian business groups and openly seek financial support for the party from them on a quid pro quo basis. He was particularly friendly with Ratanji Dadabhoy Tata (1856–1926), who collected funds for the party, Sir Purshotamdas Thakurdas (1879–1961), Gandhi's sponsor, and Sir Dinshaw Maneckji Petit (1873–1933), Jinnah's estranged father-in-law.[88] Unlike his son, Motilal favoured private property, private enterprise, and the entry of foreign capital in the Indian market. When Vithalbhai Patel demanded the nationalization of the nascent steel industry in India at a debate on the issue in the central legislature, he vehemently opposed him.[89] In the party circles he ridiculed socialists and communists.[90] When issues like granting protection to Indian industrialists from imports were hotly debated in the legislature, non-official members, including Congressmen, were anxious to protect the interests of Indian capitalists while official members stood for British interests.[91]

In fact, the position of British monopoly capitalists in India had begun to show signs of weakening during World War I and immediately after it. However, they were able to regain their old position during the period 1923–27. In the years 1926–27, British capital investment in India amounted to 474.9 million pounds, which increased to 1,000 million pounds in 1928–29.[92] British capitalists could also control vast sectors of the economy, industries and commerce worth many times their capital investment by managing their own agencies and systems. Likewise, they exercised wide control over banking and foreign trade. To top it all, their influence in the central and provincial governments allowed them to establish control over irrigation and plantations to serve their own business interests.[93]

On the other hand, Indian capitalists were also growing powerful. In 1923, there were 5,144 factories in India, which increased to 7,515 by 1927. Some of them were Indian-owned and the others were British.[94] It was only natural that Indian capitalists would endeavour to change the proportion in their favour while the British would try to hold sway over the industrial sector in general. In this competition, the government invariably adopted a pro-British stance while Indian capitalists overtly or covertly sought the help of indigenous political parties, chiefly the Congress and the Swaraj Party, to fight for their interests.[95]

In this scenario, the government decided to fix the parity ratio of the pound to the rupee at 13.5 rupees per pound instead of the prevailing rate of 15 rupees per pound.[96] There was a strong reaction from Indian industrialists and entrepreneurs against the move. The Congress and the Moderates opposed this move both inside and outside the central legislature. Likewise, issues like the protection of the steel industry came up in relation to this.[97] It was, therefore, expedient for the Indian industrial and business houses to give financial and logistical support to the

Congress and the Swaraj Party for them to organize political activities so that they could acquire administrative and legislative power by getting dominion status even if full independence was not attained.

One outcome of Motilal Nehru's induction into the government was that he was consulted about the appointment of an Indian member in the Taxation Committee. On his recommendation, Hridaynath Kunzru, a fellow Kashmiri and a member of Gokhale's Servants of India Society, was appointed to the post. He bragged about it to his son, but shortly afterwards, he had to eat humble pie when the Congress high command came to know about it.[98]

The same thing happened within a year when he accepted an offer of membership in the Indian Sandhurst Committee, popularly known as the Skeen Committee after its chairman, Lieutenant General Sir Andrew Skeen, Chief of the General Staff in India. In June 1925, the Government of India appointed this committee to select Indian officers for training in a military college to be established for the purpose. Jinnah was also appointed as one of the twelve Indian members of the committee. Motilal was scathingly criticized both inside and outside the party for cooperating with the government and had to resign from his post.

Meanwhile, Gandhi had been waiting to win Motilal fully to his fold. On the eve of the Belgaum Congress in December 1924, when C.R. Das had been calling the shots, Gandhi had taken Motilal's help to make a secret pact with him—known as the Belgaum Pact—to become the Congress president unopposed.[99] At that time, his leadership was under serious threat in the party and he had to take this measure to maintain his hold over it. Gandhi's condition for the pact was that when he became the president of Congress, the Swarajists would have to act under their own banner, outside the Congress. In return for this accommodation, he would allow the Swarajists to take over any province of their choice.[100] The Belgaum Pact had accordingly been signed between Gandhi on one side and Das and Motilal on the other; eventually, both parties kept their side of the agreement.

However, a month after C.R. Das's death, Gandhi announced his intention to abolish his spinning franchise and resign his presidency of the Congress at the general council meeting of the Swaraj Party in July 1925. A few days before this declaration, he had absolved Motilal of the conditions of the Belgaum Pact in a letter dated 19 July. On 22 September 1925, he withdrew all his earlier restrictions on the party at the AICC meeting in Patna under 'the altered circumstances', and announced that the Congress would henceforth be 'a predominantly political body',[101] i.e., it could now take part in electoral politics. He managed the whole thing in such a way that his actions were widely eulogized as a supreme example of self-abnegation.

After a few months, the Swaraj Party officially became a part of the main party. Motilal Nehru enthusiastically took part in the elections in the United Provinces that followed, but he lost his seat due to intra-party squabbles and covert propaganda that he was a beef-eater.[102]

6
PRESIDENCY FOR JAWAHARLAL

MOTILAL'S PLEA TO GANDHI

In 1926, Motilal was sixty-five years old and suffering from chronic asthma, eczema and exhaustion from overwork. Also, the heavy burden of his family, his dwindling income, his anxiety about his son, his daughter-in-law's illness, his wife's continuing sickness, his daughters' caprices, his political adversaries' tirades, and the persistent requirement for subordinating his ego to Gandhi took a further toll on him. He could feel that his life was ebbing away. So, he was desperate to fulfil his most cherished wish of seeing his son as the president of the Congress and the successor to Mohandas Karamchand Gandhi.

Maulana Azad's ascent within the party hierarchy worried him. Only a year older than Jawaharlal, he had already made his mark as party president three years ago. Another younger competitor Subhas Chandra Bose (1897–1945?), who had left the much-coveted ICS to join politics, was rapidly growing in popularity. Bose had already earned Gandhi's accolade for his organizational prowess and proficiency in Hindustani. Then there were Chakravarti Rajagopalachari and Vallabhbhai Patel—trusted aides to Gandhi—who had the support of the majority of the conservative members of the party. Any one of them was capable of upsetting the apple cart and giving Gandhi the choice of leadership.

In 1926, Motilal pleaded with Gandhi to make Jawaharlal president of the party without any further delay, but his request was ignored and the office was given to Srinivasa Iyengar (1874–1941), former Advocate General of the Madras Presidency and a veteran leader of the party. The next year, Motilal made the same request again, but this time more beseechingly. Jawaharlal was aware of this. He tested the waters by broaching the subject with Gandhi in a letter from Europe in April 1927, saying that it would be better if he were not chosen for the post this time.[1] Gandhi agreed with him. He then took a dig at Motilal in his letter to him on 14 May: 'You are living for your children. I envy you. The idea of Jawaharlal presiding has an irresistible appeal for me. But I wonder whether it would be proper in the present atmosphere to saddle the responsibility upon him.'[2] When Motilal persisted, he avoided the issue by saying that he had discussed the matter with the incumbent president and was of the view that under the prevalent circumstances, Dr Ansari would be the best choice for the office.[3] In the same letter, he said that he would write to Jawaharlal about it.[4] Accordingly, in a letter to his protégé from Nandi Hills in Mysore on 25 May 1927, he mentioned that he knew that even during difficult circumstances, Jawaharlal might unselfishly consent to put on the crown. However, he did not see the way so clearly as to put the crown on him and plead with him to wear it at that point.[5]

Gandhi knew very well that sooner or later, he would have to choose a successor from the younger generation and no one was closer to his heart than Jawaharlal. Two years ago, in his concluding speech in Belgaum, he had said the following about his general secretary: 'I say to Jawaharlal, "You are my son." What work can Panditji [Motilal Nehru] give him? I call him my son to take work from him. Who am I to venerate him? The world will venerate him, shower flowers on him.'[6] Gandhi never praised any young leader in such superlative terms before or after this. Jawaharlal had wept like a child when his mentor had said this in Belgaum.[7]

Gandhi expected his protégé to understand his predicament and have patience. The presidential election was an important issue now. Sarojini Naidu (1879–1949), a close friend of Jinnah's, suggested Motilal's name to Gandhi for the post. Motilal suspected that Jinnah was using her to supersede Ansari and Jawaharlal's claim to the president's post. Jinnah was obviously concerned about the selection of the next Congress president because the next two or three years would be critical for the Hindu-Muslim question, and he considered Ansari's outlook on the issue to be too rigid.[8] Jinnah had once told M.R. Jayakar that if Madan Mohan Malaviya, Lala Lajpat Rai and Motilal Nehru joined hands with him, he could solve the Hindu-Muslim issue.[9] He did not consider Jawaharlal with any seriousness at this stage.

Gandhi did not accept Sarojini Naidu's suggestion. He informed Motilal on 2 July 1927 that Ansari was the only possible option for the post of president. On 26 August, he said that he would watch the barometer closely but was not inclined at that point to favour Jawaharlal's election to the post. In his turn, Jawaharlal left the matter to Gandhi,[10] but, from every indication, he did not take kindly to his mentor's stand. As such, he returned to India from Europe in December as a rebel.

MADRAS CONGRESS

During his visit to Europe in 1926–27, Jawaharlal's political ideology underwent a substantial change under the influence of the radical thinker and activist Virendranath Chattopadhyaya (1880–1937), aka Chatto. He began to have doubts about Gandhi's politics. Virendranath was Sarojini Naidu's younger brother and a covert Soviet agent. Jawaharlal's frequent association with Chatto in Berlin at that time might have been an influencing factor in his attending the Soviet-inspired Congress of Oppressed Nationalities in Brussels in February 1927 as an official delegate from his party.[11] He also became a member of the executive committee of the League Against Imperialism (LAI), formed during this congress.

Later, in November 1927, Chatto organized a luxurious four-day tour of Moscow for the Nehrus with the clandestine help of the Comintern and the Berlin Communist Party. The Nehrus came down from Berlin and during the tour, Jawaharlal received lavish attention from senior Soviet leaders and was briefed by M.N. Roy. What happened behind the scenes during this visit to Moscow is not known, but Jawaharlal returned to India a confirmed socialist and an admirer of the USSR.

Earlier in Berlin and Brussels, Jawaharlal had come in close contact with A.C.N. Nambiar (1896–1986), a leftwing journalist and Chatto's brother-in-law, who the MI5 believed was a Soviet spy.[12] Nambiar ingratiated himself with Jawaharlal, who affectionately called him Nanu and offered financial support to him throughout his life. When Subhas Chandra Bose came to Europe on exile in the early thirties, Jawaharlal introduced Nambiar to him.[13] Nambiar would later play an important part as Bose's deputy at the Free India Centre in Berlin during World War II.

Returning from Europe in December 1927, Jawaharlal attended the Madras session, presided over by Dr Ansari, and proposed several resolutions based on his new ideas which went against the party's thinking. In the process, he secured the passage of a resolution on the goal of complete independence, which was a big hit with the people at large. The session was attended by Philip Spratt, an emissary of the Communist Party of Great Britain (CPGB), and the delegates of the Communist Party of India (CPI), who took part in the deliberations of the Subjects Committee and in drafting Jawaharlal's resolution on independence.[14]

The communists were apprehending a British offensive against the USSR at that time. So, Jawaharlal made a strong plea in his resolution against India helping the British war effort. Gandhi did not attend the session, but his followers removed the portions of the resolution that called for the complete control of defence, finance, economic and foreign policy, and the immediate withdrawal of the 'British army of occupation'. In effect, all that was accepted in the resolution was a general admission of the goal of independence. But even this was not incorporated in the party's constitution, which still proclaimed swaraj or dominion status as its goal.

However, the new president, Dr Ansari, retained Jawaharlal as one of the three general secretaries of the party. He also brought back Subhas Chandra Bose from a state of political obscurity following his prolonged incarceration in Mandalay, and Shuaib Qureshi, a low-profile Muslim leader and businessman from Maharashtra, for them to become the two other general secretaries.

Jawaharlal was happy when Annie Besant and the youngsters in the party (Gandhi called them 'mischief-makers and hooligans'[15]) supported him during the session, although he must have realized that he was just being humoured by his diehard Gandhian colleagues. During his stay in Madras, he presided over the first (and last) Republican Conference, though shortly afterwards he regretted having done so without knowing who were behind this conference.[16] Also, his euphoria after the Madras session was short-lived because Gandhi criticized the resolution on independence in *Young India* and remarked, 'We have almost sunk to the schoolboy's debating society.'[17]

This time, Jawaharlal protested. With his newfound courage, he sent a strongly worded letter to Gandhi. According to J.B. Kripalani (1888–1982), office secretary, the letter '...was couched in such discourteous and strong language that Gandhiji immediately destroyed it and a copy of that letter is not available anywhere.'[18] Gandhi sent a brief reply to the letter on 4 January 1928, cautioning Jawaharlal that he was 'going too fast' and that his 'plunging into the "republican army"' was 'a hasty step.'[19] He called the resolution on independence a 'tragedy'.[20] The old guard echoed the same views.[21] At this, Jawaharlal bluntly wrote back criticizing Gandhi's leadership as hesitant and ineffective, and disavowing his faith in many of his programmes that he felt were stifling him. Gandhi then offered to make their differences public and invited him to write a letter to him narrating what he thought their differences were so that he could publish them with his brief rejoinder in *Young India*. He also asked him to choose his own path if he felt this way.[22]

By this time, Jawaharlal had come to his senses. Even at thirty-eight, his political career depended on Gandhi despite his soaring popularity among the masses. Also, he had neither the ability nor the inclination to build a new party and fight for his cause. Besides, he was emotionally too attached to and dependent on Gandhi to want to break with him at this stage. So, he gave the whole thing an emotional touch and begged for Gandhi's forgiveness as his 'truant and errant child' in a letter, mentioning in it his father's ill heath and 'approaching end' which, he knew, would appeal to Gandhi.[23] Thereafter, he swept this unsavoury episode under the carpet and did not cross the line till he was able enough to do so a decade later. In his autography published nine years later, Jawaharlal painted a different picture of this episode. He wrote,

> I do not know how far the resolutions I put before the Congress met with his [Gandhi's] approval. I am inclined to think that he [Gandhi] disliked them, not so much because of what they said, but because of their general trend and outlook. He did not, however, criticize them on any occasion.[24]

ALL PARTIES CONFERENCE

One major decision taken at the Madras session, apart from the proposed boycott of the Simon Commission, was to organize an All Parties Conference for the purpose of drawing up a 'Constitution of India' acceptable to the principal political parties. This was in response to the challenge posed by Lord Birkenhead (Frederick Edwin Smith), Secretary of State for India, in the House of Lords in 1925.[25] He had challenged Indian leaders to '...produce a constitution which carries behind it a fair measure of general agreement among the great people of India...'[26] '...of whom we are the responsible guardians.'[27] Birkenhead had said:

> To talk of India as an entity is as absurd as to talk of Europe as an entity. Yet the very nationalist spirit which has created

most of our difficulties in the last few years is based on aspirations and claims of a nationalist India. There has never been such a nation. If we withdraw from India tomorrow, the immediate consequences will be a struggle a *outrance*... between the Muslim and Hindu population.[28]

It was also decided at this session that they would boycott the Indian Statutory Commission, commonly known as the Simon Commission, which had been appointed in November 1927 by the British Conservative government under Stanley Baldwin. It was tasked to report on the working of the Indian constitution established by the Government of India Act of 1919. The commission consisted of seven Members of Parliament—two Conservatives, two Labourites and one Liberal—under the joint chairmanship of the Liberal lawyer, Sir John Simon, and the Labour leader, Clement Attlee. Since no Indian member was included in the Commission, both the Congress and the Muslim League under Jinnah decided to boycott it, as did other parties.

For drafting a constitution acceptable to all political parties and groups, the Congress Party organized an All Parties Conference in Bombay chaired by Dr Ansari, which appointed a committee under the leadership of Motilal Nehru to draft such a constitution with dominion status as the ultimate goal.[29] The eminent jurist Sir Tej Bahadur Sapru was a member of the committee.[30]

In those days, British dominions enjoyed only de facto, and not de jure, independence. The Statute of Westminster, which gave the dominions the right to secede from the British Commonwealth, came into force later in 1931.[31] Though not a member of the committee, Jawaharlal became deeply involved in its secretarial work as his father's aide and also as one of the secretaries of the Congress.[32] Gandhi also roped Subhas Chandra Bose in to work on the project closely with Jawaharlal. He did this largely to do away with his opposition to his scheme.

However, when the All Parties Conference was in session in Lucknow in August 1928, a group of young nationalists staged a protest against the proposed dominion status mentioned in the committee's recommendation, disregarding the Madras resolution, although they welcomed the settlement of the communal question.[33] Jawaharlal and Subhas Chandra Bose persuaded them to withdraw their protest, while they also supported their viewpoint.[34] Together, they formed a pressure group in the party styled the Independence for India League (IIL), with Srinivasa Iyenger as president and Bose and Jawaharlal as secretaries. They aimed to carry out a struggle for achieving complete independence for India. Unknown to Bose and Iyenger, Jawaharlal also had the inspiration of his radical friends from the Berlin-based LAI in his mind as he orchestrated this move.

The proposed constitution had another snag: it enshrined the idea of private property and ownership rights, which ran counter to the socialist ideology.[35] Under pressure from the radicals, Jawaharlal made a half-hearted attempt to resign from his post as the general secretary of the Congress Party (Bose had already resigned from his post on these grounds, on his own). However, the Working Committee did not accept his resignation and allowed him to associate with the LAI on account of the fact that its goals did not fundamentally conflict with the party's policy.[36] Jawaharlal persuaded Bose also to withdraw his resignation.[37]

During this period, Jawaharlal developed a good working relationship with Subhas Chandra Bose despite Chatto's advice to beware of 'reactionaries' like him.[38] The Comintern had already assessed Bose as a 'reactionary',[39] although the latter had welcomed the bold socialist stand taken at the Madras session as a 'definite orientation towards the Left'[40] and the 'logical fulfilment of a process going on within the Congress for a long time.'[41] This was because the kind of nationalist politics with a socialist orientation ('democratic socialism', in their parlance) that Bose espoused was likely to thwart the spread of Moscow-inspired communism in India.

Meanwhile, Gandhi was desperate to ensure a smooth passage for the Nehru Report, as the All Parties Committee Report was popularly known, at the Calcutta session in December 1928. Three aspects were to be considered by the committee: first, the relations between India and Britain, second, the ratio of the representation of different religious and caste communities in the new set-up, and finally, the relations between the centre and the provinces. While a temporary settlement was arrived at on the first issue, there could be no agreement on the second and third issues. As a result, the representatives of the various caste-communal organizations, including the Muslim League, left the Conference. The constitution subsequently drafted by the committee did not envisage even dominion status, let alone full independence.[42] Along with Jawaharlal, Subhas Chandra Bose was one of the signatories to the Nehru Report.

THE NEXT PRESIDENT

In this context, the issue of the selection of the next party president became extremely important. This time, Motilal took a different path and recommended the 'crown' for Vallabhbhai Patel, 'the hero of the hour,' for his leadership of the nonviolent peasant agitations at Kheda, Borsad and Bardoli in Gujarat. 'Failing this,' he pleaded with Gandhi, 'under all circumstances Jawahar would be the next best choice.'[43]

The Bardoli struggle, as the agitations were commonly called, was a misnomer, for it did not aim at solving the problems of the peasants as a whole. The peasantry in Gujarat had three burdens: the burden of rent payable to the landlord, the burden of interest and debt repayment to the moneylender, and the burden of taxes payable to the government. The Bardoli struggle was directed only against the increased land tax imposed by the government and not against the first two issues which were equally, if not more, important. Those who led the struggle, including Vallabhbhai Patel (he earned the title Sardar ['leader'] for this), were not interested in taking up these issues as they involved taking action against the landlords and the moneylenders. They led the struggle in such a way that the interests of the rich farmers were not impacted.

In fact, Sahajanand Saraswati came to learn that the Bardoli Satyagraha was actually limited to ten to fifteen per cent of rich and middle-class farmers from the area. He discovered this during his visit to Gujarat as late as February 1938. The real peasants or tillers of the land—the Raniparaj, the Dubla and the Hali—were already dispossessed of their land by then, and their land was usurped by the same group of farmers participating in the satyagraha. As a result, the real victims were compelled to plough the same land for the usurping farmers on a half-and-half sharecropping basis.[44] The level of exploitation was such that even groundnuts and cotton were divided in half between the cultivator and the landowner. If there was a crop failure, the peasants were to pay the value of the crops lost in cash to the owners of the land.

Neither Vallabhbhai Patel nor Gandhi took any notice of these conditions. These Halis and Dublas were virtually slaves to the moneylenders and the well-to-do farmers, and they could not go anywhere without the permission of their masters. If they absconded, they were invariably brought back and then no one engaged them for work.[45] Shortly after Sahajanand's visit, the Gujarat Provincial Kisan Sabha was formed at the behest of Indulal Yagnik (1892–1972), a close associate of Subhas Chandra Bose, and a few others to fight for their cause.[46]

Nevertheless, the Bardoli struggle united the peasantry of the Bardoli taluk (administrative division) under the aegis of Gandhian politics. The peasants implemented a call to not pay the increased tax. When the government tried to attach and auction off the land belonging to those who did not pay tax, the auction was boycotted. No amount of oppressive action, including arrest, worked. The situation forced the government to come to a settlement and virtually cancel the tax increase. After Champaran, Bardoli was another feather in Gandhi's cap. It showed the world that nonviolent noncooperation, if meticulously planned out and organized on a mass scale, could definitely achieve its objective and bring about change.

Gandhi understood Motilal's eagerness to see his son as the chief of the party, but the Calcutta session, where the Nehru Report was to be passed, required an experienced leader like him to handle the whole thing. They feared opposition from younger delegates, from pro-Hindu leaders, and from minority communities, who demanded more concessions. For attaining dominion status, which he considered to be the best goal for the country at the time, it was necessary to bring both Hindus and Muslims to a common platform. He did not want to antagonize the British too much either. In such a crisis, Motilal Nehru was the only leader he could depend on.

Against this backdrop, both Jatindra Mohan Sengupta (1885–1933) and Subhas Chandra Bose requested Motilal to become the next president. Sengupta, a close lieutenant of C.R. Das and now the main leader of the Gandhi Wing in Bengal, had already been in correspondence with Gandhi on the matter[47] and probably acted on his bidding. He wrote to Motilal, 'I can well understand the feelings of a father when his son is also in the field. But most of us are in the position of your sons.'[48] He pleaded with him saying that the majority provinces, including Bengal, earnestly wanted to have him as president.[49] Bose supported Sengupta's argument by adding that it would be only proper for Motilal to accede to the request as the year 1929 was going to be very crucial for the future of the country.[50]

Motilal registered the force of their arguments, but he had his heart set on the idea of his son adorning the post. He informed Sengupta that he had recommended Jawaharlal's candidacy not because he was his son, but because he was the one person who was most likely to command the confidence of the majority of the younger members of the party.[51] He stated that both he and his son were at the service of the country and as such, it mattered little to them who actually occupied the chair.[52] The only question that had any weight for them was how to serve the country best.[53]

Strangely enough, he opposed both Gandhi's view and his own machinations and added that a climb down from independence to dominion status would make the Congress an object of ridicule. The world needed to see India as a country that was not ready to take any more nonsense from British colonizers.[54]

Motilal gave Sengupta to understand that Gandhi was likely to announce the selection of his son for the post in *Young India*, so he would just await his decision.[55] When it became clear that Gandhi wanted him and not his son on the chair, he obeyed his diktat and characteristically immersed himself in the affairs of the All Parties Committee.[56]

THE CALCUTTA CONGRESS SESSION (1928)

Soon after the All Parties Conference in Lucknow, Bose and Nehru organized several branches of the Independence for India League (in short, the Independence League) across India. The organization was formally inaugurated in Delhi in November 1928.[57] This coincided with the students' movement Bose was organizing in Bengal. In February 1928, a large number of students had participated in the movement boycotting the Simon Commission, together with the Anushilan Dal activists and communists who were just then making inroads into politics. In August 1928, Jawaharlal had presided over the first All Bengal Students' Conference held in Calcutta at Bose's invitation.[58]

There was unrest in the labour world too. In 1927, railway workers called a strike in Kharagpur, near Calcutta. In early 1928, a strike began at the Tata Iron and Steel Company (TISCO) in Jamshedpur, about 160 miles southwest of Calcutta. Almost 18,000 workers were involved in this strike.[59] Even more important was the textile strike in Bombay (Mumbai) involving no less than 60,000 workers.[60] The first stage of the strike paralyzed the city, embarrassing both the mill-owners and the government. Following this, there was a strike in the workshop of the East India Railways in Liluah, near Calcutta, then another one in the Tinplate Company in Jamshedpur, another one in the Oil and Petrol Works in Budge Budge, and in the jute mills in and near Calcutta.[61]

According to the reports of the All India Trade Union Congress (AITUC), more than 500,000 workers participated in more than 200 strikes in 1928 alone.[62] The Bombay textile strike was organized by the communists, while most other strikes were called by the more militant sections of the AITUC,[63] which was founded by Lala Lajpat Rai in Bombay in October 1920. He had done this with the help of trade-union leaders like Joseph 'Kaka' Baptista (1864–1930), Narayan Malhar Joshi (1879–1955) and Diwan Chaman Lall (1892–1973). Subsequently, the AITUC became an umbrella organization for many different trade unions, both radical and moderate.

The Comintern, which was taking a keen interest in these movements, tried to win the AITUC's loyalty by offering them financial support.[64] Its attempts, however, failed to win over a vast majority of the workers until Jawaharlal entered the scene in 1928.[65] In this, he was closely guided by Chatto.[66] Jawaharlal's interest in the labour sector was relatively recent,[67] and now he wanted to take control of the trade union movement in a planned manner.

In March 1928, Jawaharlal began to attend the meetings of the executive committee of the AITUC as an observer.[68] When the question arose as to whether the AITUC should affiliate itself with the International Federation of Trade Unions (IFTU) based in Amsterdam, he advised against it, as it would be difficult then, if not impossible, to have a formal relationship with the LAI.[69] In the same month, the AITUC's executive committee decided to send observers to the All Parties Committee of the Congress.[70]

As general secretary, Jawaharlal tried to involve the Congress in as many trade union activities as possible.[71] He was closer now to his mentor than ever before. Even Gandhi took his views on international politics seriously. Recently, he had declared that the communists were '...as patriotic as the best among us.'[72] Around this time, the moderate members of the AITUC began to endorse their delegates' participation in the deliberations of the

All Parties Committee, although the radical members continued to view the Indian bourgeoisie as an enemy on a par with the British colonial class.[73]

Shortly before the Calcutta session, Jawaharlal attended the AITUC's three-day annual conference in Jharia in Bihar, presided over by C.F. Andrews (1871–1940).[74] Back in Calcutta, he learned that he had been elected president of the AITUC after defeating Varahagiri Venkata Giri (1894–1980), the candidate pitched by the advanced workers' group, by a slender margin.[75] He appeared to be upset about being elected in preference to an actual union leader who was a railway worker himself.[76] Jawaharlal later said that his '...sympathies at Jharia were with the advanced group' who fought against N.M. Joshi, who had otherwise '...proved himself, by years of work, a sound and earnest trade unionist...'[77] Even those who considered him politically backward and moderate acknowledged the worth of his services to the Indian Labour movement. This could be said of few others, moderate or advanced.'[78]

But what actually happened at Jharia was neither fortuitous nor sudden. A lot of effort had gone into electing Jawaharlal as the president. Throughout 1928, he sought to foster a strong relationship between Indian trade unionists and the Moscow-inspired LAI.[79] All year long, he and Chatto had explored the best strategies that the LAI could deploy in order to gain affiliation with the AITUC and other Indian trade unions.[80] All this was done in pursuance of a decision taken by the LAI's international secretariat in Berlin by early 1928. It was thereby decided that facilitating international affiliations would be its most important objective.[81] Early that year, Chatto had advised Jawaharlal to 'strain every nerve' to make this affiliation possible.[82]

By April 1928, Chatto and Jawaharlal had succeeded in securing the affiliation of major Indian trade unions, such as the Bombay Mill Workers Union, the Bombay Engineering Workers Union, and the Bombay Port Trust Railwaymen's Union, with the LAI.[83] The LAI sent a fraternal delegate, J.W. Johnston, a Chicago-based American communist, to the Jharia session of the

AITUC to aid the fulfilment of this objective.[84] Before coming to India, Johnston had his talking points drafted in London by Clemens Palme Dutt, a founding member of the Communist Party of Great Britain (CPGB) who belonged to the British national section of the LAI.[85]

The All India Youth Congress (AIYC) was formed just before the Congress session; its first session in Calcutta was presided over by Khurshed Framji Nariman (1883–1948), the Parsi leader from Bombay who was extremely popular with the Congress leftwing.[86] Nariman had started his political career as a Swarajist member of the Bombay Legislative Council, where he had distinguished himself as a fighter.[87] During the Calcutta session, Gandhi neutralized any opposition that might have come from Nariman by making him a member of the Working Committee,[88] alongside Jawaharlal, much to the latter's chagrin.

Amid all these complex political games, Subhas Chandra Bose organized the Calcutta session as the chairman of the Reception Committee. He had an uphill task ahead of him because there was a group of powerful critics in the party voicing their opinions against him. This group was headed by Vallabhbhai Patel, Chakravarti Rajagopalachari and J.B. Kripalani. Motilal considered him to be his son's rival and Gandhi disfavoured his uncompromising attitude. In these circumstances, Bose made common cause with the older politician J.M. Sengupta, who belonged to the Gandhi wing but was otherwise an idealistic person.

Kripalani saw Bose's arrangements for the session as an observer from the party's side. These arrangements achieved unprecedented success. Motilal Nehru, the new president, was brought to the venue majestically in a carriage drawn by white horses[89] and given a guard of honour by well-drilled volunteers in immaculate khaki uniforms stitched by a professional firm. Bose supervised the parade on horseback as the General Officer Commanding (GOC) in full uniform. The meticulously organized show was the first (and the last) of its kind and it profoundly impressed and inspired the large group of revolutionaries who attended it.[90] They would go on to make history by raiding the British armoury in Chittagong two years later.

The well-ordered marching ranks '...in glittering Khaki uniforms' and the dazzling display of 'military pageantry' were an unthinkable spectacle in enslaved India and impressed even the British officials who were present there.[91] Gandhi, however, did not relish the explicit departure from the khadi gambit that he had introduced seven years ago. He decried this shift to khaki and called it a 'circus'.[92] He deprecated the 'military' precision of Bose's arrangements.

Before the beginning of the session, Motilal had sought Gandhi's help to pacify the rebelling Independence League.[93] Gandhi had accordingly come to Calcutta with Vallabhbhai Patel.[94] Here, he had a detailed discussion with the three leaders of the League—Srinivasa Iyenger, Jawaharlal Nehru and Subhas Chandra Bose. It was finally decided that the Congress would pass a resolution stating that if the government did not grant India dominion status and did not accept the Constitution based upon its principles that was drawn by the All Parties Conference, by 31 December 1929, the Congress would change its goal to complete independence.[95]

However, Subhas Chandra Bose and Jawaharlal subsequently reneged on this agreement. As far as Jawaharlal was concerned, the Comintern coerced him to support the move for independence, while Bose was literally mobbed by the young delegates and their sympathizers for going soft on his avowed stand.[96] Even the great Bengali novelist Sarat Chandra Chattopadhyay (1876–1938), whom Bose held in high esteem, castigated him for this.[97] As a result, he moved an amendment demanding immediate independence in the open session of the Congress three days later. Jawaharlal supported the amendment and offered his own reason for doing it in his roundabout way.

Gandhi, who had moved the official resolution, was deeply hurt.[98] Yet, he was not harsh with Jawaharlal. Rather, he sympathized with him for his 'predicament' (he probably knew why he had done so).[99] He even praised 'his call for duty to his country' and 'his tendency to plough a lonely furrow.'[100] But he lashed at Bose and his associates, saying, 'If you are not prepared to stand by your own words, where will Independence be? Independence is after all a thing made of sterner stuff. It is not made by the wriggling of words.'[101] After a stormy debate on the issue of independence during which Gandhi declared that if his resolution was defeated, he would retire from politics, it was passed by 1,350 votes to 973.

FUTURE LEADERSHIP: GANDHI'S MINDSET

The Calcutta session made Gandhi seriously contemplate the party's future leadership and he zeroed in on Jawaharlal. He alone could carry out Gandhi's wishes, execute his policies, and control the radical and revolutionary elements in the party. When the question of presidency came up in 1929, ten Provincial Committees proposed Gandhi's name, five were for Patel, and three supported Jawaharlal. Gandhi declined to accept the presidency and he made Patel do the same, and so Jawaharlal was elected to the post 'unanimously'.

In December, Jawaharlal made an announcement dropping Srinivasa Iyengar and Subhas Chandra Bose from the Working Committee. This was in spite of the fact that till August 1929, when Gandhi finally decided to give 'the Congress crown' to Jawaharlal, they were his closest allies in the Independence League and the Congress Seva Dal.

The government was keeping a close eye on these developments. In December 1928, the Home Department, Bombay, had every intention to arrest Jawaharlal, Subhas Chandra Bose and Narhar Vishnu Gadgil (1896–1966) for their seditious speeches. However, the Home Department officials were afraid that if Jawaharlal was arrested along with the other two, Gandhi and Motilal would have to defend all three, instead of Jawaharlal alone. The government would, thus, have to be unnecessarily involved in avoidable legal wrangles. In the end, the Government of India decided that the

Government of Bengal would undertake the task of looking for a valid pretext to arrest only Subhas Chandra Bose, who was the most intransigent and troublesome among them.[102] The sub-committee of the Governor-General's executive council, which made this decision, consisted of Viceroy Irwin himself, Home Member Sir J. Crerar, and Law Member Sir B.L. Mitter.

The years 1928–30 proved to be a watershed in Jawaharlal's career. Apart from being the party president for two consecutive terms (1929 and 1930), he was allowed to declare complete independence to be the party's goal during the Lahore session of the Congress (December 1929). The Swarajists were asked to resign their seats in the legislature during this session and the AICC was authorized to launch civil disobedience, whenever they found it suitable. A resolution on these points was comfortably passed, but Bose opposed it when Gandhi wanted to congratulate Viceroy Irwin on his escape from a terrorist assault on a train outside Delhi a few days ago.[103] Bose's opposition was enthusiastically supported by a vast majority of the delegates, but when the issue was put to vote, Bose lost narrowly and walked out. Very soon, he formed the Congress Democratic Party within the Congress with Iyengar's support.[104] A few days later, he was arrested and lodged at Alipore Central Jail in Calcutta. The new Working Committee, chosen mostly by Gandhi and Motilal,[105] included, among others, Vallabhbhai Patel and Chakravarti Rajagopalachari. At midnight on New Year's Eve, Jawaharlal hoisted the national tricolour on the bank of the Ravi. It was now clear to everyone that Gandhi had finally chosen his heir.

Shortly afterwards, Motilal dedicated Anand Bhavan to the nation. Needless to say, he had already constructed another house in the same compound for his family and had made a few purchases for the new house during his visit to Berlin as far back as 1927.[106] He had humorously said to Chatto while choosing a few things to buy with his help, 'I might as well buy these things and have them put up [in the new house] before Jawaharlal becomes a full socialist.'[107]

After Motilal's death in February 1931, Jawaharlal became more emotionally dependent on Gandhi. Gandhi firmly believed that whatever his personal views might be, Jawaharlal would never betray his trust. In May 1934, when he decided to wind up all forms of civil disobedience and Jawaharlal was in jail, he revealed his thoughts about the party's future leadership in a letter to Vallabhbhai Patel, 'I miss at this juncture the association and advice of Jawaharlal, who is bound to be a rightful helmsman of the organization in the near future.'[108] Jawaharlal was appointed to serve as president at the Lucknow session of the Congress in April 1936 and then the Faizpur session in December the same year. In January 1942, Gandhi put an end to all the speculation when he declared before the AICC that, as he had been saying for years, Jawaharlal would be his successor.[109]

7

A FELLOW TRAVELLER

CHATTO AND ROY

Towards the end of 1926, Jawaharlal came to Berlin with his father, wife, and younger sister, Krishna. At that time, the city was experiencing a period of renewed prosperity following a dire economic crisis after World War I. This newly regained prosperity was largely due to American investments under the Dawes Plan.[1] Indeed, in spite of 'the bitter fruits of defeat in war eaten hourly by the German people and their hatred for the conquerors,'[2] Weimar culture thrived in this period and Berlin became fertile ground for intellectuals, artists and innovators from many fields. Though still chaotic, its social environment was open and friendly, and its politics passionate but disciplined.[3] At that time, no one could imagine that in less than a decade things would change so drastically under Nazi rule.

Activities promoting the cause of Indian independence in Germany and elsewhere were aided by German funds, although the Chinese were far more active as far as organizing public meetings, protest gatherings and anniversary celebrations was concerned.[4] Germany was particularly attractive to Indian students for the low cost of living and high standard of education that was available to them there. They also went there because the social circles in Germany were better than those in England. There was greater openness and ease.[5] About seventy Indian students pursuing different disciplines lived in Berlin when the Nehrus arrived in the city.[6]

Apart from seeking medical advice, Motilal used his time in Berlin to buy artistic pieces and furniture for his new house in Allahabad with the help of Virendranath, aka Chatto,[7] who was known to the family from before their Berlin days. He was an erudite conversationalist, a polyglot, and a connoisseur of the arts and letters. He was also the head of the Berlin India Committee (BIC) and ran an informal conclave of radicals and intellectuals from his house. Jawaharlal enjoyed Chatto's company and he was drawn to his relaxed wit and sense of humour. Soon, he began to hold him in high regard.

Chatto had set up the Association of Indians of German Europe in 1921 to carry out Indian nationalist work. Towards the end of 1917, he had established contact with the Soviet government after the Bolsheviks freed Muslims in the Asian part of the Russian Empire. After that, he had become a Russian collaborator.[8] Jawaharlal probably did not know this side of him, as he would write in his autobiography, 'Chatto was not, I believe, a regular Communist.'[9] But then, one cannot be too sure about this, considering Jawaharlal's long and intimate association with Chatto and his comrades till January 1930.

Chatto had formed a number of political outfits from behind the scene, such as the Calcutta-based Indian Nationalist Party in 1917. This was constituted with no more than four members and it aimed to get Soviet funds. He was also behind the New York-based Friends of Freedom for India (FFFI), which was launched in March 1919 by a young American, Agnes Smedley (1892–1950).[10] She later came to be romantically linked with Chatto in Berlin. Smedley has offered the following pen picture of Chatto:

> He [Chatto] was thin and dark, with a mass of black hair turning grey at the temples, and a face that had something fierce about it. He might easily have been taken for a southern European, a Turk, or a Persian. To me he seemed something like thunder, lighting, and rain; and whenever he sojourned in Europe or England, he had been just about that to the

English. His hatred for the islanders who had subjugated his country knew no bounds.[11]

Agnes has stated that Chatto studied comparative philology in Heidelberg and Jena and that he spoke English like an Englishman from the ruling classes, and learned French, German, Swedish, and some Italian and Spanish.[12] He had also studied Icelandic during his stay in Sweden, assimilated Russian during his visit to the USSR, and attempted a comparative study of the languages of the Gypsies and ancient Sanskrit.[13] Chatto's aim was to establish himself as the supreme Indian leader in Europe before he took over Moscow, but he had a more resourceful contender in M.N. Roy (1887–1954), who had the ears of a powerful group in the Soviet hierarchy.

Jawaharlal's political ideology changed drastically under Chatto's influence and took a permanently leftist turn. The mental make-up of the two men were, however, completely different. Chatto was an inspirational organizer and a ruthless go-getter, while Jawaharlal was tentative, impatient and short-tempered in his approach to work. Also, Jawaharlal did not share Chatto's hatred of Britain. Nevertheless, in some matters they were alike: both of them had failed to join the ICS and subsequently criticized it; both enjoyed poetry, music (Jawaharlal had developed this taste under Chatto's influence) and good conversation in a select milieu. Inducting Jawaharlal into Soviet ideology was considered a matter of great credit for Chatto in Moscow.

During this period, Chatto believed in a united front of communists and non-communists that would usher in an era of independence and socialism in India along Lenin's strategic-tactical lines. On the other hand, M.N. Roy had no faith in bourgeois nationalism and alliance with non-communists at that time. He advocated a total communist takeover of India with the help of the Comintern. The British intelligence believed that Roy's 'ultra-left' stance was an opportunistic ploy to curry favour with the Bolsheviks.[14]

Interestingly, their views on the united front against imperialist domination in the national context reversed around 1930. Chatto abandoned this line completely and adopted the Stalinist line that advocated a total rejection of bourgeois nationalism, whereas Roy adopted Chatto's more cooperative viewpoint from the early days.[15] Around this time, Chatto started branding Subhas Chandra Bose as '...the very active National Socialist (Fascist) leader';[16] but he remained indulgent about Jawaharlal. Roy, however, berated Indian communists for criticizing the Congress leftwing under Jawaharlal and Bose.[17]

Roy's given name was Narendra Nath Bhattacharya. He came from a lower middle-class family of priests in rural Bengal. Throughout his life, he retained his orthodox faith in matters such as child marriage and the inequality of women.[18] On the other hand, Chatto (also a Bengali Brahmin) was the product of an upper-class cultural amalgamation of Hinduism, Islam, and the best of English Liberalism.[19] His life and politics had no room for bigotry, racism, and socio-economic inequalities. He could not care less if he had no more than one suit of clothing;[20] He could easily eat pork in the presence of Muslims and beef in front of Hindus.[21] Also, his personal life was austere,[22] while Roy liked to live like a prince with funds from the Soviets.

They were also poles apart in terms of their physical appearance. Roy was sleek, handsome and meticulously dressed, a derring-doer, who could be easily mistaken for a film star, and he behaved like one.[23] Both had women in their lives, but Chatto never took advantage of them sexually, as Roy did.[24] Chatto was admired for his cultured behaviour and gentleness, while Roy was often found to be overbearing, arrogant and unscrupulous.[25] In one respect they were similar: both of them were polyglots, intellectually gifted, and able organizers for their cause.

In the post-Lenin era, and up until his ouster from the Comintern in December 1929, Roy identified completely with Moscow's predominant power structure and acquired important allies in the Comintern, such as Michael Borodin, Karl Radek,

Grigori Zinoviev, Nikolai Bukharin and August Thalheimer, all of whom supported him when his political differences with Chatto became known to the Soviet hierarchy in Moscow.[26] His wife, Evelyn Trent (1892–1970), whose uncle was the American-born Irish leader Éamon de Valera, helped him greatly with the Comintern.[27] In June 1921, when both the groups fought for patronage and funds in Moscow, Roy's group won.[28] Consequently, Chatto had to maintain a façade of cooperation with Roy till the latter left for China in February 1927.

The same month, Chatto assisted Wilhelm 'Willi' Munzenberg (1889–1940), an independent-minded German communist activist, in organizing the Brussels Congress with like-minded communists and non-communists. They wanted to build a united platform to fight imperialism and non-radical forces. A former companion of Lenin's, Munzenberg was affectionately called 'the patron saint of fellow travellers'.[29] He had established the Berlin-based Workers International Aid (WIA), ostensibly to provide relief to the victims of the Russian famine but actually to carry out illegal and subversive activities on behalf of the Comintern.[30]

The Comintern had an agent, Jacob Mirov-Abramov, installed at the Russian Embassy in Berlin as the third secretary to aid their clandestine work. He was the second-ranking member of the Comintern's intelligence outfit, OMS (the Otdel Mezhdunarodnoi Svyazi or the Department of International Liaison), whose task it was to facilitate activists like Chatto.[31] The Comintern was discreetly behind the organization of the Brussels Congress and the formation of the League Against Imperialism (LAI).

In her biography of Agnes Smedley, Ruth Price assesses intelligence records and indicates that the whole thing was stage-managed by Moscow. The spies from the OMS and other outfits were keeping an eye on the developments taking place at the Brussels Congress and subsequently in the LAI. Chatto used this forum to recruit Jawaharlal and introduce him to the radical circles of interwar Germany.[32]

LEAGUE AGAINST IMPERIALISM (LAI)

When Chatto met Jawaharlal, he was already a member of the German Communist Party and a committed Soviet agent. His flat in Berlin was frequented by people following a variety of pursuits and ideologies. A.C.N. Nambiar once related an occasion when he saw Abdul Hamied, the future founder of Cipla, then a student, cooking Indian food for company that included Zakir Husain, Wajid Ali Khan, who was a relative of the Nawab of Rampur, and Huseyn Shaheed Suhrawardy (1892–1963), one of the architects of the partition.[33]

Jawaharlal came to know Nambiar closely during this time. Nambiar chaperoned him throughout the Brussels Congress where he took an active part in the deliberations[34] and met a large cross-section of nationalist and leftist activists and intellectuals from Europe, Africa, East and Southeast Asia and the United States.

Whatever Chatto's motive might have been for giving him this platform, Jawaharlal dexterously used it for his own purposes. His politics was no longer confined to nationalism after 1927.[35] Much later, in 1955, he returned to the concept of the nation-state at the Afro-Asian Conference held in Bandung in Indonesia, and subsequently joined the Non-Aligned Movement (NAM), which consisted of a bloc of nation-states working within an interstate agreement not to ally with any of the two superpowers, the USA and the USSR, during the Cold War.

Jawaharlal met the pretty leftwing intellectual and activist Agnes Smedley in Berlin and became her lifelong admirer. She, however, found Jawaharlal to be '...a quiet, unspectacular man, unlike most Indian leaders...',[36] but she kept in touch with him for political purposes. Earlier, Smedley had been involved in the Indian independence movement in the United States via Chatto's revolutionary associates, Bhagwan Singh Gyanee (1884–1962) and Taraknath Das (1884–1958), and was even jailed for some time. Later, she outgrew Chatto's influence and worked for the Russian intelligence. During the 1930s, she actively helped the legendary

Soviet spy Richard Sorge (1895–1944) to carry out espionage in Shanghai and Tokyo.[37]

As Nambiar recalled, the preliminary work of the Brussels Congress was carried out by Munzenberg, assisted by Chatto and Louis Gibarti, a resourceful Hungarian.[38] It is now known from US intelligence records that Gibarti was 'Confidential Informant T-1' of the FBI and regularly reported on the activities of Munzenberg, Chatto, Madame Sun Yat-sen, Smedley and others to the agency.[39] The FBI came to know about the activities of the LAI and its involvement with the OMS and the Comintern from him.[40]

The idea of the Brussels Congress originated in 1925 as a result of the Comintern's policy (adopted a year earlier) to support colonized and semi-colonized countries in their fight against colonial powers with the help of the leftwing sections of the Labour and Socialist International and the anti-colonial nationalist parties from the colonized world. The programme was held at Egmond Palace in Brussels, where the League Against Imperialism (LAI) was formed on 10 February 1927, in the presence of more than 170 delegates from across the world.[41] Jawaharlal (he also became a member of the LAI's executive committee and took an active role in drafting resolutions) was the only delegate from India, representing the Indian National Congress. Nambiar, Jayasurya Naidu (Sarojini Naidu's radical son), Jawaharlal's sister Krishna, Hirlekar and Bakhar Ali (later a Member of Parliament) assisted him.[42]

Among those present in the Brussels Congress were the emissaries of the Chinese Guomindang Party (KMT) in Europe, J.T. Gumede of the African National Congress in South Africa, Messali Hadj of the Algerian nationalist organization, the North African Star, and Mohammad Hatta of the Perhimpoenan Indonesia. Jawaharlal became very close friends with the latter. Many activists from the European and American Left, including Fenner Brockway, Arthur MacManus, Edo Fimmen, Reginald Bridgeman and Gabrielle Duchene were also present. All of them became Jawaharlal's contacts in the West. The delegation from

Britain included George Lansbury, the leader of the Labour Party, and Harry Pollitt, the general secretary of the CPGB.

The French writer Henri Barbusse, an active communist, delivered the inaugural address. A.C.N. Nambiar recalls that '...in a short speech with fascinating eloquence and clearly evidenced feeling he sharply condemned colonialism and vividly dealt with humanitarian virtues and requisites.'[43] Lansbury was elected as the president of the League and his eloquent address impressed Jawaharlal.[44]

During the LAI's inaugural conference, differences arose among representatives from organizations in Mandatory Palestine, the Arab nationalist Jamal al-Husayni, the Zionist labour outfit Poale Zion, and the Palestine Communist Party (PCP).[45] The PCP representative, Daniel Averbach, introduced a resolution accusing Zionism of being a tool of British imperialism and the source of racial strife and sectarian tension in Palestine.[46] The PCP and the Arab nationalists from Palestine, Egypt and Syria formed an anti-Zionist bloc at the conference. After much deliberation, the executive council of the LAI, which included Jawaharlal, barred the Poale Zion delegation from participating in the conference.

China's anti-imperialist struggle came into focus during the conference, while India's struggle for freedom was not mentioned at all. Western luminaries including Upton Sinclair, Albert Einstein and Maxim Gorky paid rich tributes to the Chinese struggle. Although Jawaharlal was not particularly impressed by the Chinese delegates in Brussels, he admitted in a letter addressed to his sister, Vijaya Lakshmi, on 12 November 1927 that Madame Sun Yat-sen, widow of the late Dr Sun Yat-sen, who had communist sympathies and was on the executive committee of the KMT founded by her husband, 'fascinated' him.[47]

Madame Sun Yat-sen did not attend the Brussels Congress but sent messages of support and accepted an honorary presidency at the conference. Jawaharlal met her nine months later during his tour of Moscow and became a China enthusiast. He wrote to Vijaya Lakshmi that she was '...delightful, look[ed] twenty-five and

[was] full of life and energy."[48] Much later, in 1938, he would be similarly fascinated by her younger sister, Madame Chiang Kai-shek, who politically opposed her elder sister. Only a few months after the Brussels conference, Madame Chiang's husband and Dr Sun's protégé Chiang Kai-shek usurped power in China and unleashed a reign of terror, imprisoning and killing thousands of communists and non-communists who opposed his dictatorship.

In July 1927, the LAI secretariat released a special report from Chan Kuen, a delegate representing the All-Chinese Trade Union Federation, which provided a gruesome first-hand account of Chiang's ruthless Northern Expedition. It appealed to the LAI members to extend their moral support to the workers of China, who were being repressed under the double yoke constituted by the Chinese bourgeoisie and foreign imperialists.[49] Busy with his European tour, meeting Chatto and Roger Baldwin among others, Jawaharlal ignored this appeal.

At the Madras Congress in December, Jawaharlal set in motion several resolutions to align the anti-colonial nationalist movement with the LAI's anti-imperialist programme. A formal resolution declaring the party's association with the LAI was adopted at his behest. This was a decision which was already approved by the AICC. Another resolution extended their warmest greetings to China, recognizing the Chinese people as comrades of the Indian people in their joint struggle against imperialism. Nowhere in his speeches and his resolutions did he indicate that he was aware of the fact that China was then in the throes of a civil war, let alone speak of his disapproval of Chiang Kai-shek's high-handedness in subduing his opponents.

Meanwhile, the executive committee of the LAI worked in earnest to preserve the equilibrium between socialists and communists by several means. The financial backing offered by key non-communists was one way of ensuring that the LAI was not dictated entirely by the Comintern. The membership rules also had provisions to ensure that as an associate of the LAI, neither camp tried to influence the other's political doctrine.

Moreover, the executive committee was formed in such a way that there was a guarantee that equity would be maintained. Two non-communists, George Lansbury and Edo Fimmen, served as chairman and vice-chairman, respectively, of the LAI, while two communists funded by Moscow, Liau Hansin and Louis Gibarti, functioned as secretaries.[50]

This arrangement, however, did not last long. Encouraged by the spectacular success of the Brussels Congress, the Comintern formed an anti-imperialist commission in Moscow in June 1927 to oversee the work of the LAI.[51] M.N. Roy was a member of this commission. The same month, the Comintern took over the financial and directional control of the LAI secretariat.[52] Soon afterwards, Lansbury resigned his chairmanship[53] probably after being pressured by his own party. A few months later, Albert Einstein gave up his membership following his disagreement with the League's pro-Arab policy as regards Palestine.[54]

Since the Brussels Congress, Jawaharlal had become one of the most coveted prizes for Munzenberg and the Comintern.[55] A small committee appointed by the Comintern's executive committee passed a resolution drafted on the basis of the report from Brussels (28 February 1927) submitted by Sen Katayama, co-founder of the Japanese Communist Party and member of the Comintern. It said that the communists in the LAI must work with Katayama to '...establish connection with prominent men in the Leftwing of the Indian National Congress.'[56] Jawaharlal, however, underplayed Moscow's hold over the LAI and wrote persuasive notes to the Working Committee highlighting the advantages of espousing anti-imperialist internationalism by associating with the LAI.[57] He underscored the importance of the Congress Party engaging with the wider world, especially in the context of the growing danger of war. He recited a now familiar Comintern warning that Britain would instigate a war in China and the Soviet Union to protect her imperialist interests. India could not afford to let this happen and imperil herself in the process.[58] The Working Committee consequently decided to remit funds to support the institution in May 1927. Shortly after the formation of the Independence for India League (IIL), Jawaharlal endeavoured to make it an adjunct to the LAI with the help of Subhas Chandra Bose without disclosing his actual intention to him. Much to his disappointment, the outfit never got going the way he wished, because Bose did not take it seriously enough as an organization that needed to be developed further.[59] He looked at it only as something to be used for pressurising the Congress executive wing to accept complete independence as the goal of the party, and perhaps for influencing the election of the Working Committee.[60] Consequently, the organization disappeared when the civil disobedience movement was launched in 1930.[61]

By 1930, the LAI had veered almost completely towards Moscow, while Jawaharlal had adopted a pro-compromise stance with the British under Gandhi's leadership. He no longer supported LAI activities with his old fervour, as he admittedly became involved in the Delhi truce between the Congress and the Government of India.[62] The LAI leadership was angry with him for signing the Congress's formal agreement, known as the Delhi Manifesto, to enter into negotiations with the colonial state for getting dominion status.

Before Jawaharlal signed the manifesto, Chatto had reminded him in a letter that '...not very long ago [he had] declared somewhere, very correctly, that no negotiations [were] possible so long as the army of occupation was in the country...'[63] and that '...the acceptance of Dominion Status in any form or under any conditions [could not] be regarded as an anti-imperialist attitude.'[64] The Delhi Manifesto set the seal on Jawaharlal's relationship with Chatto and the LAI.[65] On 20 November 1929, Chatto and Munzenberg denounced the Indian National Congress and singled out Jawaharlal as untrustworthy and hypocritical in their letter to all the affiliated and associated organizations in India.[66] This was a strong allegation and Jawaharlal's leftist image was at stake. This time too, Gandhi bailed him out by allowing him to declare the resolution for independence at the Lahore Congress in December

1929, as the president of the party.

By early 1930, the Comintern decided to expel Jawaharlal from the LAI's executive committee and dissociate the LAI from the Congress Party. His close friends in the LAI, Roger Baldwin and Edo Fimmen, who had been trying to free the organization from the Comintern's stranglehold (Jawaharlal had pledged to support them but kept aloof in the hour of their need), were expelled by this time. In keeping with the Comintern's plan, Munzenberg and Chatto launched an attack on the class character of Gandhi and the Congress Party as a whole. They fired off a letter to the Indian anti-imperialists on 29 January 1930, urging them to remember that Gandhi protected the propertied classes and the imperialist system, and that he had '...systemically acted against the interests of the workers and peasants by advocating cooperation with their oppressors.'[67]

As the president of the Congress, Jawaharlal remonstrated against these allegations in his correspondence with the LAI secretariat. He wrote a personal letter to Chatto separately in January 1930, expressing hope that the tensions between the Congress and the League might still be repaired.[68] In response, Chatto and Munzenberg advised Jawaharlal to wait until the executive council met to discuss the principle and tactics of cooperation between non-communist national colonial organizations and communists. Chatto added a personal note to Jawaharlal along with the official reply, asking him to rethink his position and not to be embittered by differences or be blind to mistakes simply because these happened to be pointed out by the communists.[69] He promised to write Jawaharlal a letter soon and offer him his personal reflections on the Congress, but no such letter arrived.

Chatto, however, had requested Moscow to stall the Comintern's impulses to purge Jawaharlal Nehru,[70] but his efforts failed. Jawaharlal later came to know that he had been expelled by the League through a resolution of some sort,[71] but it mattered little to him now. In a letter dated 9 April 1930, he asked the LAI secretariat to accept his resignation and remove his name from its committee, assuming that he had not already been expelled. He sent copies of the letter to his associates Fimmen, Baldwin, Reginald Bridgeman and also Shiv Prasad Gupta (1883–1944), the founder of Kashi Vidyapith, who had once represented the Congress Party at a LAI convention in Berlin.[72]

VISIT TO MOSCOW

When the Nehrus were in Europe in November 1927, Chatto arranged to send an invitation to Motilal to take part in the celebrations of the tenth anniversary of the October Revolution with his family, through the surrogate organization the Soviet Society for Cultural Relations. The German Communist Party assisted him in the matter. M.N. Roy facilitated the Nehrus' luxurious travel to and from Moscow and other arrangements.[73]

To make the invitation look inconspicuous, a few other Indians like Shapurji Saklatvala (1874–1936) were also asked to join the celebrations by the organization. The invitation extended to the Nehrus was reported in the Soviet national daily *Pravda* on 5 November.[74] Before making this move, Chatto had written to Roy that the presence of the Nehru family would mean that 'the big guns of the Congress' were well represented in Moscow.[75] Chatto's real target, of course, was Jawaharlal.

Initially, Motilal was not inclined to accept the invitation due to his asthma and other ailments, but his son's keenness prevailed upon him to change his decision. Chatto and Nambiar firmed up their logistical arrangements from Berlin.[76] Saklatvala, Chatto's contact, was present at the Moscow railway station to receive the Nehrus.[77]

The Nehrus took the train to Moscow from Berlin. Their passage had been booked by their hosts. At the station, they were fed sumptuously by the Russians in spite of them having had their dinner earlier. They simply could not refuse their hospitality and had to comply with their wishes.[78] The Russian train had only one class, but it had a few special sleeping cars and the Nehrus were provided with these.[79] They had a very comfortable journey to Moscow,[80] passing through the whole of Poland.[81]

Poland had freed herself in 1920 after a grim battle with the Red Army. From the train, Jawaharlal found the Polish countryside desolate, cheerless and dismal, primarily for the lack of industrialization.[82] The idea of Soviet-type industrialization and the collective leadership of the proletariat was close to his heart by now. His account of his travels gives one the impression that he was of the opinion that Poland would perhaps have done better under the Soviets.

Interestingly, Agnes Smedley, who travelled in the common class on the same route about the same time next year, had a different tale to tell. She wrote:

> For years there has remained deeply etched in my memory the scene that confronted me as I entered the Soviet Union in 1928. My train had passed through Poland, and at railway stations I had watched fashionably dressed Polish ladies, painted and elegant, bid farewell to Polish officers in smart uniforms gaudy with gold braid. On a late wintry October day our train drew up at the Soviet-Polish frontier and I approached the custom station of the first socialist country.[83]

The Nehrus' visit received extensive coverage from the Russian media. The newspapers carried a detailed account of Jawaharlal's activities at the Brussels conference. During this three-day visit, M.N. Roy met him in an exclusive session and greatly impressed him.[84] Jawaharlal was received in the Kremlin by Mikhail Kalinin, the chairman of the Central Executive Committee of the USSR.[85] Stalin, however, did not meet the guests. To him, both Jawaharlal and Gandhi were counter-revolutionaries serving British imperialism.[86] He viewed India's fight for independence as a bourgeois conspiracy connived by the imperialists behind the backs of the Indian people.[87]

During his brief stay, Jawaharlal attended Moscow court

proceedings, visited factories, the Museum of the October Revolution and the Bolshoi Theatre, and watched the film *The End of Saint Petersburg* directed by Vsevolod Pudovkin and Mikhail Doller, before its official release. On 8 November 1927, he and his father took part in a ceremonial meeting dedicated to the October Revolution. When they were introduced to the audience, they were given a standing ovation. They loved the attention.[88]

Soon after returning from Moscow, Jawaharlal published an exuberant account of his visit in a series of articles in various newspapers, chiefly *The Hindu* published from Madras. One article, captioned 'Education', appeared in Gandhi's *Young India*. The articles were primarily based on the handouts he received from the Soviet government during the visit. In 1929, he compiled them in a slender volume titled *Soviet Russia: Some Random Sketches and Impressions*, which was his first published work. In Moscow, he found the second leg of the tripod—the Comintern's support—on which his future career would stand to a large extent.

Nine years later, Jawaharlal described this visit to Soviet Russia in just a couple of sentences in his autobiography and then he moved on to his meeting with Sir John Simon in London, for which he accompanied his father.[89] By now, he had learned to be cautious. Besides, he was now in search of the third leg of the tripod—the support of British Liberal politicians—to fulfil his ambitions.

8

CONSOLIDATION AND COMPROMISE

THE DELHI MANIFESTO AND AFTER

Following the Madras session of the Congress held in December 1927, Jawaharlal began concentrating on consolidating his influence within the Congress Party, particularly among the progressive elements. He wanted to use the Independence for India League (IIL) as a weapon to achieve his objective. However, ground realities did not favour Chatto's grand scheme, or even his modest attempt to link the IIL with the LAI and build up an anti-imperialist nucleus in India.[1] When the initial momentum of the IIL faded soon after its inaugural meeting in Delhi in November 1928, Jawaharlal blamed it on Subhas Chandra Bose.[2] The latter had lost interest in the organization after independence became the stated goal of the Congress Party.

Throughout 1928 and in the first six months of 1929, Jawaharlal remained close to Bose. Their relationship waned after Gandhi made him the president-elect for the Lahore session. Bose was always concerned that the lure of office would wean Jawaharlal off leftist politics.[3] This was indeed what happened. In November 1929, Gandhi literally bullied Jawaharlal into signing the 'Delhi Manifesto,' as witnessed by Dr Balakrishna Shivaram Moonje (1872–1948) and Tej Bahadur Sapru.[4] He was told that he would lose his position as secretary of the Working Committee and next year's presidency if he did not obey Gandhi and sign the manifesto.[5] The manifesto was, in fact, Gandhi's way of settling for a compromise after the British government announced its intention to hold a Round Table Conference in London to discuss ways and means to grant self-rule to Indians. The British initiative was part of a plan to frustrate the Congress's demand for independence. It was hatched by the British premier Ramsay MacDonald, acting on the suggestions of Muhammad Ali Jinnah. Following the plan—finalized with Jinnah in Simla and approved by London—Viceroy Irwin issued a statement on 31 October 1929 that His Majesty's Government was willing to discuss the possibility of dominion status at a Round Table Conference in London after the publication of the Simon Commission Report, as suggested by Sir John Simon himself.

Jinnah had assured MacDonald that this ploy would wean Gandhi and the Congress off the path of a movement and would show them in a bad light at the All Parties Conference in London. Accordingly, the viceroy had asked Gandhi and Motilal Nehru—apparently on the suggestion of Vithalbhai Patel, the president of the central assembly and a close friend of Jinnah's—for a meeting in December to discuss the matter.[6] Gandhi had called the November conference in Delhi to prepare the manifesto for presentation to the viceroy at the time of the meeting. The manifesto proposed that the Round Table Conference in London should frame a scheme for a Dominion constitution for India, instead of merely discussing when it could be established.[7] It laid down three conditions for the conference: the adoption of a more conciliatory policy by the government, granting amnesty to all political prisoners (which Gandhi later dropped as a gesture of goodwill to the viceroy), and the recognition of the predominant position of the Congress Party vis-à-vis other political organizations.[8] The manifesto relied greatly on their belief in the goodwill of the viceroy and the Labour government, which later proved to be ill-founded.

Subhas Chandra Bose suspected the viceroy's motives and appealed to Gandhi to exercise caution in the matter. When his words of caution were ignored, he opposed the Delhi Manifesto, resigned from the Working Committee, and put forward an alternative manifesto with S. Kitchlew and Abdul Bari. It proposed that only the contending parties participate in the Round Table Conference for a fruitful discussion and that the Indian representatives be selected by the Indian people, and not by the British government as planned. The alternative manifesto warned that the viceroy's declaration was a trap, similar to what the British government had offered Ireland some years ago, when Prime Minister Lloyd George had suggested that an Irish Convention comprising all parties should be held to frame a Constitution of Ireland. However, the Sinn Fein had seen through the scheme and boycotted the convention.[9]

During the discussions, the alternative manifesto was defeated and Gandhi's manoeuvres won. Jawaharlal persuaded Bose to withdraw his resignation. Shortly thereafter, Gandhi allowed Jawaharlal to declare independence at the Lahore session symbolically, in an emotionally charged function at midnight on 31 December 1929. This would help him regain his position among the leftwing elements in India and abroad. The Lahore session also saw Bose depart from the venue in a gesture of protest against Gandhi kowtowing to the viceroy. This led him to be excluded from the Working Committee for the next seven years. He went on to form the Congress Democratic Party as a faction within the national body with the support of Srinivasa Iyengar, and then he got arrested on charges of sedition and sentenced to one year's rigorous imprisonment on 23 January 1930 and was lodged in Alipore Central Jail.

In the end, the Congress did not take part in the first Round Table Conference. It was held from November 1930 to January 1931. Instead, largely to put pressure on the government, Gandhi started the Salt Satyagraha and began a march to a remote coastal village named Dandi in Gujarat. This was scheduled just a few months before the conference as a direct-action campaign of tax resistance and nonviolent protest against the repressive British salt policy. It was a brilliant move. Salt was among the cheapest and the most essential items of human consumption. So the movement (the Dandi March) almost immediately drew global attention to the colonial question. It lasted twenty-four days, from 12 March to 6 April 1930, and developed into an all-encompassing mass movement against the British Raj in different parts of the country. Jawaharlal was initially sceptical, as was Vallabhbhai Patel, especially about the subject of the Satyagraha. They were both surprised when the movement spread like wildfire across India.

However, the movement soon became violent and Gandhi began to avoid active involvement in it, although he kept in close touch with the developments till his arrest on 4 May 1930. In early 1931, he was released from prison and ended the movement. Thereafter, he made a pact with Viceroy Irwin—the Gandhi-Irwin Pact—on 5 March. Consequently, he decided to attend the second Round Table Conference from September to December 1931 in London as the sole representative of the Congress. Jawaharlal was not happy about his decision, but he kept quiet about it. Subhas Chandra Bose, however, met Gandhi in Bombay immediately after his release from prison and tried in vain to dissuade him from attending the conference, which was bound to be controversial.

Indeed, the conference ended in a quagmire of controversy and quite dismally brought into focus, much to the delight and the advantage of the British, that India was 'a house divided' and that there were differences not only between Hindus and Muslims, but also among Hindus themselves. The dalits or the 'depressed castes' had serious grievances against upper-caste Hindus and the Congress Party that was dominated by them.[10] It was a setback from which the party never recovered.

Back in Bombay after the conference, Gandhi sought an interview with the new viceroy, Lord Willingdon, on 29 December. The viceroy was then on a visit to the city. Gandhi wanted to discuss with him, among other things, the police atrocities that were being committed in Bengal, the United Provinces and the North-West Frontier Province. He had ignored this issue during his pact with Irwin as a gesture of goodwill to the viceroy. The interview was a face-saving measure after his dismal performance in London and he probably also intended to build a relationship with Willingdon, as he had done with Irwin before him.

A diehard imperialist and a former governor of Maharashtra, Willingdon had other ideas. He refused the request on 31 December. A dismayed Gandhi sent a long rejoinder to the viceroy on the same day, conveying that the operation of the pact would be suspended unless they had a dialogue immediately. His usual tactic of compromise-confrontation-compromise did not succeed this time. Willingdon was an old hand at the game and had high-level connections among Indian politicians. On 2 January 1932, he replied that an interview under the threat of civil disobedience was out of the question.[11] This was the end of the much-touted Gandhi-Irwin Pact.

The government had foreseen this eventuality and had a plan of action ready. The very next day (3 January), Subhas Chandra Bose was arrested from the train in Kalyan, thirty miles from Bombay, under Regulation III (the Bengal State Prisoners Regulation) of 1818 and thus began his long odyssey in prison followed by exile. The next day (4 January), the Government of India issued a public statement justifying its actions against the threat of the Congress Party. Orders were separately but simultaneously issued to local authorities throughout India to strike at all the Congress organizations at once.[12]

On the same day, Gandhi, Vallabhbhai Patel, Rajendra Prasad, Maulana Azad, Jawaharlal and many other Congressmen in Bombay, Delhi, Allahabad and Calcutta were arrested.[13] The four ordinances promulgated on this occasion had been prepared during the period of truce. Dr Mukhtar Ahmed Ansari had forewarned Vallabhbhai Patel, the then Congress president, about it, but the latter did not pay any heed to the alert. These ordinances now began to wreak havoc on the Congress Party and the various organizations under it.[14]

VISIT TO EUROPE: ESTABLISHING CONTACT WITH RADICALS

On his release from jail on compassionate grounds, Jawaharlal came to Europe in September 1935 to visit his critically ill wife in Lausanne in Switzerland. He was received in Basel on 8 September by Subhas Chandra Bose. He took him straight to the sanatorium by car early next morning.[15] Three months earlier, on 4 June 1935, he had similarly received Kamala and Indira in Vienna and had made arrangements for their stay in the city and Kamala's medical treatment, first in Germany and then in Lausanne.[16]

Jawaharlal's plan was to utilize this trip to make political connections in London and Paris so that he could play a bigger role in Indian politics on his own. Gandhi had agreed to make him the president at the next session of the Congress to be held in Lucknow in April 1936, though none of his colleagues knew that yet. His autobiography was about to be published in London. V.K. Krishna Menon (1896–1974), his new radical friend, was taking all the necessary steps to have it published. The book was expected to establish him as a sensitive and fair-minded politician with intellect and a sense of purpose.

In Lausanne, Jawaharlal met Ben Bradley (1898–1957) and Rajani Palme Dutt (1896–1974) from the Communist Party of Great Britain (CPGB). Bradley was an activist, but Dutt was a leftist intellectual and a reputed author and in charge of Indian affairs on behalf of Moscow. Dutt's beautiful Finn-Austrian wife, Salme Annette Murrik (1888–1964), was one of the founders of the CPGB and a very high-level operative in the Soviet hierarchy. Dutt and Jawaharlal spent three days together in a guest house in Lausanne; Dutt found the 'Professor', as Jawaharlal was known in the Comintern circles, very receptive to his ideas.[17] Rajani Palme Dutt took over from where Chatto had left off.

A month after shifting from Badenweiler, Kamala died on 28 February 1936 at the sanatorium in Lausanne. Jawaharlal took her death rather stoically, expending only a single sentence on it in his autobiography before he moved on to other subjects like his future presidency and a request from Mussolini to see him.[18] Not even once did he mention Bose, who had stood by him in this distressing time and arranged his wife's funeral. From A.C.N. Nambiar's account, it is known that it was in Lausanne that Jawaharlal received the news of his selection as the next party president from Rajendra Prasad. At that time, he was struggling with a dilemma: whether to leave Kamala in her current state of poor health, or to neglect an important public duty.[19] Kamala was aware of her husband's dilemma.[20] Since she felt at home in Nambiar's company, Jawaharlal requested him to find out what she would like him to do. In Nambiar's words, 'When I entered her room, she said: "I know why you have come, my wish is he should go." I was most surprised. Jawaharlal did not have to make the hard choice, though for a very sad happening.'[21] She died within a couple of days of the conversation.

Jawaharlal was actually worried that Gandhi might change his mind about his presidency due to the influence of intra-party politics. Kripalani said in his memoir that Jawaharlal had approached Gandhi at the Faizpur Congress (December 1936) to request him to grant him the presidency instead of Vallabhbhai Patel,[22] on the grounds that just a single term spanning eight months had not been enough to revitalize the Congress. Gandhi had deliberated for a while and then said, 'I shall see what can be done.' The conversation took place in J.B. Kripalani's presence.[23] Vallabhbhai Patel knew about this, but he did not express his resentment except to a few confidants long afterwards.[24] In Lausanne, neither Bose nor Nambiar had any idea about the real reason for Jawaharlal's anxiety.

Later, when Jawaharlal returned to India, he issued a public statement saying, inter alia,

> Nominations for the presidentship have now been made and as the time for election draws near, I feel that I cannot remain silent any longer and I must tell my countrymen what my feelings are. I shall gladly welcome the election of any of my

colleagues and cooperate with him in another capacity in the great enterprise we have undertaken. Should however the choice of my countrymen fall upon me, I dare not say no to it; I shall submit to their pleasure. But before they so decide, they must realize what I stand for, what thoughts move me, what the springs of action are for me in speech and writing. I have given enough indication of this and from this I want to be judged.[25]

Kripalani and others, who knew the real story, were not amused.

Once Jawaharlal was sure of his presidency, he stayed in Europe till March 1936. He did not visit Russia or Ireland, which were both regarded as anti-British. He similarly avoided visiting Italy and Germany, which were associated with Fascism and National Socialism respectively. His autobiography, well received by both the radical and the liberal sections by now, had established his long-yearned-for identity as a staid and cerebral politician. A year earlier, in 1935, Lord Lothian (Philip Henry Kerr), an influential British Liberal politician and newspaper editor, had established a strong relationship with him.[26] Sir Stafford Cripps, Ellen Wilkinson and Edward Thompson were among a few other important British personalities who had befriended him and who remained his well-wishers throughout his life.[27]

On the other hand, Krishna Menon, who was in close touch with Soviet officials in London, became his dedicated spokesman and ally. Jawaharlal picked up the threads of his past relationship with the LAI in London without directly participating in its activities. From Badenweiler, he travelled to London twice and each time, he visited the LAI secretariat.[28] The time was ripe for his return to the League when he reached Europe. The LAI's international secretariat had shifted from Berlin to London as the Nazis had begun persecuting communists and anti-colonial activists in Germany. Moscow's policy had also shifted in favour of the revival of cross-party alliances between communists and non-communists.[29]

Although Bose kept in close touch with him, Jawaharlal did not discuss his political activities with him. A.C.N. Nambiar recalls one occasion when C.F. Andrews came to Lausanne with Bose to meet with the Nehrus. During their visit, Bose spoke to Jawaharlal about the memorandum recently presented to the League of Nations in Geneva on the question of Abyssinian independence. It exposed the efforts of four imperialist powers—Britain, France, Japan and Italy—to carve out areas of influence in this free, ancient country and encroach upon its sovereignty. Bose strongly felt that a similar kind of memorandum should be sent to the League of Nations, stating the true nature of Britain's imperialism and exploitation in India. He sought Jawaharlal's signature on the memorandum to add weight to their demands.[30] However, Jawaharlal was completely unaware of the issue and avoided Bose's request on the grounds that his parole restrictions did not allow for any participation in political activities.[31]

However, when Jawaharlal came back to India, he became a champion of the Abyssinian cause and received appreciation from both party men and people in general. What actually happened was that during his visit to London shortly after his discussions with Bose, his LAI colleagues—Krishna Menon, Reginald Bridgeman, Shapurji Saklatvala and Ben Bradley—had called upon him to raise awareness about the Abyssinian crisis in India. Jawaharlal did not disappoint his comrades this time.[32]

In spite of such setbacks, Bose went out of his way to try to win Jawaharlal to his side in the years 1935–37. He was prepared to play second fiddle to him to bolster the Congress leftwing. This was because he was certain that another World War was imminent, and during this India would get a golden opportunity to pressure Great Britain to yield to her demands and grant her freedom in return for her support in terms of manpower, industry and weaponry-manufacturing resources to fight the War. Bose knew that owing to his proximity to Gandhi, Jawaharlal's role would be crucial in making decisions on the issue. He did not believe that his integrity could ever be questioned.

Therefore, he accommodated Jawaharlal in every way possible. He appreciated it when Jawaharlal pointed out a possible error about a date in his book, *The Indian Struggle,* and agreed that there could be several other mistakes, as the book was written abroad in a hurry, largely from memory and without any archival help. Enclosing a copy of his letter on Abyssinia that he sent to the *Manchester Guardian* on 1 October 1935, he wrote to Jawaharlal that as the War had just begun, it remained to be seen if it would develop into a war between England and Italy, indicating that it would then give an opportunity to Indians to reinforce their demand for freedom.[33] When Jawaharlal used the Abyssinian issue to bolster his own image in India, he kept quiet. He even took his counsel about returning to India, defying the embargo imposed by the government, in spite of Romain Rolland cautioning him against doing it.[34] Moreover, at his request, he issued a public statement giving him full support for his decisions surrounding the proposed rejuvenation of the Congress.[35]

The relations between the two leaders, thus, remained cordial, cooperative and even affectionate during this period. Jawaharlal got Bose's untainted cooperation on every conceivable issue during his presidency in 1937. This included Hindu-Muslim unity, the use of 'Bande Mataram', group alignments in Tripura, Sylhet and Faridpur, party discipline and so on.[36] He made it quite clear that he was prepared to follow Jawaharlal's lead. But when Gandhi declared Bose to be president of the Congress for the following year, Jawaharlal's relations with him grew strained, once again.

PRESIDENCY, 1936-37

In 1936, Jawaharlal's political ideas and perspectives were tilting towards socialism. Gandhi did not mind his ideological peregrinations as long as he was willing to accept his leadership and party discipline. During his presidency, Jawaharlal allowed communists and fellow travellers working in different committees and subcommittees to use their opportunities to organize leftwing activities in the country. Communists had, however, no illusions about the Congress's largely feudal, autocratic and sectarian character under Gandhi.[37]

After becoming president in 1936, Jawaharlal consciously admitted communists to various committees of the Congress to strengthen his position. They came not as communists, but as representatives of trade unions or similar organizations. At this point, Jawaharlal believed in the unified control of the economy and not in competitive market. He never said that he was a communist in his speech and writings; quite the contrary. But he had admitted to his preference for communism in multiple places, particularly before independence. The Lucknow session of the Congress, presided over by Jawaharlal on 12–14 April 1936, was significant in more than one sense. Having returned from Europe with a new ideological determination a month ago, he included three ardent socialists, Jayaprakash Narayan, Narendra Deva, and Achyut Patwardhan, in the Working Committee. Sarojini Naidu was kept out of it. She had to be called back under popular pressure when a casual vacancy arose in the middle of the year. Subhas Chandra Bose, who was in prison then, was also inducted into the Working Committee.

Jawaharlal sought to strengthen the AICC office with four foreign-educated radical young men—Dr Ram Manohar Lohia, Dr K.M. Ashraf, Dr Z.A. Ahmed and Sajjad Zaheer. Ram Manohar Lohia was to look after foreign affairs, K.M. Ashraf was put in charge of the department of communal amity, and Z.A. Ahmed was assigned economic affairs. Sajjad Zaheer, an Urdu poet and Marxist ideologue, held no particular portfolio and attended the office occasionally. Jayaprakash Narayan was in charge of labour, but he neither stayed in Allahabad nor attended the office.[38]

The old guard at the Working Committee was unhappy about these arrangements. Towards the end of June, matters came to a head at a Working Committee meeting in Wardha. Seven members of the committee (Rajendra Prasad, Vallabhbhai Patel, C. Rajagopalachari, Jairamdas Doulatram, Jamnalal Bajaj,

J.B. Kripalani and S.D. Dev) jointly sent a letter to Jawaharlal on 29 June, expressing their desire to resign from the committee.[39] Gandhi had seen the letter before it was sent. When an anxious Jawaharlal approached him for help to deal with the crisis, he gave him a mild hint that he must behave and then proceeded to take care of the issue.[40]

Thereafter, Jawaharlal's job became increasingly difficult due to the interference by the old guard. He repeatedly felt like resigning his presidency, but did not do so. Later, he justified his actions by saying that he did not resign because 'the news of General Franco's revolt in Spain' had upset him and he '...could not afford to weaken [their] organization and create an internal crisis by resigning just when it was essential for [them] to pull together.'[41]

One major achievement of the Lucknow session was that it could influence the opinions of a considerable number of people who had stayed away from leftwing ideas for a very long time. A few things that happened outside the conference also had far-reaching effects on its internal functioning. For instance, an 'anti-imperialist rally' organized by the CPI (banned since 1934) and the CSP attracted a large section of delegates and helped to lay an ideological-political foundation for the anti-imperialist front that communists, socialists, and other leftists had been trying to build for quite a long time. Significantly, a CPI leaflet explaining the party's stand on various issues was distributed at the venue and in the delegate camps by a section of Congressmen.[42]

The All India Kisan Sabha (AIKS) was formed at the Lucknow session under the leadership of Swami Sahajanand Saraswati and Indulal Yagnik (1892–1972), both of whom were prominent peasant leaders. No serious attempt had been made so far to form a peasant organization to address their needs. Moreover, the All-India Progressive Writers Association (AIPWA) also came into being at that time. The initiative was strongly supported by Rabindranath Tagore, Sarat Chandra Chattopadhyay, Sarojini Naidu and Josh Malihabadi, among others. Munshi Premchand (1880–1936) presided over their first conference.

JAWAHARLAL'S FASCINATION WITH CLASS STRUGGLE

Class struggle was Jawaharlal's favourite subject now. He published his second book, *Glimpses of World History*, in 1934 from Allahabad (its revised and much enlarged second edition came out in England in 1939). In the book, he dismissed non-Marxist schools of socialism in a single chapter and devoted two chapters to Marx and Marxism. His ideas largely guided the formation of the Congress Socialist Party (CSP) within the Congress in 1934, although he kept away from the organization for fear of displeasing Gandhi.

In his book, he severely criticized the leaders of the Second International (1889–1916) and praised the Third International, i.e., the Communist International (the Comintern), without going into the relative merits of one compared to the other. The Second International, created on 14 July 1889 by the socialist and labour parties of Europe, was an offshoot of the International Workingmen's Association (IWA) or the First International, founded in London in 1864 and dissolved in 1876. Its professed goal was to work towards international socialism. Vladimir Lenin (1870–1924) was a member of the Second International since 1905. Among the major achievements of the Second International were the declaration of the first of May as International Labour Day in 1889 and eighth March as International Women's Day in 1910. The Third International or the Comintern was founded by Lenin on 2 March 1919. It advocated world communism. It held seven World Congresses between 1919 and 1935 and conducted thirteen Enlarged Plenums, which had much the same function as the somewhat larger and more grandiose Congresses. Stalin officially dissolved the Comintern in 1943 to accommodate the sentiments of the United States and Britain.

Jawaharlal's charge against the Second International was that its leaders had usurped power and become prime ministers and presidents and deserted the common people who had helped them come to power. Subsequently, when the masses, forced by desperation, rose in protest and demanded action, they were kept down by force. Among the usurpers, according to him, were the Social Democrats in Germany, Aristide Briand in France, Ramsay MacDonald in England, Benito Mussolini, the Duce of Italy, and József Piłsudski, the dictator of Poland. After Independence, however, Jawaharlal remained noncommittal about communism, but people close to him in the party and the government knew that he took the CPI's criticism of his actions seriously and tried, wherever possible, to accommodate its viewpoint. This was despite the fact that communists were a special target for the Indian intelligence during his premiership. As the Mitrokhin Archive reveals, the secret correspondence between Moscow and the CPI was frequently intercepted by the IB in the early years after Independence and the organization had many 'assets' in the CPI, including Promode Dasgupta, who became the state secretary of West Bengal in 1959.[43]

When the Soviet prime minister Nikolai Bulganin and the party secretary Nikita Khrushchev visited India in November 1955, Jawaharlal took personal care to make their sojourn memorable. He requested Dr Bidhan Chandra Roy, the chief minister of West Bengal, to give the dignitaries a warm welcome in Calcutta. Their visit went exceedingly well, so afterwards he expressed his gratitude and appreciation to both the chief minister and the police commissioner of Calcutta.[44] His efforts went on to reap dividends later as India received Soviet support in the United Nations on the Kashmir issue. Moreover, on his return from India in December, Khrushchev asked the Presidium to discontinue their 'primitive' portrayal of India in Soviet publications and films.[45]

BOSE'S OUSTER FROM THE PARTY

Jawaharlal was not happy when Gandhi declared that Subhas Chandra Bose was going to be his successor in September 1937. He did not like the idea and saw it as a symptom of the rise of fascism in Indian politics.[46] On 1 October, he wrote to Gandhi suggesting Pattabhi Sitaramayya's name as an alternative.[47] A few days earlier, Rajkumari Amrit Kaur, Gandhi's favourite personal secretary, had sent him a note asking if Jawaharlal would not feel neglected if Bose became president.[48]

A few days after Jawaharlal, Vallabhbhai Patel also objected to Bose's selection. Gandhi wrote to him in a letter dated 1 November that although he shared his unhappiness about Bose, the fact remained that only he could be the president of the Haripura Congress. Vallabhbhai Patel accepted the leader's decision and organized the Congress session in Haripura, which was near Kadod, a town in the Surat district of Gujarat, from 19 to 22 February 1938. And he did it with such efficiency and finesse that it earned the praise of all the delegates present. Rajendra Prasad wrote in his memoir, 'There was unprecedented enthusiasm at the Congress session, which was presided over by Subhas Chandra Bose.'[49]

Soon after Bose became president, Jawaharlal decided to go to Europe. Bose offered him the post of general secretary, but he declined and reluctantly agreed to be a member of the Working Committee. A month ago, his mother had died after a long illness and his daughter was in Oxford. So, his desire to go abroad struck a sympathetic chord with his colleagues in the Working Committee. Much later, he would disclose that 'the real reason' he went to Europe '...was to freshen up my tired and puzzled mind.'[5] En route to Europe, he met Nahas Pasha, with whom he had been in regular correspondence, as well as the leaders of the Wafd Party in Alexandria. He invited them to attend the next annual session of the Congress on his own. Later, during the Tripuri Congress (1939), he prevailed upon Bose to use party funds to make elaborate arrangements for them.

After landing in Italy, Jawaharlal went straight to Spain, where a violent civil war was raging at that time, and spent five days in Barcelona as the guest of the republican government. Indira and Krishna Menon joined him there from London. From Spain, Jawaharlal and Indira went to Czechoslovakia and met A.C.N.

Nambiar in Prague. Jawaharlal told Nambiar that his assessment was that the socialist republican government in Spain would hold out and stay in the saddle. He got this impression from the leisurely disposition of the socialist mayor of Barcelona who spent a great deal of time with him having lunch in Madrid. He was flummoxed when General Franco marched into Madrid a few days later and formed a new government there.[51] His assessment of the Czechoslovakian situation, which he thought was not alarming, was similarly proven wrong.[52]

From Prague, Jawaharlal and his daughter travelled to Vienna by train via Bratislava, the principal town of Slovakia, which was not far from the Austrian capital. Nambiar accompanied them till Bratislava. For four days, Jawaharlal toured German minority areas, accompanied by Nambiar, Indira, and a pretty Oxford-educated interpreter, Dr Sylvia, whom Indira found to be pleasant company.[53] In September 1938, when he and his daughter were in Geneva, Jawaharlal met the Soviet intelligence official T. Maisky, to whom he expressed his desire to visit the Soviet Union.[54] Jawaharlal wanted Nambiar to be with him in Geneva, but the latter was busy shifting to a new apartment in Prague.[55] During this time, Jawaharlal gave him some financial help.[56]

A.C.N. Nambiar was with Jawaharlal and his daughter in Paris and Munich.[57] According to some accounts, Jawaharlal had a secret meeting with Nazi leaders in Munich.[58] This contradicted his biographer's contention that he went to Munich as a tourist and declined to meet any Nazi officials.[59] According to Sarvepalli Gopal, Jawaharlal had received an informal request to visit Germany as a guest to the Nazi government before his European tour, but he turned it down.[60] Jawaharlal's movements in Munich were kept under watch by the British intelligence; and he was spotted meeting Nazi leaders in secret.[61] The surveillance report could not throw any light on what transpired during the meeting.

During this European tour, Jawaharlal met Viscount Halifax, Foreign Secretary; the Marquess of Zetland, Secretary of State for India; and Viceroy Linlithgow, who were all Conservative politicians. These meetings in London, apparently for making connections,[62] could mean more than what met the eye. While he was in England, T. Maisky strongly urged him to visit the Soviet Union, but he expressed his inability to do so.[63] Gopal has stated that Jawaharlal could not visit Moscow because he did not get a visa on time, but Maisky's overtures contradict this contention.[64]

Before Jawaharlal's return to India in November 1938, Subhas Chandra Bose offered him the chairmanship of the Congress Planning Committee that he had set up a month earlier.[65] This pet project of Bose was inaugurated on 17 October in Bombay; Dr Meghnad Saha, a prominent scientist, was a member of the committee and Hari Vishnu Kamath, who had resigned from the ICS, was secretary. Gandhi was not enthusiastic about it, but he did not oppose its formation either. Jawaharlal was initially reluctant to accept the chairmanship of the Planning Committee. But very soon it caught his interest. Later, he took credit for setting it up in his book, *The Discovery of India*, when Bose was no longer in the Indian political scene.

The same thing happened with the medical mission sent to China during Bose's presidency. Jawaharlal took all the credit for it, and after Independence, he even indirectly insinuated that Bose was opposed to the idea. What actually happened was that in November 1937, Agnes Smedley, who was then with the Chinese Eighth Route Army (Red Army), motivated Chu Teh (Zhu De), the commander-in-chief, to write to Jawaharlal, the then Congress president, to send them funds from India for the revolutionary war. On 23 November 1937, she requested Jawaharlal to send a bank draft to the Sianfu branch of the Bank of China, to her address in Sianon.[66] Zhu De made the same request three days later.[67] Jawaharlal presented Zhu De's letter to the Working Committee and sat on the matter.

Three months later, the issue was discussed at the Haripura Congress (February 1938) when Subhas Chandra Bose was the president. Bose went about the matter with his usual thoroughness and formed the China Aid Committee, with G.P. Hutheesingh,

Jawaharlal's sister Krishna's husband, as secretary, and Dr Bidhan Chandra Roy, Dr Sunil Chandra Bose and Dr Jivraj Mehta as members.[68] On 12 June, an 'All-India China Day' was organized across India with great success. On 28 June, Bose made an appeal through the press for people to donate funds for the cause. Following this, a 'China Fund Day' was observed from 7 to 9 July all over the country with great enthusiasm. Bose organized a number of meetings in Calcutta and elsewhere to popularize the cause.[69] He also sent a letter to Chinese leaders, expressing India's solidarity with the people of China in their fight against Japanese aggression.

In September 1938, a medical mission was sent to China with the funds raised in the campaign. Bose personally took care of the nitty-gritty of the arrangements. The medical team was headed by Dr Madan Lal Atal, Kamala Nehru's brother, and consisted of Dr Moreswar Ram Chaudre Cholker, professor of surgery at the Nagpur Medical School, Dr Dwarkanath Shantaram Kotnis from Solapur, Maharashtra, Dr Bijoy Kumar Basu from Calcutta, and Dr Debesh Chandra Mukherjee from Dibrugarh, Assam.[70]

Agnes Smedley was only in touch with Jawaharlal and she had no way of knowing these developments. She had the impression that Jawaharlal had formed what she described as 'the first China Medical Committee of the Indian National Congress.' She kept the Congress Party informed about the progress of the war and of China's plight via Jawaharlal from time to time.[71] Subhas Chandra Bose was no longer in the picture then, so he was conveniently forgotten.

In the meantime, the government was keen on creating a rift between Bose and Gandhi. Bose's movements and activities were kept under close scrutiny by the Indian intelligence. Through its high-level contact K.M. Munshi, a Congress minister in Maharashtra, Gandhi was informed and shown photographs of Bose's recent clandestine meeting with a German official in Bombay.[72] At this time, Gandhi was increasingly feeling that his method of containing people, which had worked so well with

Jawaharlal, was not that successful with Bose. In fact, they had nearly fallen out over the issue of the formation of the Bengal ministry.

In the elections held in January 1937 under the Government of India Act of 1935, the Congress had secured the majority of seats in five major provinces—Bihar, Orissa, Madras, the Central Provinces and Berar, and the U.P.—and was the single largest party in four other provinces—Bombay, Bengal, the North-West Frontier Province and Assam. Only in Sind and the Punjab did it fail to become the single largest party. The party was, thus, in a position to form ministries in the five majority provinces and be in a dominant coalition in the four others where it was the single largest party. The Bengal Congress under Sarat Bose was keen to form a coalition government with the non-communal and radical Krishak Praja Party (KPP) led by Abdul Kasem Fazlul Huq (1873–1962), but Jawaharlal, then the president of the party, showed no interest.

In Bengal, where Muslims were in a slight majority compared to Hindus (the ratio of their populations would be 52:48), the seat allocation was such that the general franchise could elect only forty-eight out of the 250 seats in total. As many as 117 seats were exclusively reserved for Muslims, and in such cases, the candidates as well as the electorate had to belong to this religious community. Eleven seats were reserved for Europeans; three for Anglo-Indians; two for Indian Christians; nineteen for the representatives of commerce and industry; eight for labour; five for landowners; two for universities; two each for general-category women and Muslim women; and finally, one for Anglo-Indian women. Another thirty seats were reserved for the depressed castes who were basically Hindus, but were listed in a Schedule to the Act.[73] This is how the category of the 'Scheduled Caste' was identified as an independent political entity in India for the first time.

The Congress won forty-three out of forty-eight general seats (the party did not contest any of the Muslim seats). The regional radical Muslim party, the Krishak Praja Party (KPP) led by Fazlul Huq, which won the majority of the seats, was willing to form a coalition government with the Congress. But the central Congress leadership under Jawaharlal Nehru was not interested in teaming up with them. So, Fazlul Huq formed the ministry together with the Muslim League.

After Subhas Chandra Bose became the president of the party, he reasoned with Gandhi in Wardha that it would be strategically important to have a coalition with a Muslim party in Bengal at this critical time in order to present a united front to the British. No one could be better for the purpose than the radical, non-communal KPP. This measure would not only rob Britain of a major propaganda point in the developing war scenario as the USA was already breathing down its neck to grant independence to India, but also put the Muslim League on the back foot.

Bose and Fazlul Huq had decided among themselves that Nalini Ranjan Sarkar, the finance minister of the Huq ministry, would resign and this would present them with an opportunity to step out of the coalition with the Muslim League and form a new one with the Congress Party.[74] Gandhi approved of Bose's plan, but soon, however, G.D. Birla and Maulana Azad, who had got wind of the plan, met Gandhi in Wardha. They took Nalini Ranjan Sarkar with them and convinced him that it would be unwise to bring down a communal Muslim ministry. G.D. Birla was Gandhi's man of confidence in Bengal and Maulana Azad was almost the last word in Muslim affairs in the Congress at that time. Each of them had a stake in the matter. G.D. Birla's business interests in Bengal were thriving under the present political dispensation. Moreover, the government, of which he was a reliable contact, disfavoured a coalition ministry with the Congress in which the Bose brothers would play a pivotal role. As for Maulana Azad, he apprehended losing his hold among liberal Muslims and Hindus due to Bose's plans for a coalition.[75]

Subsequently, Gandhi dictated a letter to Bose in their presence, asking him to discard the proposed plan and carry out the desired reforms with the help of the existing ministry. G.D. Birla himself delivered the letter to Bose, who was then in Bombay.[76] Maulana Azad and G.D. Birla both knew that the letter would serve a dual purpose: the acceptance of this diktat would damage Bose's reputation and initiative while opposing it would ruin him politically. Gandhi's volte-face, which came abruptly when everything was almost as good as settled, dismayed Bose. He understood that his proposed move was going to be futile as Nalini Ranjan Sarkar was now on the opposing side. Besides, Gandhi's letter had put an effective seal on it as far as his party was concerned. Any other leader would have kept quiet, but not Bose. He wrote back to Gandhi, 'It has astonished me that you did not feel it necessary even to consult me before you arrived at a decision on such a serious matter.'[77]

In hindsight, it appears that had Bose's plan succeeded, the communal holocaust of 1946 might not have happened under the Suhrawardy ministry in Bengal and Jinnah might not have got enough support to create Pakistan. This is because after this, the charismatic Fazlul Huq soon joined the Muslim League and rejuvenated the party at the grassroots level in Bengal. Two years later, he took a leading role in the Lahore Resolution, which ultimately led to the Partition.

During his presidency, Bose became increasingly convinced that the right-wing leaders in the Congress would compromise with the British government on issues like the formation of a federation with the princely states and the question of cooperation with Britain's war effort, and would effectively put the issue of independence on the backburner. On the contrary, if the Congress launched a struggle now, it could attain independence within eighteen months at the most and the country could still remain intact.[78] He was even prepared to step down as president if it meant that a struggle would be launched at that moment.[79] However, Gandhi and Jawaharlal did not share his view of the situation.[80] Their coterie selected an official candidate behind Bose's back to ensure that he did not become president in the next term.

Frankly speaking, Bose's suspicion about the right wing's intent to compromise on the plan to form a federation with the princely states in a truncated India was not as baseless as it was made out to be during the anti-Bose campaign. The Government of India Act of 1935 called for a federal structure for the nation of India, consisting of the provinces and the princely states, which meant that the country was to be divided into several parts. While the federal sections of the Act dealing with the princely states had not become operative at that point, the sections on provincial autonomy had. Though the Congress Party was officially dead against the federation and a truncated India, Lord Lothian quoted Bhulabhai Desai, a Congress leader from Bombay, who mentioned in his press statement that the party was ready to compromise on the federal elements of the Act.[81] G.D. Birla also gave such hints.[82] The British press also indicated that Gandhi was behind Desai's remarks.[83] There were even rumours that a tentative list of central ministers had already been prepared on the basis of the proposed federation.[84]

During his electoral campaign, Bose's opponents approached the press and quoted him as having said on several occasions that there was a possibility of the right wing compromising on the issue of the federation and that he, as a staunch anti-federalist, would stand against a right-wing candidate. Jawaharlal and others from the Gandhian coterie propagated this as 'aspersions' on Gandhi. Jawaharlal harped on it even when the issue had become dormant after the election. During the campaign, Gandhi stayed away in Delhi and Gujarat, although his name was freely used against Bose. He did not attend the annual conference at Tripuri, a village near the historical city of Jabalpur in the Central Provinces (now Madhya Pradesh), where Bose defeated Pattabhi Sitaramayya, the official candidate, and won the election.

In Tripuri, the Congress rank and file were told by the coterie that they would have to choose between Gandhi and Bose in their future fight for independence. The issue of 'aspersions' became a major propaganda point against Bose. Govind Ballabh Pant

(1887–1961) used this to get his resolution passed among the confused delegates in Tripuri and Bose was unable to counter their propaganda because of his high fever. This effectively reaffirmed their faith in Gandhian 'fundamental policies' and 'programme,' and they expressed their confidence in the previous Working Committee, asking the president to accept Gandhi's wishes for the formation of the new Working Committee. During this fracas, the Congress Socialist Party and the other leftist groups withdrew their support from Bose at the behest of Jayaprakash Narayan and Narendra Deva—Jawaharlal's close allies—who stated, contrary to the stand they had taken earlier, that Gandhi's leadership was necessary to preserve national unity at this time. Govind Ballabh Pant and others launched a lurid mud-slinging campaign against Bose on this occasion. Vallabhbhai Patel took part in it directly and Jawaharlal did the same, again indirectly.

Personally, Jawaharlal continued to be outwardly solicitous of Bose, and the latter still wanted to keep the older politician on his side. By this time, the manoeuvres to remove Bose from the Congress hierarchy were already in motion with Gandhi and Jawaharlal's full knowledge and approval. Knowing that Bose was sick in Calcutta, the old guard of the Working Committee (J.B. Kripalani helped in these manoeuvres as the secretary) called a meeting in Wardha, near Bombay, on 22 February 1939, just before the Tripuri session (10–12 March). This time, Bose was cautious not to allow the meeting to take place in his absence in view of a bitter experience in the past when Gandhi and his cohort had chosen the presidential candidate for the Congress without his knowledge. He demanded that the meeting be delayed.

In a premeditated move, the old guard took umbrage at the postponement of the meeting; on 22 February, thirteen out of the fifteen members of the Working Committee, including Jawaharlal, resigned on the grounds that Bose had expressed no confidence in them by this action. Twelve Working Committee members signed the resignation letter together, while Jawaharlal sent in his resignation separately. While the joint resignation letter, drafted by Gandhi himself, was 'decent' and 'straightforward', Jawaharlal's letter was 'accusatory'.[85] Jawaharlal had wanted his own version of the letter to be adopted by the others, but they did not agree to this.[86]

Bose sought to resolve the crisis with Gandhi's help but to no avail. He sent him telegrams and four long letters—three in March and one in April—besides an eight-page letter on 10 April 1939, explaining himself and suggesting three alternative ways to come out of the impasse. First of all, he requested him to resume the nationalist struggle, which would automatically resolve their differences. Alternatively, he sought Gandhi's vote of confidence in him if he were to form a cabinet according to his advice. If these two proposals were not acceptable to him, he suggested that Gandhi assume direct control of the Working Committee, in which case many obstacles and difficulties would be automatically removed.[87] Bose also informed Gandhi that he would not form a homogeneous cabinet including only the members from his faction, as he had suggested,[88] because the existing political situation demanded a cohesive struggle to achieve independence.

On Gandhi's advice, Bose met with Rajendra Prasad at the Sodepur ashram where Gandhi was staying. He also had discussions with both Rajendra Prasad and Maulana Azad in the latter's house in Calcutta for two consecutive days to solve the problem of forming the Working Committee before the AICC meeting. But he was humiliated during the discussions (Maulana Azad was particularly offensive). Even when he agreed to accept that all the candidates would be chosen by the other side, Gandhi refused to accommodate him when Maulana Azad and Rajendra Prasad finally discussed the matter with him in Sodepur (Bose was asked to wait in a separate room). Bose understood that it would not be possible for him to get along with this coterie; he resigned his presidency at the AICC session held on 30 April 1939. A few days later, on 3 May 1939, he announced the creation of the Forward Bloc at the mammoth Ramgarh Conference in Bihar.[89]

After Bose's resignation, Gandhi sounded both Maulana Azad and Jawaharlal out for the post, but they both declined. So, Rajendra Prasad was made president for the remaining term. Two months later, on 21 June 1939, Bose formed a Left Consolidation Committee (LCC) in Bombay with a few heterogeneous leftist parties and organizations. Shortly afterwards, the AICC adopted a resolution in Bombay prohibiting party men from criticizing Congress ministries. A few days later, on 9 July 1939, the LCC successfully organized an all-India protest day against this undemocratic diktat.

Consequently, in an unprecedented move, the Working Committee removed Bose from the BPCC presidency with immediate effect, and barred him from holding any elective office for three years. This resolution was also drafted by Gandhi and the order was issued by Rajendra Prasad as the interim president. Following this, Bose resigned from the Congress Party and Jawaharlal was finally able to get rid of his greatest rival in the party.

Years later, Jawaharlal told a British correspondent that he had let Subhas Chandra Bose down. He justified his actions by saying, 'I did it because I had realized that, at that stage, whatever one's view might be about the way India should develop, Gandhi was India. Anything which weakened Gandhi weakened India. So I subordinated myself to Gandhi, although I was in agreement with what Subhas was trying to do.'[90]

9

JINNAH AND CONGRESS POLITICS

AN ANIMUS THAT HARMED

When Gandhi joined Indian politics, Muhammad Ali Jinnah was already a famous Gujarati public figure. Gandhi revealed his complex about him in their very first meeting. When Jinnah was presiding over a reception arranged for him by a Gujarati association in Bombay,[1] he customarily welcomed him in English. However, in response, Gandhi remarked in Gujarati that in South Africa when people talked of Gujaratis, '...Parsis and Mahomedans were not thought of, but now he had returned to find a Muslim chairing the meeting.'[2] This communal and offensive remark, which must have shocked the sophisticated Jinnah like many others, was reported in *The Bombay Chronicle* on 15 January 1915.[3]

In April 1918, Gandhi and Jinnah got into an open conflict at Viceroy Chelmsford's War Conference over the issue of recruiting of Indians into the British army (Bal Gangadhar Tilak and C.R. Das were not invited).[4] Jinnah raised a number of issues, especially the denial of commissioned ranks to Indians, and wanted these to be addressed before India sent more men to the army. Also, he demanded the immediate introduction of a parliamentary bill to institute Home Rule so that Indians could fight the war as equal citizens of the Empire, not mercenaries. On the other hand, Gandhi was keen to help procure volunteers for the British,[5] believing that loyalty and goodwill would persuade Britain to grant self-government to Indians.

The difference between their approaches stemmed from the difference in their understanding of the problem. To Jinnah, swaraj meant responsible Home Rule on the Canadian model. To achieve this, one would require a political arrangement that had to be argued over in detail and arrived at in stages. It could not be attained by begging for charity. The war provided a good opportunity to hasten the demand for Home Rule. Therefore, throughout 1918, Jinnah remained belligerent towards the British. He opposed the Raj when the Montagu-Chelmsford Report and the Rowlatt Report were published in July, and even led a mass protest in December against a civic function organized in Bombay to commemorate the conclusion of Governor Willingdon's term.[6]

At this point, Jinnah's popularity eclipsed Gandhi's. He had just married the beautiful eighteen-year-old heiress Rattanbai 'Ruttie' Petit, and was acclaimed the uncrowned king of Bombay. In contrast, the end of the year 1918 found Gandhi both demoralized and ill. His health did not recover till 1920, but he managed to make a recovery in the political arena before then, riding on the wave of outrage against the Rowlatt Act(s) and the massacre in Amritsar.

By the middle of 1919, Gandhi and Jinnah disagreed on several areas related to policy and tactics. Although he was seven years younger than Gandhi, Jinnah was a relatively experienced and more typical Congressman (he had joined the party in 1906). He enjoyed the implicit trust and support of eminent leaders like C.R. Das, Bal Gangadhar Tilak, M.R. Jayakar and even Lala Lajpat Rai, all of whom thought more or less along the same lines as him at that time. But Gandhi was fast consolidating his position within the party with the help of Madan Mohan Malaviya, Motilal Nehru and Annie Besant. He was maintaining an interface with C.R. Das and Bal Gangadhar Tilak as well. He had acquired the title of Mahatma ('great soul') in 1915, on which Tagore put a seal of approval in an open letter to him dated 12 April 1919.[7]

At the Nagpur Congress (December 1920), Gandhi brought about an irreversible change in the field of Indian politics by convincing the party to agree to join the Khilafat movement and officially adopt nonviolent noncooperation as a creed. By the latter half of 1920, the mood of the nation had become rather militant and there was a tremendous upsurge of Muslim interest in the Congress. The Nagpur session witnessed a clash between the ambitions of the two men.

Gandhi had taken meticulous care in selecting his supporters as delegates prior to the Nagpur session and had come up with planned strategies to humiliate Jinnah. A few days ago, he had asked Ruttie to 'coax' Jinnah to learn either Hindustani or Gujarati in an unsolicited letter.[9] Afterwards, when she took her seat with her husband on the podium during the session, Gandhi's supporters made her step down on the grounds that her clothes were 'improper' (though from all accounts, she was decently and tastefully attired). Subsequently, there was a lot of booing and catcalling, as well as a barrage of insulting words from the audience during the debates, which '...drove Jinnah from the platform.'[8]

Jinnah had brought his wife to Nagpur all the way from Bombay to acquaint her with Indian politics. So this humiliation left a deep scar on both their psyches. The events of 1920 convinced Jinnah that the Congress could no longer be the vehicle for ensuring equality for Muslims in Indian politics. Gandhi was dismayed as well when the Khilafatists ceased to be genial and drifted apart from the Congress even before the conclusion of the noncooperation movement. In August 1921, the Muslim Mappila community from the Malabar region initiated a jihad against wealthy Hindus and resorted to murder and forced conversions.

As a face-saving measure, Gandhi planned to start a satyagraha on the issue of taxation in Bardoli in Gujarat and informed Lord Reading about this. But before the plan could be executed, word got around that twenty-two policemen were killed by Congress activists in a small town called Chauri Chaura (UP). The incident gave him the opportunity to call off the movement on the grounds that the principle of nonviolence had been violated. His own arrest in March 1922 came to him almost as a reprieve from this sticky situation. He remained in prison till February 1924 and then reluctantly returned to Congress politics. By this time, the Khilafat-noncooperation alliance was long gone. At the AICC meeting held in Ahmedabad in June 1924, it became clear that his hold over the party was waning and he wept publicly for the people's lack of commitment to nonviolence.[10]

As for Jinnah, he resumed his legal practice and observed the noncooperation campaign from a disapproving distance. After the failure of the campaign, he decided to return to politics in 1923, contested and won the Muslim seat from Bombay at the Central Legislative Assembly. He found himself leading a faction of 'Independents' in the Assembly which was large enough to hold the balance of power. He then alternately worked with and against the Congress and adopted the same approach with the government. The Swarajists under C.R. Das and Motilal Nehru did well in the 1923 elections, winning forty-two out of 101 seats in the Central Assembly, where they took their place alongside Jinnah and the Independents. An informal alliance sprang up between them, and when they voted together they called themselves the Nationalist Party.

The alliance was not a stable one. The Swaraj Party was dedicated to wrecking the system from within and Jinnah's Independents preferred to take each measure on its merits. Although together they could command a majority in the Assembly of 1923–26, the government neutralized the advantage using its reserved power. After 1926, another group of dissident Congressmen, led by M.R. Jayakar and N.C. Kelkar, formed the Responsive Cooperation Party, which cooperated with the British and aimed at counterbalancing the Muslim influence in politics.

Jinnah was still in search of a middle path in order to achieve dominion status through the united struggle of like-minded parties and a political scenario where Muslim interests would be secure. In 1924, he was appointed to the Muddiman Committee, a body set up by the viceroy to assess the mechanics of the new 1919 constitution. The nine-man committee, headed by Sir Alexander Muddiman, the Home Member of the Government of India, included Sir Sivaswami Aiyar, Dr R.P. Paranjpye, Tej Bahadur Sapru and Bijay Chand Mahtab. The majority report submitted by government officials and loyalists held that the diarchy had not been given a fair trial and recommended that only minor changes be made to the constitution. The minority report, largely penned by Jinnah, scathingly criticized the system and recommended its immediate scrapping, as well as wider popular representation.

In the years 1923–27, the field of national politics remained fragmented. Gandhi chose to maintain silence and stayed at his ashram in 1925–26. He was in poor health, as was often the case when he felt politically sidelined. He used this time to finish his autobiography, write letters and articles for publication, many of which were about stray dogs. But he kept his ears to the ground.

Jinnah was trying to consolidate his influence in the Muslim League at this time, along with finding a basis for Hindu-Muslim cooperation. In March 1927, he called a meeting of important Muslim leaders, including members of the Central Legislature, to develop a programme for unity. The following proposals, known as the Delhi Proposals, were made at the meeting: (a) the separation of Sind as an independent province, (b) the extension of reforms to the North-West Frontier Province and Baluchistan, (c) population-based representation in Punjab and Bengal so as not to reduce the Muslim majority to a minority, (d) the reservation of one-third of the seats in the Central Legislature for Muslims, and (e) a system of reciprocal weightage to be followed in other Muslim-majority and Hindu-majority provinces.[11] It was stipulated that if these demands were met, then mixed electorates would be accepted not only in elections to the provincial assemblies, but also in those to the Central Legislature.[12]

The Delhi Proposals were welcomed by most Congressmen, but Motilal and Jawaharlal Nehru dismissed them and convinced Gandhi that politically, Jinnah was of no consequence. Sarojini Naidu, who was Congress president a year ago, was enthusiastic about the Delhi Proposals and thought that Jinnah had risen against all odds and had nearly come up with a resolution to the Hindu-Muslim problem. On 22 March 1927, she wrote to her daughter, Padmaja, from inside the assembly: 'Jinnah has absolutely risen to his height and carried the better mind of the people with him. I am very proud of Jinnah.'[13]

The CWC appreciated the proposals, especially the idea of joint electorates with reciprocal concessions in favour of minorities; it selected a small committee to iron out the details with both Muslim and Hindu leaders. However, Lajpat Rai and Jawaharlal refused to acknowledge the fundamental divide between the two communities, and their influence within the party stood in the way.[14] What ultimately wrecked the initiative was their failure to understand that the mere union of hearts was an illusionary objective if one were to ignore the question of power.[15]

During the All Parties Conference, Jinnah's Muslim League agreed to cooperate with the Congress while devising the Swaraj Constitution, while the faction led by Muhammad Shafi (1869–1932) kept away from it. The draft report, popularly known as the Nehru Report, was published in August 1928. It was not really based on consensus because it represented only a common measure of agreement among three or four predominantly Hindu factions within the All Parties Conference, namely a dominant group from the Congress represented by Motilal Nehru, the Hindu Mahasabha group represented by M.S. Aney, and the liberals represented by Tej Bahadur Sapru. The Muslim point of view was not adequately represented in the report.

Consequently, the Nehru Report drew an adverse reaction from Muslim legislators. Plans were afoot to call an all-embracing conference of the representative Muslims to face the challenges posed by the Nehru Report. The Congress ignored the signs of danger. On 28 October, the AICC session in Calcutta endorsed the Nehru Report and passed only two resolutions on the Hindu-Muslim question relating to (a) conversion and cow protection, and (b) the prohibition of music in public processions. A committee was formed to look into the problems, but it lost steam soon after its formation.

Before publishing the report, Motilal Nehru had requested Jinnah in a letter dated 2 August to return from Paris (Jinnah had gone there to attend to his wife who was admitted in a nursing home) to take part in the final deliberations on the Report in Lucknow to be held from 27 to 31 August 1928. He knew that the report would not be accepted by a vast majority of the Muslims without Jinnah's support. He had sent Jinnah the draft report, assuring him that the committee was still open to any suggestions that he might have.[16] Jinnah, however, could not leave his wife behind in Paris.

The Nehru Report was welcomed by M.C. Chagla (1900–81), who was left in charge of the League in Jinnah's absence. When Jinnah returned in October, he was furious with Chagla for not keeping him posted about the developments and for accepting the 'Hindu position' as he called it.[17] At the meeting of the All Parties Conference in Calcutta on 22 December 1928, Jinnah's Delhi Proposals, which most people had thought would finally resolve Hindu-Muslim differences, were heavily opposed by the Hindu Mahasabha led by M.R. Jayakar.[18] He even questioned Jinnah's credentials as a Muslim leader. Even the liberals, who had initially favoured the League's amendments, became hostile. Tej Bahadur Sapru, the co-author of the Nehru Report, called him 'a spoilt child'.[19]

Though deeply hurt, Jinnah appealed to the convention again and again, 'not as a Mussalman but an Indian,' to accept these small concessions for the sake of unity. When his persuasive and conciliatory speech failed to convince Hindus and Sikhs to accept the Muslim position, he still appealed to the convention to '...part as friends...' and give up any 'bad blood'. But his appeal fell on deaf ears. When M.R. Jayakar, who had known him well enough and long enough as a secular nationalist, called him a 'communal zealot', Jinnah abruptly left the conference.[20] He left Calcutta around half past eight the next morning. His friend Jamshed Nusserwanjee Mehta recollected the last time they met: 'I went to see him off at the railway station. He was standing at the door of his first-class coupe compartment, and he took my hand. He had tears in his eyes as he said, "Jamshed, this is the parting of the ways."'[21]

Jinnah did not go back to Bombay directly, but stopped in Delhi to attend the All India Muslim Conference organized by Muslim hardliners. He had not planned to attend it before, but after his failure in Calcutta, he decided to put in an appearance at their open session. This raised the hardliners' hopes that they had won him over to accept their views at last. But shaken as he was by his Calcutta experience, Jinnah still did not think of crossing over to their camp.

A few days later, Gandhi moved the resolution on the Nehru Report at the Calcutta Congress, which ratified it as party policy.

JINNAH IN RETREAT

Jinnah was now on the verge of being eclipsed in the world of Muslim politics. The leaders from Punjab, who held the key to power, had little interest in his goal of having a strong central authority and a joint political platform with the Congress. They were also not keen on securing freedom from the British and preferred to have provincial autonomy in as loose a federation as possible. With this end in view, Fazl-i-Husain (1877–1936), their chief, formed the All-India Muslim Conference and directed Aga Khan to head it. In January 1929, the outfit rejected the Nehru Report and continued to demand weighted representation at the centre and separate electorates in the provinces.

Though temporarily ill and tired, Jinnah was, however, not ready to admit defeat. He drew up a list of demands, known as the Fourteen Points, in an attempt to create a new national pact. The Points were basically an elaboration of the Delhi Proposals in light of the Nehru Report. They included a demand for a federal government, with residuary powers vested in the provinces, and a uniform degree of autonomy for all provinces. Minorities were to be represented adequately and effectively in all provinces, but majorities—of any kind—were not to be reduced to a minority status or a state of parity. A few of his other demands were: at least one-third Muslim representation in the central legislative body, Muslim ministers constituting at least a third of any governing body, freedom of worship and belief, separate electorates which could be amended or revised by mutual agreement, no changes in the boundary of provinces that would affect existing Muslim-majority communities, a reasonable share of government jobs and preferment to Muslims, and the protection of and respect for Islamic cultures, languages, education and charitable institutions. Nevertheless, Jinnah could not get his Fourteen Points adopted at the Muslim League meeting in Delhi in March 1929. This was a greater blow to him than his defeat in Calcutta last December.[22] He did not quite recover from it till he took control of the revitalized Muslim League after nearly half a decade.

As usual, the Congress ignored Jinnah's proposals. Motilal described the Fourteen Points as 'preposterous' in a letter to Gandhi and advised him to ignore Jinnah.[23] He was guided by Jawaharlal's views in the matter. To Jawaharlal, there was as much difference between Jinnah and the Indian masses as between Savile Row and Bond Street on the one hand, and the Indian village with its mud huts on the other.[24]

Gandhi, however, did not put Jinnah in the waste bin of history. In August 1929, he travelled to Bombay to talk to him in private. Jinnah came and met him, but the talks were inconclusive. In May 1929, a Labour government came to power in Britain under Ramsay Macdonald, with whom Jinnah had a fairly good rapport.[25] Jinnah wrote to Macdonald about his ideas for India's future. He explained to him that if Britain pledged a fully responsible government to India now, the efforts of the Congress Party, which was going to demand independence, would be thwarted effectively.[26] He suggested that they convene a round table conference in London, in which Indian and British leaders would discuss India's advance towards a future constitution.[27] He travelled to Simla shortly afterwards to discuss his plan with Viceroy Irwin. He worked on it with him and the British premier for the next few months.[28]

In November 1930, a Round Table Conference was held in Westminster Hall without the Congress's participation. But there was substantial participation by all other social and political groups from India. As many as fifty-eight representatives from British India and sixteen from the princely states took part in the deliberations. Though Aga Khan led the Muslim delegation, Jinnah also made his presence felt. He declared that Indians expected action and looked forward to the creation of a new 'Dominion of India' to join the others in the British Commonwealth of Nations.[29]

That December, while the first Round Table Conference was in progress in London, the poet Sir Muhammad Iqbal (1877–1938) spoke to an audience of less than seventy at the annual session of the Muslim League in Allahabad about a possible Muslim homeland in northwest India, as an alternative to what had been envisaged in the Nehru Report and the Simon Commission's recommendations.[30] His idea later became famous as the 'Iqbal Plan'. However, at that time Muslims from neither Sind and the NWFP nor the Punjab favoured his opinion. Sind and the NWFP were unwilling to lose their separate identity in the bigger geopolitical entity called Punjab, whereas the Muslim-majority province of Punjab was eager to have regional autonomy.[31]

Later, Iqbal corresponded with Jinnah on this issue and met him several times till his death in 1938. He was instrumental, together with Liaquat Ali Khan (1895–1951), in bringing Jinnah back from his flourishing legal practice in London, in which he had been engaged in the meantime, and from his temporary retirement from politics to assume the leadership of the rejuvenated Muslim League in 1934. The Muslim League had mended internal conflicts and differences by 1933 and was now ready to accept him as their leader. When Aga Khan and the other loyalists failed to launch another Muslim party, Jinnah's position became secure among India's Muslims.

SHIFT TO COMMUNAL POLITICS

Even after securing this strong position in India's political arena, Jinnah did not abandon his old idea of forming a united nationalist front against the British. He negotiated with Rajendra Prasad, the then Congress president, to work out a joint approach to the new Constitution. Rajendra Prasad tells us that there was a significant breakthrough in these efforts in the early part of 1935.[32] However, Jawaharlal strongly disapproved of Jinnah and the Muslim League and his influence;[33] additionally, Jinnah's insistence that Madan Mohan Malaviya and the Hindu Mahasabha should also be a party to the agreement[34] scuttled it. Jinnah was convinced that without their support, the Congress alone could not achieve the unity that he desired. Jinnah's eagerness for unity was viewed by Jawaharlal as a symptom of his lack of a powerful political support base.

In early 1937, Jawaharlal refused to have an electoral alliance with the Muslim League in the United Provinces although he had promised his friend Chaudhry Khaliquzzaman that he would do so. The Muslim League lacked party infrastructure at the block level and nor did it have funds like the Congress to win elections. Moreover, the Congress had its traditional vote bank among Muslims. As a result, the party failed to get even a majority of the provincial reserved Muslim assembly seats and could only win 109 seats out of 482. In contrast, the Congress won all the general seats open to it, plus sixty per cent of the reserved seats, bagging a total of 716 seats.[35]

Sir Muhammad Iqbal was quick to understand what had happened. The Congress had reached out to the Muslims masses, bypassing their aristocratic leaders, during its 'mass contact' campaign in March 1937. In his letter dated 28 March 1937, he urged Jinnah to leave 'the old League' consisting of the upper classes and reach out to the masses[36] by appealing to 'the law of Islam'.[37] Jinnah also realized that he must have a powerful and effective voice in Delhi in order to secure the allegiance of regional Muslim parties and groups.

However, he was still reluctant to give up his long-held beliefs. But when Chaudhry Khaliquzzaman, who was third in the League hierarchy, failed to obtain even two berths in the Congress Party government and could not forge a coalition in the United Provinces, in spite of Nehru's past promises,[38] and B.G. Kher could not form a coalition and induct some League leaders into his ministry in Bombay[39] because Jawaharlal, as Congress president, saw no reason to accommodate the Muslim League,[40] he finally made up his mind to make a momentous choice.

Soon, Jinnah started a negotiation with Sir Sikandar Hayat Khan and Fazlul Huq, chief ministers of Punjab and Bengal respectively, to represent them at the central level. Both of them were initially opposed to the concept of a Muslim nation, but they came to accept it later. Sir Sikandar granted Jinnah the authority to speak for Muslims at the national level on the condition that he would not interfere in the politics of Punjab. Jinnah kept this promise till 1947.

He now began to ramp up his anti-Congress rhetoric at every congregation he attended, branding it an 'authoritarian' and 'totalitarian' party that only represented Hindu interests. Soon, he was able to capture both the ears and the hearts of common Muslims in India and whip up a communal frenzy of sorts. This was precisely what he had condemned in Gandhi's politics earlier.

Jinnah gathered competent lieutenants like Liaquat Ali Khan and Huseyn Shahid Suhrawardy around him to help him organize his followers and build a following. He was now hailed as 'Quaid-e-Azam', the great leader—a title by which Gandhi also started calling him on Sarojini Naidu's suggestion. However, Jinnah always addressed him as 'Mr Gandhi'. For a person who had been suffering from tuberculosis from the 1930s and later from severe lung cancer (he lived for only thirteen months after Independence), this was an inhuman feat. Jinnah kept his poor health a closely guarded secret, so much so that Mountbatten commented many years later, perhaps in jest, that had he known Jinnah was so ill, he would have stalled the process of Partition.[41]

Jinnah now demanded complete equity with the Congress in all national affairs and also the exclusive right to speak for Muslims. His claim was recognized by the British government. In early 1938, he made a new constitution for his party, dividing the country into wards, divisions and provinces on the lines of the Congress Party. There would be a Central Board consisting of 465 members and a Working Committee of twenty-one members. The annual subscription fee for membership of the party was two *anna*s (sixteen annas = one rupee), which was exactly half of what the Congress charged.

His progress was not lost on the Congress leadership. Jawaharlal began corresponding with him from January to April 1938 in order to come to an understanding, but he failed in his efforts because of his lack of clarity and his refusal to adopt a straightforward approach.[42] In late April 1938, Gandhi went to Bombay and met Jinnah, this time at the latter's residence. During this meeting, Jinnah demanded that the Congress must accept that he and his party alone spoke for India's Muslims. This claim was central to Jinnah's agreement with Sikandar Hayat Khan and became a vital part of his own strategy. Gandhi, tired and ill, put up a jaded performance. The discussion remained inconclusive, yet again.

Since the matter was important to the party, as Congress president Subhas Chandra Bose tried, from May to December 1938, to work out an agreement with Jinnah on Hindu-Muslim unity. Their parlay progressed cordially, but a problem arose when Jinnah insisted that the League must be considered to be the 'authoritative and representative organization of the Mussalmans of India'.[43] Jinnah pointed out on 2 August that this position had been accepted by the Congress-League Pact in 1916 and during their talks with Rajendra Prasad in 1935. The matter was relevant because '...the very existence of the League had been questioned by Pandit Jawaharlal Nehru, the then President of the Congress, in one of his statements, wherein he asserted that there were only two parties in the country, viz. the British Government and the Congress.'[46]

Jinnah then added two more conditions for holding the talks: (a) the Congress must not include any Muslim member from their party to participate in the talks, and (b) the Muslim League shall freely deal with other minorities. Bose's correspondence with Jinnah continued till 16 December 1938 when the Working Committee decided to proceed no further.

That August, Jinnah confidentially proposed to the acting viceroy Lord Brabourne that he would fully support the government if he was accepted as the sole representative of the Muslims of India.[45] Brabourne declined, but a year later and with a war to consider, his successor, Lord Linlithgow, thought otherwise.[46]

10

THE POLITICS OF PARTITION

THE PROMISED INDEPENDENCE

Two days after Germany invaded Poland, on 3 September 1939, Britain and France declared war on Germany, jump-starting, in the process, World War II. A day later, Viceroy Linlithgow invited Gandhi to Simla for consultations. Gandhi proceeded to Simla without consulting the Working Committee and did not disappoint the viceroy.

After the meeting, Linlithgow wired Lord Zetland, Secretary of State for India, in London:

> Mr Gandhi explained to me in moving terms the depth of his affection for England and told me that the idea of any enemy defacing Westminster Abbey or Westminster Hall or any other monuments of our civilisation was one which was intolerable to him and he contemplated the present struggle in his own words with an English heart. I was greatly struck with the depth of his real feeling, his emotion being at times so marked as to make it impossible for him to continue with what he was saying.[1]

But the viceroy's optimism was short-lived. Gandhi could not translate his feelings into an effective policy for his party at the Working Committee's meeting in Wardha from 8 to 15 September that year. Jawaharlal, unhappy that he was called back from his tour of China, vehemently opposed the move. He gave vent to his anger towards several things, including the British premier

Neville Chamberlain's 'connivance with' General Franco, the appeasement of Hitler in Munich, and the suppression of the activities of socialists in Britain.[2] Subhas Chandra Bose, who was invited to attend the meeting, also took a combative stand, demanding the declaration of independence as a pre-condition for his support. Gandhi could not turn the tide against Jawaharlal's emotional appeal and Bose's logical one. Besides, he did not want to expose to the British how divided the party was on the issue of the war and much else by shooting their views down publicly.[3]

It was, therefore, decided that the Congress would cooperate with the British against fascism, provided that they declared their aims for the war and pledged to free India in its aftermath. It took Jawaharlal four days to draft the statement, full of platitudes about democracy, the fight against oppression, and the condemnation of Nazism and Fascism, and release it, together with his colleagues, on 14 September.[4] He would later call it his September Manifesto.[5]

When Gandhi met Linlithgow on 26 September with these recommendations, he found him cold and unresponsive. The viceroy told him brusquely that there was simply no possibility of him agreeing to these demands. Besides, the views of the other prominent groups, particularly the princes and the Muslims, were equally important. Gandhi's claim that if the British '...could make up [their] minds to buy Congress [they] should buy the finest propaganda machine in the East...' did not impress him.[6]

In fact, the viceroy had met Jinnah immediately after Gandhi on 4 September and Jinnah had pledged them 'the loyalty of Muslim community everywhere.' Referring to the Congress ministries in the provinces, he had advised Linlithgow to '...turn them out at once. Nothing else will bring them to their senses. Their object, though you may not believe it...is nothing less than to destroy both you [the British] and us Muslims. They will never stand by you.' And then, he had revealed his ideas: 'Muslim areas should be separated from "Hindu Area" and run by Muslims in collaboration with Great Britain.'[7]

The reason Jinnah was able to speak to Linlithgow so

emphatically was because a few months ago, his associate, Chaudhry Khaliquzzaman, had met Lord Zetland and told him about the strategic benefits of creating autonomous Muslim states in the Indian subcontinent, which would be linked with Britain and act as a bulwark for Britain's defence in Asia. The minister had been deeply impressed by Chaudhry Khaliquzzaman's arguments, which, in fact, touched on the traditional British fear of the 'Great Game', to use Rudyard Kipling's phrase that he used in his novel *Kim* to describe Russian ambitions to move towards the warm waters of the Indian Ocean, Afghanistan and the Persian Gulf through the northwestern part of India.[8]

Unaware of this background information, Gandhi now requested Linlithgow to meet Rajendra Prasad, the Congress president, and Jawaharlal Nehru to discuss the issue. The viceroy did so on 3 October 1939. During the meeting, Rajendra Prasad argued that if India were to play her part in the war she must feel satisfied that she had something to fight for. He asserted that the Muslim League did not represent the mind of Islam. Jawaharlal asked for a declaration of their war aims to enthuse the people about the war, dilating at length on how the changes brought about by the war would modify the concept of the Empire itself.

In doing so, Jawaharlal had touched a raw nerve.[9] The viceroy firmly believed, like Winston Churchill and many other Englishmen at that time, that the Empire was here to stay (Churchill had, in fact, used intermediaries to travel to India and persuade the princes to stay out of the federation with a view to undermining the freedom effort).[10] Linlithgow retorted that if the war was to transform the British Empire, it might make a difference to the fortunes of the Congress too. The party would therefore be well advised, in its own interests, to avoid such a transformation.[11] Rajendra Prasad has mentioned this meeting in his memoir, but has omitted several details.[12]

Gandhi met the viceroy again on 5 October and unveiled before him a plan to bypass the obstacles created by some of his colleagues and help Britain's war effort. He criticized Jawaharlal's ideas without mentioning his name and indicated to Linlithgow that he would try his best to sway the party leaders to his side. Meanwhile, he suggested that the viceroy go ahead quietly, following the path that he had already chosen.[13]

Interestingly, Linlithgow met Jinnah later the same day. Jinnah assured him that he would refuse to reach an agreement with either the Congress or the government unless the plan to create a united India was abandoned and effective protection given to the minorities in the provinces. This should enable Linlithgow to deflect the Congress Party's demands as well as those of the Labour Party circles at home.[14] Indeed, the Labour Party leader, Clement Attlee, had suggested that the viceroy respond to the Congress's demand for Britain to declare its post-war policy on India 'with imaginative insight'.[15] Stafford Cripps had also advised Jawaharlal to stand firm on this demand in a letter intercepted by the state department.[16]

Boosted by Jinnah's pledge, Linlithgow issued a statement on 17 October 1939 declaring that after the end of the war, consultations would be held with the representatives of various communities, parties and interests in British India, as well as Indian princes, in order to make such modifications in the stalled federal scheme as might be agreed upon by all the stakeholders. This was intended to rattle the Congress leadership and force it to make an error of judgement. The ruse worked and on 23 October, the Congress Party decided to quit the ministries on the grounds that Britain had dragged India into war without consulting its elected representatives.

Subhas Chandra Bose appealed to the party leadership to refrain from this 'suicidal step' and Jinnah privately called it a 'Himalayan blunder'.[17] He took advantage of this development and publicly rejected the demand for the publication of Britain's war aims and post-war policy regarding India. Also, he declared 22 December (the day the Congress quit the ministries) as Deliverance Day as it marked the day India got deliverance from Congress rule. He thus strove to achieve by backroom politics and blistering propaganda what he could not do by popular votes.[18] Under pressure from London, Linlithgow proposed to expand the Viceroy's Executive Council by including two political members to appease the Congress.[19] But the party went ahead with its programme of mass resignation.

The Congress's actions were construed as a refusal to support Britain in her life-and-death struggle against the Axis powers and created a bad impression in London.[20] On the other hand, it gave the Indian government an opportunity to recruit men for the army and produce arms and ammunition, among other things, without any political interference.

A BEND IN THE ROAD

In January 1940, Linlithgow sought Jinnah's help to install a Muslim League ministry in the NWFP. He was being pressurized by London to ensure popular participation in the government. He also asked Jinnah to help him counter the propaganda Jawaharlal Nehru was spreading in the United States with the help of his radical friends. Jinnah was non-committal about the first issue and avoided the second by saying that he did not have enough money to counter such propaganda.[21]

On 5 February, Linlithgow met Gandhi and offered to negotiate for the All India Federation, which he had refused to set up earlier. He aimed to establish it now to offer the Congress a means to achieve the goal of self-government within the Empire. It would also function as a reward of sorts if the Congress chose to return to the ministries. But Gandhi did not show any interest in his proposal.[22] Later that day, Jinnah told Linlithgow when they met that there would be a civil war in the subcontinent if the Congress returned to the ministries. This time, he agreed to help the viceroy install a Muslim League ministry in the NWFP if the local governor, Sir George Cunningham, supported his endeavour.[23] As a matter of fact, the idea of a Congress ministry in a province whose population was over ninety-five per cent

Muslim was embarrassing to him vis-à-vis his scheme for the partition. The viceroy promised to ask the governor to assist him.

In February 1940, the Congress revived the threat of civil disobedience.[24] Shortly afterwards, from 17 to 19 March, the party passed its most radical resolution to date, at its annual session in Ramgarh, Bihar (now Jharkhand). The resolution refused to support the war and demanded the immediate election of a constituent assembly.[25] At the same time, Subhas Chandra Bose was holding a mammoth All-India Anti-Compromise Conference under the banner of his newly formed party, the Forward Bloc, at the same place. In this, he was assisted by radical leaders like Sahajanand Saraswati and they were demanding complete independence and mandating a policy of noncooperation with the British war effort.

It appears, in retrospect, that had the Congress Party resorted to civil disobedience at this juncture, Jinnah might have run out of steam and the British government might have beaten a retreat. Nevertheless, in less than a week, Jinnah proclaimed at the League's Lahore conference on 24 March 1940 that the Muslims were a separate nation and must have their own homeland, their own territory and their own states. The following features of the Lahore Resolution demonstrate how fragile the party was even at this late stage:

> Resolved that it is the considered view of this Session that no constitutional plan would be workable in this country or acceptable to the Muslims unless it is designed on the following basic principles, viz. that geographically contiguous units are demarcated into regions which should be so constituted with such territorial readjustments as may be necessary, that the areas in which the Muslims are numerically in the majority as in the North-Western and Eastern zones of India, should be grouped to constitute 'Independent States' in which the constituent units shall be autonomous and sovereign.

That adequate, effective and mandatory safeguard shall be specifically provided in the constitution for minorities in these units and in these regions for the protection of their religious, cultural, economic, political, administrative and other rights and interests in consultation with them; and in other parts of India where the Mussalmans are in a minority....

This Session further authorizes the Working Committee to frame a scheme of constitution in accordance with these basic principles, providing for the assumption finally by the respective regions of all the powers, such as defense, external affairs, communications, customs and such other matters as may be necessary.[26]

The words 'Pakistan' and 'partition' did not appear in the Resolution. Nor was there any mention of any kind of central body, or federating power, or of any kind of timeframe for the execution of any of these provisions. What it harped on was a series of unspecified concepts such as units, regions, areas, zones and states which were all undefined. The only positive references were to 'this country' and 'the constitution', in sharp contrast to definitive terms such as 'independent', 'autonomous' and 'sovereign'. This vagueness was necessary at this stage to achieve a broad unity within the party and to win the backing of its main rivals in the provinces. Fazlul Huq from Bengal moved the motion, and it was supported by Sikandar Hayat Khan from Punjab.

Historians generally believe that the British government was surprised by Jinnah's actions. The Congress Party certainly was. However, records now reveal that eleven days before this happened, on 13 March 1940, Jinnah had informed Linlithgow of his plans. He had even hinted that the League was prepared to use violence in order to establish a separate homeland for Muslims.[27] Linlithgow had informed Zetland about this the same day.[28]

Two months later, in May 1940, Winston Churchill, who had spent his early years in India, replaced Neville Chamberlain as the prime minister of England. An inveterate imperialist, he had gone on record saying, 'I hate Indians—they are a beastly people with a beastly religion.'[29] In fact, his senior schoolmate from Harrow, Leopold Amery, who became the Secretary of State in place of Lord Zetland, wondered whether Churchill was really quite 'sane' on the subject of India.[30]

Amery had a soft corner for Jawaharlal Nehru because of his Harrow background. He pinned his hopes on winning him over to the British side sooner or later. After assuming office, he sent a telegram to Linlithgow asking him whether there was any chance of recruiting Jawaharlal as 'the recruiter in chief' for the British.[31]

By June 1940, the Congress's capacity for negotiating with the government deteriorated further. Gandhi became a bit too loud while preaching nonviolence during the summer of 1940, partly to meet the challenge posed by Bose.[32] On 29 June, he advised Linlithgow on his own that Britain should resist Hitler's invasion through nonviolence, even if it meant self-annihilation for the British. He took an impish delight in the viceroy's utter amazement at his words and gloated over it to his colleagues.[33] The next day, he wrote to Linlithgow offering his services as an emissary to negotiate peace with Hitler, who, according to him, was not a bad man and would be amenable to reason. He received a polite refusal in response.

Around this time, there was a noticeable change in Jawaharlal's attitude towards the British. After the fall of France, he impressed upon his colleagues the risks to India and the world if Hitler were to overwhelm Britain. He reneged on his earlier stand and devised a formula by which a dialogue could be opened between the government and the Congress about the latter's cooperation with the war effort. Accordingly, in July 1940, the Congress passed a resolution laying aside the creed of nonviolence in the sphere of national defence. Gandhi probably saw a threat to his leadership in this development, or perhaps he did not like Jawaharlal's altered position. So contrary to the stand he had taken earlier, he withdrew his unconditional support to the war effort and resigned from the Congress over this violation of the principle of nonviolence. By this time, his leadership had lost its relevance to Jawaharlal Nehru, though he did not openly talk about an alternative leader like Bose. Nevertheless, he indicated that Gandhi's withdrawal from politics closed a definite period in the history of the national movement.[34]

As for Linlithgow, he felt no need to pursue the Congress now. Every month, around 200,000 recruits were offering themselves for military service, out of whom only 50,000 could be absorbed by the defence forces.[35] Also, Indian industrialists, including G.D. Birla, were fully engaged in producing goods for the army, which was an immensely profitable business.[36] Against this backdrop, Jinnah met Linlithgow on 27 June 1940 and apparently received information that Amery had plans to come up with a declaration about India. He demanded a guarantee that '...the likes of Cripps and Wedgewood Benn [both socialists and close to Jawaharlal] in England at some future date would not sell the Muslims to the Hindus.'[37]

Jinnah's views were accepted by the War Cabinet, though Churchill warned against making any far-reaching declaration. The upshot of all this was Linlithgow's declaration on 8 August 1940—which was repeated by Amery on 14 August at the House of Commons at Jinnah's request—offering dominion status to India after the war. It also mandated an expansion of the Viceroy's Executive Council to accommodate representatives from political parties and the creation of a War Consultative Committee, which could include some of the princes and offer a few specific guarantees to the minorities. Later, the government would interpret the declaration as a firm commitment not only to the Muslims of India, but also to Jinnah as their sole spokesman, and would thus virtually give him the power of veto over future constitutional developments.

The August Declaration, particularly the power of veto that was given to Jinnah, came as a rude shock to the Congress. Gandhi protested against it to the viceroy in his letter dated 29 August and during his meeting with him on 27 September. Finding the viceroy unmoved, he launched an 'Individual Peaceful Disobedience' campaign against the British war effort on 17 October 1940. This involved important Congress leaders speaking in public against the recruitment of Indians into the army and getting arrested one after the other. The first to be arrested was Vinobha Bhave, followed by Jawaharlal Nehru and then Vallabhbhai Patel. When Jawaharlal was sentenced to three years of rigorous imprisonment, both Amery and Churchill enquired of Linlithgow whether the sentence was not too harsh. This apparent concern for an Indian leader was quite out of character for Churchill.[38]

After a large number of leaders were thus arrested, Gandhi retired to his ashram and devoted himself to social work and spinning. Louis Fischer characterized this move as a face-saving measure of Gandhi. But the director of Intelligence Bureau had a different view of the matter. He cited Jawaharlal Nehru's words: 'No one expects Gandhiji's movement to bring success, but its moral value is what counts.' Drawing on this, he said in his report that this move had the twin intents of embarrassing the government morally at present and reaping great benefits and success at the polls after the war.[39]

The number of arrests during the movement reached 15,000 by the summer of 1941, though it attracted little attention due to the ongoing censorship of the press.[40] It went on for a year as participation dwindled, while the strength of the armed forces rose from about 190,000 at the beginning of the war, to almost two million towards the end.[41] On 3 December 1941, both Jawaharlal and Maulana Azad were released from prison. They would play a valuable role for the British during the Cripps Mission and the Cabinet Mission. Churchill called it a 'surrender at the moment of success.'

When the Congress's civil disobedience campaign was afoot, the Muslim League made rapid progress in building a support base in the villages and cities of India. Believing that violence would ultimately win the day, the League mobilized a force called the Muslim National Guards whose volunteers escorted Jinnah to public functions with swords in their hands.⁴² Linlithgow believed at heart that the empire was here to stay; he repeatedly turned down Jinnah's plea to accept the concept of Pakistan in principle. But he also made concessions to Jinnah primarily to keep the Congress in check. These concessions went on to create a political condition in India that made the partition a possibility in the future. Linlithgow's day-to-day reports to London on the Indian political situation—a useful backgrounder for the viceroys after him—showed the Congress leadership in a bad light while simultaneously projecting Jinnah as a leader of integrity and reliability. This 'good boy' image helped Jinnah and his party a great deal in the days to come.⁴³

Japan's surprise attack on Pearl Harbour on 7 December 1941 as well as its advance towards India's eastern borders changed everything for British as well as Indian politicians. It also brought the USA into the global political arena. Subhas Chandra Bose's presence in Europe and later in Southeast Asia caused both Jawaharlal and the government a great deal of anxiety. And it also brought them closer together. The political imperatives of the Congress changed accordingly.

THE CRIPPS MISSION

Churchill received news of the Pearl Harbor attack on the night of 7 December. It was a Sunday and he was already in bed. The news filled him with relief and elation as he realized that the United States would no longer remain a spectator, watching the war from the sidelines. It had no choice but to get directly involved in the war. He wrote in his memoirs: 'Being saturated and satisfied with emotion and sensation I went to bed and slept the sleep of the saved and thankful.'⁴⁴ The first thing he did on waking up was to plan to go to Washington and conduct a review of the situation with President Roosevelt. They would examine '...the whole war plan in the light of reality and new facts as well as the problems of production and distribution.'⁴⁵

A month later, on 7 January 1942, Churchill was on board the battleship *Duke of York*, en route to the United States. It was during this visit that Roosevelt '...first raised the Indian problem with [him] on the usual American [i.e. anti-Empire] lines...' He went on to say, 'I reacted so strongly at such length that he never raised it verbally again.'[46] After getting back to London, Churchill asked the War Cabinet to develop a policy to forestall any pressure that the USA might put on them to grant self-government to India.

The Secretary of State, Leopold Emery, recommended a status quo on the basis of Congress-Muslim League differences.[47] From India, Linlithgow advised that it was not the best idea to offer concessions in a time of military reverses. Also, India and Burma (now Myanmar) had no natural association despite being within the Empire, being alien by race, history and religion. They did not share a relationship of mutual affection.[48] Amery and Linlithgow's views were after Churchill's own heart, but his deputy in the War Cabinet, Clement Attlee, was the one discordant note in this political symphony, as it were.

Attlee criticized the 'hand-to-mouth policy' followed by the Secretary of State and asserted that it was 'not statesmanship'. He pointed out the necessity of re-examining India in view of the changed relationship between Europeans and Asians. This change was signalled by the defeat of Russia in the hands of Japan in the beginning of the century, followed by the belated recognition of China as an equal and of the Chinese as fellow fighters for civilization against barbarism, and finally, the success of the Russians (who were an amalgamation of the East and the West both geographically and culturally) against the Axis powers. In this context, India could naturally demand to be treated differently now. His suggestion was to send a representative to India, either as a special envoy or as a replacement for the present viceroy, with the requisite power to negotiate within broad limits. A Cabinet Committee could draw up his terms of reference and list of powers.[49]

Churchill cleverly used both Amery and Attlee's viewpoints to forge a policy that would ease the pressure the USA was putting on England to grant self-government to India immediately. It would also appease the coalition partners of the Labour Party, and confuse the Congress into making mistakes. In a masterstroke, he selected the flamboyant Labour Party leader Sir Stafford Cripps (1889–1952), a member of the War Cabinet and the leader of the House of Commons, to head a mission to India on behalf of His Majesty's Government. A brilliant barrister, Cripps was the same age as Jawaharlal Nehru and likewise, he was a dilettante and a politically ambitious man. He knew Gandhi well and was Jawaharlal's guest in Anand Bhavan back in 1939.[50] Churchill also roped in Attlee to play his games and made him the head of the newly constituted India Committee within the War Cabinet.

Churchill discounted Cripps's recent success as the British envoy when he brought the Soviet Union closer to Britain, for which he was rewarded with an appointment to the War Cabinet. In fact, he had once remarked, 'The trouble is his [Cripps's] chest is a cage in which two squirrels are at war, his conscience and his career.'[51] So this time, he nurtured no hope about the mission. Nor did he wish him success. On the other hand, Cripps had his eye on 10 Downing Street and he desperately wanted to succeed. He pinned his hopes on Jawaharlal Nehru, Gandhi and Maulana Azad, the then Congress president, who he thought could help him.

The Cripps offer, which was devised by the India Committee in early 1942, consisted of the following goals: the constitution of a new Executive Council with Indian politicians as members and British officials as secretaries to nudge the Indians a little closer to self-rule, a promise to address the question of Indian independence after the war and providing the provinces and the princely states the right either to remain in or to opt out of the Indian Union in case of independence, and finally, a solution to the communal question to be devised by Indians themselves after independence. The proposal, thus, amounted to nothing more than the formation of an Executive Council with an ostensible, but not empowered, Indian representation.

No promise was made in the proposal about granting independence after the war. What was the most striking was that the proposal left the door open for communal dissension, secessions and the creation of Pakistan. Churchill approved this line of action on 26 February; the War Cabinet, with Attlee in the chair, adopted it on 27 February 1942. Churchill and his colleagues stuck to this line of thinking, despite American pressure and even after the failure of the Cripps Mission. The fragmented Congress leadership did nothing to obstruct their plan. The right of the provinces to walk out remained a consistent feature of British policy in the Cabinet Mission plan of 1946 and even in Attlee's announcement about British withdrawal on 20 February 1947. Even the British Labour Party could not rise above parochial national interests.

Two days before the Cripps Mission's strategy was whipped out in the War Cabinet, General Chiang Kai-shek had wired to Roosevelt from Chungking that his recent visit to India had convinced him that if Britain did not change her policy towards India fundamentally, it would be like presenting India to the enemy. If Japan invaded India now, she would be virtually unopposed. Since Chiang and his wife were quite fond of Jawaharlal and vice versa, it can be presumed that the latter might have contributed to this perspective. At this time, Subhas Chandra Bose was organizing an effective anti-British campaign from Germany.[52] Japanese propaganda against the British occupation of India was also gaining intensity. Bose's propaganda from Germany created a deep impact in India in spite of British vigilance.[53]

The US was unhappy with Britain's India policy. Twice in 1941, the US Secretary of State Cordell Hull had raised with the British government the issue of the prompt recognition of India's free existence and its membership to the British family of nations. The US government had suggested that India be made a full member of the United Nations in order to secure her total commitment to defence production. Roosevelt was particularly under pressure from the Senate's powerful Foreign Relations Committee with regard to this particular issue.⁵⁴ He thought that Indian self-government would evolve through a process of trial and error and a date should be fixed for granting them independence.⁵⁵

Chiang Kai-shek's telegram on 25 February prompted Roosevelt to wire the US ambassador in London the same day and enquire about Churchill's thoughts on the matter.⁵⁶ Earlier that month, he had decided to send an Economic and War Supplies Mission to India, which would be headed by Colonel Louis Johnson (1891–1966), the erstwhile assistant secretary of the War Department, as his personal representative.

When Averill Harriman, the president's special representative in London, broached the subject with Churchill on 26 February, he was told a lie that approximately seventy-five per cent of the Indian troops were Muslim (the actual figure was around thirty-five per cent), who largely opposed the Congress movement, and so no political step should be taken that would alienate them at that point. Churchill also said that there was no dearth of men in India who were willing to fight. The only problem was how to train and equip them.⁵⁷

On 4 March, Churchill followed up this conversation with Roosevelt with a telegram. It said that his government was considering whether a declaration of dominion status after the war, carrying with it the right to secede, should be made at this critical juncture. Britain had already made a commitment to a hundred million Muslims who were the main constituents of the army and thirty to forty million 'untouchables' (use of this term has since been banned by the Constitution of India), and it had treaties with the princely states. To buttress his point, he sent him a memorandum written by the military secretary of the India Office, which stated that Indian soldiers were voluntary mercenaries, and also that they were proud of their calling and owed their allegiance to the British Raj. It added that any indication of a fundamental change in their service conditions would adversely affect their performance in the war. Churchill also enclosed a note from Jinnah to convince the Americans.⁵⁸ The whole exercise was intended to divert the US's attention from the issue.

Churchill followed this up with another telegram on 7 March conveying to Roosevelt the views of the governor of Punjab. The latter was of the opinion that the responsible section of Muslims desired Britain to continue to rule India till an acceptable constitution was devised to ensure that Hindus, who had pro-Japanese tendencies, did not usurp all the power.[59] Roosevelt understood Churchill's perspective and did not pursue the matter any further. So on 10 March, he wired back to Churchill, 'Of course all of you good people know far more about [the problem] than I do.'

He proceeded to relate how the thirteen American colonies had federated through a process of trial and error during the American Revolution from 1775 to 1783. Likewise, a temporary dominion government could be constituted with the representatives of different Indian groups that would function till a year after the war. And thereafter, they could form a more permanent government.[60]

Against this backdrop, Cripps landed in Delhi on 22 March 1942 and made his offer eight days later. Interestingly, in his broadcast from the All India Radio, New Delhi, on 30 March, he used the expression, 'peoples of India' instead of 'the people of India.' Gandhi opposed the Cripps Proposal on all counts;[61] Jawaharlal and Chakravarti Rajagopalachari accepted it in toto;[62] Maulana Azad maintained that independence or at least a definite promise of freedom must be the prerequisite for accepting the proposal. The Cripps Mission ultimately failed because of its inherent problems. Maulana Azad later said that Gandhi's new-found admiration for Subhas Chandra Bose, who vehemently opposed the proposal in his broadcasts from Berlin, influenced the latter's decision.[63]

On 6 April 1942, Cripps was still in India when the first Japanese bombs fell on Indian soil, in Visakhapatnam and Kakinada on the eastern coast of India. At that time, only eight anti-aircraft guns were available in the whole of India and there were no planes to counter the raids. The Japanese were in complete control of the Bay of Bengal and had sunk a good many British ships. In Burma, British forces were in full retreat. They were making their way back into Northeast India through dense forests and mountains. After the ineffective resistance that they put up in Malaya and Burma, the British had little confidence in their ability to defend India against the Japanese.

It was in such a scenario that Colonel Louis Johnson, Roosevelt's personal representative, arrived in New Delhi. He immediately entered into a dialogue with Jawaharlal Nehru and persuaded him to support the war effort by compromising on favourable interim arrangements, and forgetting the long-term 'provincial option'. In his turn, Cripps found in the course of time that Congress politics was not easy. He stayed with his wife, Isobel, at Anand Bhavan for two days as Jawaharlal's guests, surviving mostly on fruits.[64] The Nehrus sent for melons from Kabul and grapes from Quetta to supplement what little the local markets could provide in that season.[65] Cripps had talks with Maulana Azad, the Congress president, and Gandhi for several weeks.[66]

In his desperation to succeed, he went beyond his brief and dangled before Nehru and the other leaders the possibility of an immediate cabinet-type government with a restricted viceregal veto. Jawaharlal agreed to these arrangements and did try, with Johnson's help, to work out a compromise on the contested issues, though, as he told Cripps and Johnson, he could not count on his colleagues from the party to back him. However, he failed in his efforts when Gandhi decided to oppose him. Finally, the matter was abandoned when Linlithgow protested to Churchill against Cripps's new ideas which would lead to a virtual transfer of power into Indian hands. Baffled and dejected, Cripps abruptly left India on 11 April 1942.

Meanwhile, Colonel Louis Johnson had briefed Roosevelt and Cordell Hull, the US State Secretary, about Churchill's real intentions in his reports from New Delhi. On 4 April, he had wired to Hull: 'Unless the President feels that he can intercede with Churchill it seems the Cripps mission is doomed to failure...' He then added, 'Cripps so believes too.'[67] As negotiations collapsed on 11 April, Johnson informed Hull: 'Cripps with embarrassment told me that he could not change [the] draft [of the British offer] without Churchill's approval.' He added, 'Churchill had cabled him that he will give him no approval unless Wavell [the commander-in-chief in India] and Viceroy endorsed the change.' Johnson then concluded: 'London wanted a Congress refusal.'[68]

Johnson's impressions were corroborated by the reports sent by two other US sources, namely, Edgar Snow and Louis Fischer. Snow, best known as an expert on China and the author of *Red Star Over China* (1937), had been visiting India regularly since 1931. He was encouraged by Roosevelt to visit the country again in 1942 as a war correspondent and report anything of interest that he could find there.[69] Snow was a radical intellectual and thus was acquainted with Jawaharlal Nehru. Roosevelt instructed him before he left for India that he must tell Jawaharlal to write to him to specify what help he expected from the United States. Similarly, Louis Fischer, who later wrote *The Life of Mahatma Gandhi* (1950), was directed by Summer Wells, the Under Secretary of the US State Department, to report on the Indian political situation.[70] Fischer spent a week with Gandhi in Sevagram in June 1942.

The Indian intelligence viewed Johnson's activities as suspect. Sir Maurice Hallet, the governor of the United Provinces, wired to the viceroy, 'America will compel us to hand over [power] to Congress...it is extremely dangerous that the idea should get around that Roosevelt disapproves of HMG policy in regard to India and is even willing to interfere in that policy.'[71] Linlithgow forwarded this telegram to London with the comment, 'A difficult people and we are bound to have a great deal more difficulty I think once the war is over... I of course and you are only too well aware of the difficulties presented to us by American sentimentalism and ignorance of the Indian problem.'[72]

Around this time, Roosevelt's economic adviser, Lauchlin Currie, passed through India on his way back from China and found that Americans were being identified with British policy in the country. On being alerted by him, Roosevelt, who was extremely conscious of the global image of the US and its future role in Asia, passed a directive to his countrymen to keep away from India's internal political problems.

Churchill was trying to block Jawaharlal Nehru's connection to the US in the meantime. He was able to do so substantially by August 1942 when he had Louis Johnson recalled from India with the help of Harry Hopkins, the president's friend and his most influential adviser.

THE QUIT INDIA MOVEMENT

While Cripps was in India, a section of Congressmen, headed by Chakravarti Rajagopalachari, introduced two resolutions at an AICC meeting on 2 May 1942. They demanded that the Muslim-majority provinces be allowed to secede as a positive move towards a Congress-League settlement and that the Congress re-enter the government. Both the resolutions were defeated and Chakravarti Rajagopalachari quit the party.[73]

From 10 May, Gandhi began to sound an alarm against a possible partition of India in *Harijan* and proclaimed that British presence in India was an invitation to Japan. Jawaharlal tried to pacify him and simultaneously mobilize Congressmen and Indian masses against Japan. A day after Cripps's departure on 12 April, Jawaharlal assured Roosevelt in a letter he sent secretly through Johnson: 'Though the way to our choice may be closed to us and we are unable to associate ourselves with the activities of the British authorities in India, still we shall do our utmost not to submit to Japanese or any other aggression or invasion.'[74]

He pinned his hopes on the Americans and the Chinese to persuade Britain to give self-government to India (i.e., Congress Party). Therefore, he convinced Gandhi that in case India was given independence, Britain and America should still be allowed retain their forces in the country to fight the Japanese. He induced him to write to both Chiang Kai-shek and Roosevelt soliciting their support for the Indian cause.[75] In his reply to Gandhi, Chiang Kai-shek advised him to wait for a favourable development before acting, and not to precipitate the situation by launching an agitation now.

However, Gandhi had already decided to launch the 'Quit India' movement. So, when the Working Committee met on 14 July, it gave the British government time till 7 August to accept their demand for independence. It so happened that a few days later, on 25 July 1942, Chiang Kai-shek sent a three-page telegram on the Indian situation to the US President, in which he urged Roosevelt to stand on the side of justice and equity. Chiang's resourceful foreign minister, T.V. Soong, who was in Washington at that time, delivered a personal message to Roosevelt. He also paid a visit to Summer Wells, the Under Secretary of State, in person. He explained to him that the Indian Congress represented the desire of the Indian people, and that the Indian question was regarded by all of Asia as a test case, and that the US and China, acting together, could influence the outcome.[76]

Accordingly, on 29 July, Wells recommended a joint Sino-American intervention to come up with a satisfactory arrangement. Roosevelt, however, transmitted Chiang Kai-shek's entire message to Churchill to learn his views on the matter.[77] Churchill was then on tour in the Middle East and his deputy, Attlee, forwarded the message to Amery, the Secretary of State, to handle. In his turn, Amery sent for the US ambassador and told him that if the Congress executed its threat to revolt after 7 August, the government would take firm action and arrest Gandhi and other political leaders. He assured the envoy that the war effort or recruitment would not be affected by the agitation.[78] Roosevelt did not press the matter further, although the United States continued to raise the issue from time to time.

By this time, Gandhi was convinced that the British had no intention of ever transferring any power to Indians. He had very little to leverage with the ruling power now. On 8 August 1942, the AICC decided to launch a new satyagraha, as government security forces watched it closely; the next day, right before dawn, almost every Congress leader in every corner of the country was carted off to jail. Spontaneous and severe disturbances followed everywhere in the country despite the fact that the Congress had not officially called for any action. This disproved Gandhi and Jawaharlal's repeated assertions that the country was not ready for action. At the end of August, Linlithgow cabled Churchill that it was the most dangerous rebellion since 1857.[79]

The movement was mostly violent and not Gandhian at all in character. However, the government was much better prepared this time around and more ruthless than it ever had been under Reading or Irwin. There was a lack of national coverage of the movement due to the severe censorship of the press and the radio. The army also stayed loyal to the colonial government. In the absence of an able leadership, the movement gradually lost its momentum and was over by March 1943. Conservative diehards like Churchill and Amery were proved right. The Congress was unable to oust the British; the war could still be fought without their cooperation.

Jinnah was, as ever, the one who reaped the benefits of an ill wind. The Congress Party was outlawed; most of the Congress leaders—Gandhi, Jawaharlal, Vallabhbhai Patel and Maulana Azad, among others—stayed locked up until the end of the war. Meanwhile, the Muslim League rapidly consolidated its strength and influence in the country.

All was, however, not lost. The Indian National Army (INA), around 50,000 strong and led by Subhas Chandra Bose, fought the British on the Northeastern front. When their deeds came to be known by all and sundry after the war, India's political atmosphere was charged like never before. It eventually led to revolts in the Indian Navy and some Air Force and Army units in February 1946.[80] The British government was facing the worst financial crisis since the Great Depression. This irretrievably hostile milieu necessitated a re-examination of its future course of action concerning India.

Meanwhile, following Churchill's orders dated 5 May 1945, the Post-Hostilities Planning Staff of the War Cabinet in London had prepared an appraisal of long-term British interests in India on 19 May. It stated that the subcontinent was extremely useful as a base for the deployment of forces in the Indian Ocean area, the Middle East and the Far East. It was also useful as a transit point for air and sea communications, as a large reservoir of manpower of good quality, and as a vantage point in the NWFP for British air power vis-à-vis Soviet military installations. The report had also highlighted the advantage of detaching Baluchistan from India to take advantage of its unique location in the north of the Gulf of Oman that led to the Persian Gulf. This view was reiterated in all subsequent appraisals and the idea of partitioning India in some form had thus finally germinated in Whitehall during Churchill's premiership.

In post-war India, the rising trend of violent civil disorder, the widespread exodus of demoralized European ICS officers, and the keenness of the Indian officers of the Indian Police (IP) and subordinate services to shake off their inglorious past under colonial rule were all causes for concern.

WAVELL TAKES CHARGE

The new viceroy, Archibald Percival Wavell, who took charge in the summer of 1943 wanted to appoint a new representative council to defuse some of the tension simmering in the subcontinent. But Amery felt that a broad declaration of intent on the subject of independence would suffice to calm the situation. Attlee was unenthusiastic about Wavell's proposal probably also because of his personal dislike for the erstwhile commander-in-chief's crisp manners. Indeed, Attlee removed Wavell from the position of viceroy at the first available opportunity after becoming prime minister. As for Churchill, he preferred to wait till the post-war elections in July 1945, which he was confident he would win.

He wanted to deal with India's future with a strong hand, after the fresh mandate. India's independence, however, was far from his mind.

The Labour Party's landslide electoral victory and the unprecedented mass upsurge in India following the trial of the soldiers of the INA at Red Fort and the consequent insurrections in the Indian armed forces in February 1946 completely altered the state of security in India. In March 1946, the new British premier Clement Attlee expressed support for Indian independence in the House of Commons and sent a three-member Cabinet Mission to India to find ways and means to hand over power to Indians. Attlee gave a clear indication that a settlement would be engineered one way or another and that a constituent body would be set up in India and an interim executive formed.

The Cabinet Mission consisted of Lord Pethick-Lawrence, the new Secretary of State for India, A.V. Alexander, First Lord of Admiralty, and Sir Stafford Cripps, who was now the president of the Board of Trade. They arrived in New Delhi on 23 March and stayed there for three months. The Mission outlined two plans, one in May which was on the constitution, and another in June which was about the establishment of an Interim Government. Gandhi barely took part in the Mission's consultations, most of which were carried out by Jawaharlal and Maulana Azad, who represented the Congress.

On 30 March 1946, Jinnah demanded the creation of a viable Pakistan, including Punjab, Bengal, Sind, the NWFP, Assam and Baluchistan. To press home this demand, the Muslim League met in Delhi in April and modified the Lahore Resolution of 1940 and added a demand for a separate state of Pakistan comprising all these regions. It accommodated, however, Bengal's demand for a separate and independent status.

Jawaharlal and Vallabhbhai Patel were prepared to negotiate the precise boundaries of any Pakistan that would be created, but they were more interested in the British withdrawing from India as swiftly as possible, as well as the formation of a sovereign constituent assembly to iron out the details of an independent India. They were confident about their ability to sort things out in their favour by the force of sheer majority once the British left the scene. According to Ram Manohar Lohia, Jawaharlal had been collaborating with the British since 1942,[81] and now he had Patel as his companion.

In this situation, the Cabinet Mission decided to work on the basis of two broad models. Scheme A was a loose federal system—the 'three-tier' India—in which the existing eleven provinces would be assembled into three regional groups. Group A would be the central Hindu-majority area, Group B the north-west Muslim-majority area, and Group C would include Bengal and Assam. These groups would carry out the bulk of the legislative and executive functions in the new Union, which would be held together by a federal government responsible for defence, foreign affairs and communications. There would be no central legislature.

This scheme was a near-match to Jinnah's demands, as it would ensure that a Hindu Raj was not imposed on Muslims and leave them to decide all important matters for themselves locally, in the fields of law, culture and religion. The other proposal, Scheme B, was for a truncated Pakistan, without the Hindu and Sikh 'hostages' left inside its boundaries. It was to be a fully sovereign state living alongside a separate, sovereign Hindustan. When the Mission sought London's guidance on the Schemes on 11 April, it was told unequivocally to go for Scheme A, and only if this was not at all possible, they were to move on to Scheme B.

The Cabinet Mission discussed the Schemes threadbare with the Indian leaders at a conference in Simla from 5 to 12 May 1946. At one point during the course of the heated discussion, Jinnah declared that he would accept the Union only if the Congress accepted the groups. Gandhi did not like the idea of 'grouping' at all, while Jawaharlal and Patel felt that Jinnah could use the groups to secede at a later stage. Overall, there was a great deal of misgivings on both sides about the details of the system and there were capable lawyers on both sides to argue over the many anomalies of the system. Therefore, on the basis of the Simla discussions, the Cabinet Mission announced their decision as an 'award' on 16 May 1946, going for a modified Scheme A with a central legislature.

According to the scheme, an Indian Union was to be created and it was to include the princely states. The Union would handle defence, foreign affairs and communications, and have an executive arm and a legislature, with powers to raise finance. All residuary powers were to be vested in the provinces, which were to be organized into the three aforesaid groups. All the eleven provinces were to meet within the three groups to sort out detailed provincial and group constitutions, after which all the provinces, plus the princely states, were to assemble to draw up a Union Constitution. The final transfer of power would come only after this constituent assembly had completed its deliberations. The provinces could vote to drop out of a group but not out of the Union. A review of the scheme was to be conducted after ten to fifteen years. Moreover, an Interim Government of India was to be formed as soon as possible.

This award did not satisfy either party fully. The Congress wanted to have independence immediately, along with the formation of a sovereign constitutional assembly to make decisions on the developing issues. Jinnah was unhappy about having to settle for two Muslim entities instead of a united Pakistan. He was also displeased that the central government had the power to raise taxes and not the provinces, which had only residuary and not sovereign rights. Moreover, there were no rights of secession and Muslims were to be in a minority in the central legislature.

The award was, however, acceptable to Hindus and Muslims in general. Some leading Bengali and Punjabi Muslims saw in it a desirable balance between communal and national interests. After some more discussion, Jinnah and the League accepted the award in a resolution dated 6 June 1946.

The Congress was not as forthcoming as the Muslim League.

Jawaharlal and Patel were more interested in the precise composition of the Interim Government. Wavell assured them that he would treat the new executive as if it were of a dominion state. Now, a squabble began in the Congress over the number of posts and the specific portfolios in the Cabinet. The party wanted to have a 7:4 ratio in favour of the Congress in a twelve-member Cabinet headed by the viceroy. Finally, the Congress got a 6:5 ratio, which was close to the parity demanded by Jinnah.

The Congress insisted on the right to nominate Muslim ministers if it so wished. Jinnah was carefully watching the Congress's reactions before making his move, while Jawaharlal and Patel chose not to deal with Jinnah just yet. So they decided to test the waters. In a resolution dated 25 June, the Congress affirmed its acceptance of the Plan proposed on 16 May, but it declined to join the Interim Government because of the restrictions on its right to have Muslim members.

Wavell was in a fix as the Plan would not work without Congress participation. He refused to form the Interim Government with only the Muslim League and requested Jinnah to accommodate the Congress's demand for the inclusion of Muslim members in the Cabinet. Jinnah refused to do so. The next day, on 26 June, the viceroy announced the appointment of a caretaker government. Two days later, the Cabinet Mission flew home to England.

JINNAH'S CALL FOR DIRECT ACTION

In the League's resolution on 6 June, Jinnah had made it clear that he was only supporting the process because he saw the 'groups' as a helpful step towards the eventual creation of Pakistan. The Congress's own attitude was also uncertain. After taking charge as the Congress president succeeding Maulana Azad on 7 July, Jawaharlal said at a press conference on 10 July that the Congress would not be restricted by its acceptance of the Cabinet Plan and would enter the constituent assembly '...completely unfettered by arguments and free to meet all situations as they arise.' When asked if this meant that the Cabinet Mission Plan could be modified, he replied emphatically that the Congress regarded itself free to change or modify it as it thought best.[82]

Jawaharlal's statement alarmed Jinnah about the bona fides of the negotiations. He was already facing a lot of disapproval from his own party men for agreeing to the Plan. Now, he quickly took advantage of Jawaharlal's declaration and issued a statement that this declaration by the Congress called for a review of the whole situation. He called a meeting of the League Council and issued a statement that the Muslim League had accepted the Plan with the assurance that the Congress had also done the same, and that the Plan would be the basis for the future Constitution of India. The declaration by the Congress president meant that the party could change the scheme through its majority share in the Constituent Assembly and place the minorities at the mercy of the majority.[83] Jinnah interpreted it as the Congress Party's rejection of the Plan and demanded that only the League form the government.[84]

On 29 July, the Muslim League adopted a resolution rejecting the Cabinet Mission's Plan. This followed many a behind-the-scenes confabulation in which Huseyn Shaheed Suhrawardy, who had once been Chatto's radical disciple in Berlin and who was now the rabidly communal Prime Minister of Bengal, played a prominent part. On this issue, Jinnah called upon Muslims throughout India to observe 'Direct Action Day' on 16 August 1946.

A section of Congress leaders, including Maulana Azad, who had taken great pains to see the Cabinet Mission Plan through, was unhappy with Jawaharlal's actions. On Maulana Azad's insistence, the Working Committee met on 8 August to review the situation. Jawaharlal pleaded at the meeting that they not embarrass him publicly for his remark. Accordingly, the Working Committee passed a resolution reaffirming the party's adherence to the Plan, without making any references to Jawaharlal.[85]

On 16 August, a hartal called by the League led to an unprecedented degree of looting, murder and arson carried out by

Muslim rioters in Calcutta—'the Great Calcutta Killing'. Around 5,000 people were believed to be killed and 16,000 injured. The governor Sir Frederick John Burrows had declared the day as a public holiday at Suhrawardy's request and on the advice of Ronald Leslie Walker, the chief secretary. This was in spite of the vehement opposition they received from Prafulla Chandra Ghosh, the leader of the Congress at the Bengal Legislative Assembly.[86]

Later, a three-member Calcutta Disturbances Commission of Enquiry was constituted to look into the riots in November 1946, under the chairmanship of Sir Patrick Spens, the Chief Justice of India. It came to light during its proceedings that Suhrawardy and his henchmen—Raghib Ahsan, Syed Abdullah Farooqui, Elian Mistry and others—were behind this carnage, which was planned to create enough of an uproar for the idea of a separate Muslim state to be taken seriously.[87]

Meanwhile, on 6 August 1946, Wavell had invited the Congress into the Interim Government, ignoring Jinnah's rejection of the Plan. The Working Committee, in consultation with Gandhi in Wardha, accepted the offer on 8 August and finally formed the ministry on 2 September. This development put Jinnah in an awkward position. In mid-October, the Muslim League negotiated with the viceroy to have five seats in the ministry, including the prized position of finance minister, which ultimately went to Liaquat Ali Khan. Jawaharlal Nehru headed the government, while Jinnah stayed out of it as Wavell had not accepted his request for the vice-presidency.

Initially, the Finance Department was offered to the Congress, while the Home Department was allotted to the League. But Vallabhbhai Patel refused to part with the Home Department,[88] little realizing that the Finance Department held the key to the effective functioning of all the other departments. Soon, Liaquat Ali Khan began to reject or, in the very least, delay every proposal put up by the Congress members of the Executive Council. He did this with the help of a few very capable and senior Muslim officers in the Finance Department.[89] Vallabhbhai Patel discovered that in spite of being the Home Member, he could not even create the post of a chaprasi or office messenger without Liaquat Ali Khan's concurrence.[90]

When Louis Mountbatten came to India as viceroy in March 1947, he took full advantage of this discord to have his own way in India. He gave these political wrangles a new twist and led both the Congress and the League down a path towards partition.[91]

TOWARDS PARTITION

Unlike many Conservatives, Wavell did not believe that Britain should leave India disunited and fragmented, if it had to leave at all. By late 1946, he drew up the 'Breakdown Plan' to hand over power gradually to the democratic provinces and the Indian princedoms in localized groups, retaining British control at the centre.[92] But when the Constituent Assembly held its first session on 9 December, the League members did not attend it. This led to a dysfunctional government. Wavell sought to remedy the situation by arranging a mini-conference for both the parties in London. Jawaharlal Nehru, assisted by Baldev Singh (Vallabhbhai Patel had opted out of it), and Jinnah, assisted by Liaquat Ali Khan, attended the conference in late December. It was being chaired by Attlee. However, four days later, their efforts proved to be futile.

Three months later, the suave go-getter Mountbatten replaced Wavell as viceroy. He was the King's cousin and Churchill's protégé, and very proud of his royal lineage. He managed to secure full power to negotiate with Indian leaders. After being nominated for the office, he did his homework meticulously, pouring over files and acquainting himself with the Indian situation as extensively as possible. The King privately instructed him to make India a member of the British Commonwealth in order to preserve Britain's military and economic interests in South Asia.[93]

In London, Mountbatten recruited Krishna Menon, Jawaharlal's friend and the main interlocutor with the Labour Party leaders in London, and sent him to Delhi to act as his 'mole' and make the idea of the partition acceptable to him. Krishna Menon came to Delhi to stay with Jawaharlal before Mountbatten arrived in India.[94]

By all accounts, Krishna Menon had a peculiar hold on Jawaharlal. Earlier, the latter had wanted to appoint him as the Indian high commissioner in London, but failed to do so due to Wavell's objection. All this changed with the arrival of the new viceroy. Krishna Menon's frequent invitations to the Viceroy's House pleased Jawaharlal, but it aroused Maulana Azad's suspicion that he was acting as a spy.[95] About Krishna Menon, Mountbatten reported to the secretary of state: 'He [Krishna Menon] was a close friend of Pt. Nehru… I would ask him to tell me what was in Pt. Nehru's mind. He would keep me informed of the background of what was going on in Congress circles generally: I would recruit his assistance to "put over" any points I find too delicate to handle myself and at all events to prepare the ground for me.'[96]

Before taking over as the viceroy, while he was still in London, Mountbatten had received a note from V.P. Menon (not related to Krishna Menon), the reforms commissioner in the viceroy's office. It said that Vallabhbhai Patel might agree to accept the creation of a Pakistan of the truncated variety as well as independence on the basis of dominion status if power was transferred to Indian hands immediately.[97] But he did not pay much attention to this note at this stage. He was most eager to meet two Indian leaders after arriving in India—Gandhi and Jinnah. He requested them to meet him,[98] but both of them stayed away.

Mountbatten faced many odds upon his arrival in India. The European community in general was unhappy about Wavell's sudden removal and replacement by a royal 'playboy'. Many Indian princes pressed for independence and presented the prospect of dozens or more private kingdoms. The Maharaja of Bikaner blamed the Nawab of Bhopal for dividing the princes along communal lines, while the Nawab of Bhopal insinuated that the Maharaja of Bikaner was just a patsy of the Congress. Both of them begged

Mountbatten not to leave India at all.[99]

Only a week before the beginning of his viceroyalty, the British intelligence services had reported the first clear case of direct financial aid from the Soviets to the CPI. The same week, Stalin had told the British Foreign Secretary in Moscow, Ernest Bevin, that Russia would not interfere in India's independence, but Bevin remained doubtful about his intentions.[100] Pethick-Lawrence, the Secretary of State, had also advised Mountbatten not to take Stalin's words at face value, for there had recently been certain signs that pointed to the contrary.[101] The focus of US President Truman's campaign against communism had also suddenly shifted from Greece and Turkey to India.[102]

In spite of these developments, Mountbatten asserted his 'ostensibly frank, inclusive and open-minded' style immediately. He developed an affectionate relationship with Gandhi and got on tolerably well with Jinnah. But the person he really came to attach himself with socially and politically was Jawaharlal Nehru. At fifty-seven, the latter had become a close admirer of this handsome and well-groomed man of forty-six. Mountbatten also developed a good working rapport with Vallabhbhai Patel and found him more reliable and effective in matters of administration than Jawaharlal. His wife, Edwina, helped her husband by developing close friendships with the female relatives of these leaders. One of Edwina's most important friendships was with Vijaya Lakshmi. But it was her brother who was the most valuable connection of all. Jawaharlal and Edwina took to each other almost immediately. According to Shahid Hamid, private secretary to Field Marshal Sir Claude Auchinleck, their relationship was '...sufficiently close to have raised many eyebrows...' by 31 March, just nine days after the arrival of the viceregal couple in Delhi.[103] Subsequently, this relationship influenced Nehru's political activities in a powerful way.

Two days after reaching Delhi, Mountbatten had a detailed talk with Jawaharlal for the first time on 24 March and he perceived a glimmer of hope for the fate of his project.[104] Jinnah was, of course, harder to read. Three days later, on 27 March,

Jinnah alleged in his speech that the British had been deliberately conspiring against Muslims and trying to force them into staying in India by refusing to create Pakistan,[105] although he knew that the real picture was quite different.

On 1 April, Gandhi advised Mountbatten to solve the Indian problem by handing over the reins to Jinnah and the Muslim League. When Mountbatten told Jawaharlal about it the next day, the latter made light of the whole thing and thereafter ensured that Gandhi did not take part in any of the subsequent talks on the matter as he was 'out of touch'.[106] Later, when the viceroy floated Gandhi's idea to Maulana Azad, the veteran Congressman found it quite feasible and opined that if they executed the idea, Jinnah might even come around and they could put an end to the communal bloodshed once and for all.[107]

By 10 April, Mountbatten began to tell his staff that partition was the only way forward. A few days later, when he tabled the idea at a conference of his provincial governors, they were all concerned about the collapse of public order that this would result in, and wanted reinforcements to handle the situation. They did not recommend a partition. But Mountbatten was determined to forge ahead with his plans for the partition of India more rapidly.

Jawaharlal was already with him in this. Mountbatten now found that Vallabhbhai Patel was also quite amenable to the idea.[108] Indeed, at that time, Patel was openly saying that he was prepared to settle for just a part of India if he could get rid of the Muslim League that way.[109] In his private conversations, Mountbatten always referred to Vallabhbhai Patel as the 'Walnut'—hard on the outside but soft on the inside once the shell was broken.[110] He started making detailed plans for the partition with the help of select officials in early May, but publicly, he continued to deplore the idea of the partition as 'sheer madness'.[111]

At this time, Jinnah favoured the idea of partition along provincial boundaries and not the internal partition of the provinces. Before Mountbatten's arrival, the League had organized a violent campaign to dislodge the Unionist ministry in the Punjab, which had led to its resignation on 2 March 1947, followed by a serious three-day communal conflict. This had prompted the Congress to call for an 'administrative' partition of the province in a resolution on 8 March. Jawaharlal had then suggested to Wavell that this principle would probably have to be extended to Bengal as well.[112]

Jawaharlal had a strange dislike of East Bengal. It was a region which he could not associate with the rest of India as he disclosed to Ram Manohar Lohia during their private conversation in Noakhali in 1946.[113] By 20 April 1947, he conceded that the League could have Pakistan in public, provided that the regions it wanted to have were willing to join it.[114]

Meanwhile, the Hindu Mahasabha, which was quite strong in West Bengal, had begun to call for a partition of the province as a way of curing its chronic political instability due to a very large Muslim population in East Bengal.[115] Again, there was a cross-party alliance in Bengal at the behest of Huseyn Shaheed Suhrawardy and Sarat Chandra Bose, and it began to float the idea of a united and independent Bengal outside both Pakistan and India.[116] When Mountbatten broached this subject with Jinnah, he did not object to the idea.[117]

The Congress, however, vehemently opposed the idea of an independent Bengal[118] primarily because the party apprehended that Jinnah would find a way to include it in Pakistan at a later stage. By this time, there was a scramble to recruit the support of the Sikhs in Punjab. In this, the Congress had a slight edge over the Muslim League. Due to the Punjab factor, the Congress leadership was in a hurry to have an early settlement.

Between 16 April and 2 May of the same year, a withdrawal plan for the British was drafted and redrafted at least a dozen times by General Sir Hastings Ismay, the viceroy's chief of staff, and his colleagues. First, the plan provided choices to individual provinces to be independent, and then it gave the princely states the autonomy to determine their own future.[119] This meant the likely vivisection of India into many miniscule parts. Ismay's plan later gained some notoriety as 'Plan Balkan' as it aimed to fragment

India irredeemably. When the viceroy's principal secretary showed its broad outlines to Jawaharlal and Jinnah, they both approved it.

On 2 May, Ismay left for London with the plan. Four days later, he wired back saying that preliminary responses to the plan at home were favourable. Mountbatten now embarked on the second phase of his task, namely to tackle Jawaharlal on the issue of India joining the Commonwealth. This was crucial to prove that Indian leaders had accepted the partition of their own free will. Moreover, this step would help him curry favour with the Conservatives and help pass the Indian Independence Bill in the Parliament. Also, this would ensure that Britain's defence and economic interests in the subcontinent were preserved even after independence.

With this end in view, Mountbatten invited Jawaharlal and Krishna Menon to be his guests at 'the Retreat', the viceroy's cosy private English cottage in Mashobra in Simla district, from 7 May.[120] This was Edwina's favourite place in India and she would later have Jawaharlal spend a few idyllic days with her here when things got a bit more stable in early 1948. Presently, Mountbatten's sole objective was to secure Jawaharlal's cooperation in order to get the plan accepted by the Congress. He was not worried about Jinnah's acquiescence.

On 10 May, London returned the plan without any major amendments, except that they altered the language to an extent that it further diluted the concept of Indian unity. Only six weeks after claiming his viceroyalty, Mountbatten was elated by this success. He immediately issued a statement that he was ready to present the plan to Indian leaders and formally invited Jawaharlal, Jinnah, Vallabhbhai Patel, Liaquat Ali Khan and Baldev Singh to attend a meeting to discuss the plan, at 10.30 a.m. on 17 May at the Viceroy's House in Delhi.[121]

In his elation, Mountbatten had handed the plan over to Nehru in Simla, on the night of May 10, to gauge his reaction to it. He did this in spite of the advice of his staff, who felt that the plan should be shown either to all the parties or to none at all.

Mountbatten would later say that he had done this on a 'hunch' and that his 'hunch' had saved his viceroyalty from failure. However, he had had another plan outlined to him a few days ago by his reforms commissioner, V.P. Menon, just in case.

The Ismay Plan, which Jawaharlal had glanced through earlier and approved, now had a bewildering effect on him and kept him awake till 4 a.m. in the morning. The next day, the viceroy got a hand-written note from Jawaharlal, followed by a longer type-written one a little later, rejecting the plan. Mountbatten would later recall that Jawaharlal was 'white with rage.' He said, 'You know, he used to get this tantrum, having been in prison. He took a long time to control himself.'[122] Mountbatten was upset with Jawaharlal's reaction, but he soon realized that this had effectively saved him from a great *faux pas* in both India and London. He immediately cancelled the announcement and postponed the meeting with Indian leaders in Delhi from 17 May to 2 June. Also, he had V.P. Menon prepare a new draft in two to three hours,[123] well before Nehru was set to leave Simla. The second plan, soon to be known as 'Plan Partition', became the Independence settlement.

Eight days later, on 18 May, Mountbatten flew to London with the new plan. He explained to the British government that Indians' willingness to accept the partition and Britain's transfer of power on a dominion basis within the British Commonwealth would kill three birds with one stone. He emphasized that the transfer of power should happen immediately in order to secure the Congress Party's support. As regards the NWFP, a referendum would be engineered in due course to remove it from the Congress Party's control. Similarly, Bengal under the Muslim League would provide an advantage to British enterprises in the future. However, when Mountbatten was in London, the Congress nullified the idea of an independent Bengal.

Mountbatten's plan was still not without a few hiccups. On 22 May, Jinnah informed the Reuters correspondent in London that he would resist the separation between Bengal and Punjab, and would demand a corridor between East and West Pakistan, passing through Delhi, Rampur, Lucknow and Patna.[124] Mountbatten met him in London on the same day. During their discussion, Jinnah yielded on the issue of Bengal and the corridor, but he demanded six months of joint control of Calcutta. Mountbatten sought Vallabhbhai Patel's view in the matter via V.P. Menon, arguing that this might help them avoid trouble in the city during the partition. Patel replied: 'Not even for six hours.'[125]

On 3 June, the Congress Working Committee endorsed the decision that Jawaharlal Nehru and Vallabhbhai Patel had already taken on the Partition.[126] The only member who opposed the division was Abdul Ghaffar Khan.[127] Ram Manohar Lohia and Jayaprakash Narayan were invited to the meeting as special invitees. Lohia later wrote:

> Maulana Azad sat in a chair throughout the two days of this meeting in a corner of the very small room which packed us all, puffed away at his endless cigarettes, and spoke not a word...Acharya Kripalani was a pathetic figure at these meetings. He was president of the Congress party at that time [...]. Mr Jayaprakash Narayan spoke some brief but definitive remarks against Partition in a single stretch and was silent for the rest of the meeting...[128]
>
> I would like to make two points that Gandhiji made at this meeting. He turned to Mr. Nehru and Sardar Patel in mild complaint that they had not informed him of the scheme of Partition before committing themselves to it. Before Gandhiji could make this point fully, Mr. Nehru intervened with some passion to say that he had kept him fully informed. On Mahatma Gandhi's repeating that he did not know of the scheme of Partition, Mr. Nehru slightly altered his earlier observation. He said that Noakhali was so far away and that, while he may not have described the details of the scheme, he had broadly written of Partition to Gandhiji.[129]

According to Lohia, both Jawaharlal and Patel were offensively aggressive towards Gandhi at this meeting.

On 14 June, Govind Ballabh Pant moved the resolution for Partition at the AICC meeting and Maulana Azad supported it.[130] Thirteen amendments to the official resolution were discussed at the meeting, of which eight were ruled out by J.B. Kripalani as substantive amendments and the rest were either withdrawn or voted out.[131] Gandhi addressed the meeting for nearly forty minutes and supported the resolution. He told the AICC delegates that it was their duty to stand by the Working Committee's decision and accept the plan.[132]

A FULL BASKET OF APPLES

On 19 July, the King signed the Indian Independence Act in London, while the Mountbattens celebrated their silver wedding anniversary in Delhi, twenty-five years after their engagement in the same city. By this time, Jinnah had started disliking Mountbatten. In a breach of protocol, he was late to the official dinner and left it at the same time as the viceroy. When Mountbatten suggested that the new dominions retain the Union Jack in the upper cantons of their national flags like a few other members of the Commonwealth, both Jinnah and Jawaharlal rejected the suggestion. Again, when Mountbatten had the flags designed for the Governor-Generals of the new dominions, that were to be flown on top of their residences and car bonnets, Jinnah disapproved of his designs.[133]

The Indian Independence Act of 1947 gave a wide range of options to the princely states, and remaining independent was one of them. Attlee did not clarify British intentions towards the princely states and only asked Mountbatten to '...aid and assist the states in coming to fair and just arrangements with the leaders of British India as to their future relationships.'[134] Mountbatten interpreted this directive liberally and promised to help Vallabhbhai Patel sort out the accession of 565 princely states, each of which had a separate agreement with the government. He assured him that he would deliver him 'a full basket of apples' before 15 August. To London, he wrote: 'I am positive that if I can bring a basket-full of States before the 15th August, Congress will pay whatever price I insist on for the basket. I can hardly say that unless we can pull this off, India will be in a bit of a mess after the 15th August.'[135]

Vallabhbhai Patel was in charge of the States Department, which was created in June 1947 for processing the integration of the princely states. He had V.P. Menon as his secretary. A three-pronged programme was devised between them and Mountbatten for the purpose of bringing the princely states into India's fold: first, Menon would meet the diwans or chief ministers of the princely states to bring home to them the advantages of joining the Indian Union; thereafter, Patel would meet the rulers and assure them of fair treatment in free India; finally, Mountbatten would disabuse the princes' minds of any misgivings that they might have. An Instrument of Accession was prepared and kept ready for their signature.

On 9 July 1947, the representatives of the princely states met in New Delhi to discuss all possible courses of action following independence. A majority of them were inclined to join India. However, four of the most important states—Hyderabad, Kashmir, Bhopal and Travancore—preferred to become independent. Mountbatten and Vallabhbhai Patel described the princes as their 'personal friends' and offered them ambassadorships, honorifics and privileges for joining the Indian Union.[136] Mountbatten also used his royal connections to exert pressure on the princes.

The result of these endeavours was that 559 out of the 565 princes signed the Instrument of Accession before 15 August 1947. The six unwilling princely states were Junagadh, Hyderabad, Bhopal, Indore, Kalat and Kashmir. Of them, Bhopal and Indore soon acceded to India and Kalat ultimately went to Pakistan. As Jinnah adopted a laid-back policy in response to this, none of the ten princely states which were expected to go to Pakistan ultimately acceded to it.

In less than a year, Vallabhbhai Patel and Mountbatten had carved out a larger India, which was much more closely integrated than what could be forged in ninety years of British rule, 180 years of Mughal rule, or by Ashoka and his predecessors in 130 years of Mauryan rule. Since Jawaharlal desired to handle Kashmir himself and described it in emotional terms as his 'first priority', Vallabhbhai Patel left the matter to him.[137]

11

THE KASHMIR IMBROGLIO

STRATEGIC IMPORTANCE

Mountbatten had already cleverly placed the NWFP in Pakistan's hands by using Jawaharlal's idea that it could not stand on its own as an independent nation.[1] The referendum was manipulated in such a way that the Muslim League, never popular in the province, had the support of the majority. Gandhi had assured him before the referendum (29 June) that Ghaffar Khan's followers would not interfere with the proceedings.[2] London expected Mountbatten to repeat the performance in Jammu and Kashmir, which was equally important strategically as a gateway to Central Asia and as a buffer zone between India and the Soviet Union.

In October 1946, the India Office had informed the Chiefs of Staff Committee in New Delhi that if India were to split up in two or more parts, the Muslim areas and the princely states should be motivated to remain in the Commonwealth.[3] As time progressed, the British Foreign Office realized more and more the necessity of making Pakistan a part of Britain's defence strategy. On assuming the viceroyalty, Mountbatten had indicated to the Congress and the League leaders the advisability of retaining the Commonwealth link as well as the services of British officers in the armed forces. Within a day of joining, he had impressed upon Jawaharlal the importance of retaining British officers to prevent a complete breakdown of law and order.[4]

Jawaharlal was initially unhappy about British officers being at the helm of the Indian Army in free India, but when the army chief explained to him that the process of rearrangement and nationalization of the forces would take time, he willy-nilly accepted his advice. He also dithered over the issue of joining the Commonwealth. On the other hand, Liaquat Ali Khan promptly agreed to both the suggestions from the viceroy.[5] Jinnah even confided in Mountbatten: 'I do not wish to make any improper suggestion to you, but you must realize that the new Pakistan is almost certain to ask for dominion status within the Empire.'[6]

By August 1947, British authorities were convinced that Pakistan would serve their strategic interests, although they did not give up the hope of making a defence treaty with India as well. Jawaharlal's dilemma about joining the Commonwealth and his uncertain and ever-changing foreign policy ideas and attitudes made Mountbatten's colleagues in London and even Prime Minister Attlee feel that Jawaharlal Nehru's India could not be trusted with regard to future cooperation. They were aware that in September 1946 Nehru had sent Krishna Menon to meet Vyacheslav Molotov, the Soviet foreign minister, with a letter conveying India's earnest desire to establish friendly relations with the USSR. Krishna Menon had transcended his brief and asked the Soviets if a team of military experts could be sent to India, much to Vallabhbhai Patel's consternation.[7]

In July 1947, Mountbatten mentioned 'the possibility of Kashmir joining Pakistan' in his personal report to the Secretary of State.[8] He had got this impression from his six-day tour to Srinagar in June. Maharaja Hari Singh (1895–1961) was an old acquaintance as they had served together as aides-de-camp during the Indian tour of the Prince of Wales (later King Edward VIII) in 1921.[9] Singh's premier, Ram Chandra Kak, was distinctly pro-Pakistan. From the very beginning, Jinnah and his party believed that Kashmir would logically join Pakistan and that Britain would ensure this in her own interest. Jinnah had even commissioned an architect to design a house for him in the Valley.[10]

Before his visit to Srinagar, Mountbatten had asked Jawaharlal to prepare a detailed note on Kashmir to enable him to hold fruitful discussions with Singh.[11] In Jawaharlal's note, the following was mentioned: 'The State consists of roughly 3 parts: Kashmir Proper, Jammu and Ladakh (Baltistan, Skardu and Kargil)...'[12] He omitted the strategic Gilgit Agency, probably because it was leased to the British then. In any case, this document coming from India's future prime minister had the potential of creating a wrong impression in London that Indian leaders did not consider Gilgit to be a part of Jammu and Kashmir.[13]

In Srinagar, Hari Singh had avoided discussing the issue of accession with Mountbatten on one pretext or another because he had heard of Jawaharlal's intimate relationship with Edwina and was afraid that the viceroy would help his adversary.[14] He had not even allowed Mountbatten to visit Jawaharlal's political ally, Mohammad Abdullah (1905–1982), in prison.[15] Edwina had also found it impracticable to meet Begum Abdullah. Mountbatten had not met or sought the views of any other Kashmiri leader, but he told Ram Chandra Kak that Kashmir would have to accede to either India or Pakistan and could not remain independent.[16] He also hinted to Hari Singh that Indian leaders had assured him about not taking it amiss if he chose to join Pakistan.[17]

Around the same time, in July 1947, Field Marshal Claude Auchinleck, the commander-in-chief of the army, had passed an order with the viceroy's concurrence that in the event of hostilities breaking out between the two would-be dominions (which was considered to be a distinct possibility), the British officers serving in the dominions would not take active part in them and instead resort to 'Stand Down' (that is, resign) if they were asked to do so. This order would be flagrantly violated by the British officers in Pakistan during their incursion into Kashmir soon after the Partition, in collusion with their counterparts in the Indian Army. While the British government was privy to everything, the Indian government was intentionally kept in the dark.

The fragility of India's security situation became evident on 15 August 1947 when Sir Shah Nawaz Bhutto, the diwan of Junagadh and a Muslim League politician, announced the state's accession to Pakistan.[18] India sought an immediate response from Pakistan in the matter, but none was available in spite of several reminders. Then, on 13 September, Pakistan announced a Standstill Agreement with Junagadh.[19] The announcement caused tensions in the Kathiawar region where the rulers of the other states sought India's intervention.[20] Mountbatten regarded the accession as valid, even if morally indefensible. He advised Jawaharlal and Vallabhbhai Patel to refrain from taking military action in Junagadh on 17 September.[21]

On the same day (17 September), the Indian cabinet decided, largely on Vallabhbhai Patel's initiative, to send V.P. Menon, Secretary to the States Ministry, to Junagadh to persuade the state authorities to merge with India.[22] V.P. Menon's visit to Junagadh the next day (18 September) was not fruitful in the sense that the Nawab did not meet him on the grounds of illness.[23] But it induced the Sheikh of Mangrol to sign the Instrument of Accession to India, which was then accepted by Mountbatten. This action prompted the Nawab of Junagadh to send troops to intimidate the neighbouring Babariawad, which had also volunteered to join the Indian Union. Vallabhbhai Patel wanted to rid Babariawad of the invaders at once, but Jawaharlal chose to ascertain its constitutional position first.

On 22 September, it was decided in a high-level meeting that the army and navy chiefs would prepare an operational plan for Babariawad and Mangrol. In the meantime, the Indian government would send a telegram to the diwan of Junagadh, demanding the immediate withdrawal of their troops from Babariawad. On 25 September, Junagadh communicated their refusal to do so. On the same day, Pakistan turned down India's proposal for a referendum on the grounds that this was a matter between the Nawab and his subjects. In the meantime, Mountbatten had informally ascertained from a leading British constitutional lawyer who was familiar with Mangrol that the state's accession to India was legally valid.

Two days later, on 27 September, the three service chiefs— General Sir Rob Lockhart, Admiral John Talbot Hall and Air

Marshal Sir Thomas Walker Elmhirst (represented by Air Commodore Subroto Mukherjee)—submitted a joint memorandum to the defence minister, Baldev Singh, expressing concerns over the possible fallout from the contemplated military measure and suggested that the matter be settled through negotiations with Pakistan.[24] Vallabhbhai Patel and his cabinet colleagues viewed this as an invasion of the political domain by the military, and as an act of disloyalty committed by British officers. When Nehru informed Mountbatten of the matter, he persuaded General Lockhart to withdraw the memorandum and write a letter of apology to the government and thereby averted the crisis.[25]

Shortly after this incident, on Mountbatten's suggestion, it was decided that a Cabinet Defence Committee would be formed to deal with military operations. Normally the prime minister would head a committee which included the three service chiefs. However, Jawaharlal allowed Mountbatten to become its chairman in view of his military experience. The Indian government had to pay dearly for this decision in the future because it allowed Mountbatten to have a say on every important matter of the state.

OPERATION GULMARG

Meanwhile, Hari Singh was exploring the possibility of remaining independent with the help of Britain and Pakistan. Mountbatten persuaded Gandhi to meet the Maharaja and convince him to accede to India, as he was sure by then about this being the best option. On 1 August 1947, Gandhi met the Maharaja at his palace in Srinagar and advised him to release Sheikh Abdullah, remove Ram Chandra Kak from his post, and make up his mind about accession.

Hari Singh sacked Kak on 11 August and got him arrested at Srinagar airport while he was attempting to flee in an aircraft with his English wife, Margaret, with the help of Richard Powell, inspector-general of police, and Major General Henry Lawrence

Scott, the chief of the state armed forces.[26] Singh, however, dithered about the advice on accession.

By mid-September 1947, Hari Singh realized that it was not possible to have an independent Kashmir. He decided, therefore, to accede to India on the condition that he would not have to hand over power to Sheikh Abdullah immediately, as demanded by Jawaharlal. He appointed Justice Mehr Chand Mahajan as the new diwan and instructed him to secure an agreement with New Delhi on these lines. Nehru, on the other hand, insisted that Hari Singh install a fully representative government under Sheikh Abdullah before they could contemplate any further step for the future. He argued that this would help India in a future plebiscite, but this had no basis in fact. The negotiations thus kept dragging on.

Vallabhbhai Patel and Jawaharlal Nehru had different approaches towards the Kashmir issue. Vallabhbhai Patel sought to befriend the Maharaja and persuade him to join the Indian Union instead of harassing him, since it was he who would decide on the accession under the Indian Independence Act. Vallabhbhai Patel tried to calm the fears that arose in his mind due to Jawaharlal's support for the 'Quit Kashmir' movement against him. He wrote to Hari Singh on 3 July, urging him to accede to India 'without any delay' and assured him that '...the Congress is not only not your enemy, as you happen to believe, but there are in the Congress many strong supporters of your State. As an organization, the Congress is not opposed to any Prince in India.'[27]

Towards the end of September, Jawaharlal and Vallabhbhai Patel closed ranks sensing the approaching crisis vis-à-vis Pakistan. Jawaharlal was aware through his secret contact in the Indian Army, Lieutenant General Roy Bucher, that Pakistan was planning to mount an attack on Jammu and Kashmir and that the chief of the Indian Army, General Lockhart, had come to know about it from his British counterpart in Pakistan. But instead of cautioning the army chief (and sacking him if necessary) and taking countermeasures to check the aggression, his first thought was to use the situation to get the National Conference, which was led by his friend Sheikh Abdullah, in power in Jammu and Kashmir. He wrote to Vallabhbhai Patel:

> It is obvious to me from the many reports I have received that the situation there [in Kashmir] is a dangerous and deteriorating one...I understand that Pakistan's strategy is to infiltrate into Kashmir now and to take some big action as soon as Kashmir is more or less isolated because of the coming winter...It becomes important therefore that the Maharaja should make friends with the National Conference so that there may be this popular support against Pakistan... Once the state accedes to India it will become very difficult for Pakistan to invade it officially or unofficially without coming into contact with the Indian Union...It seems to me urgently necessary therefore that accession to the Indian Union should take place early.[28]

The letter was more argument for empowering the National Conference than a genuine attempt to save the territory from the clutches of Pakistan by immediately accepting Maharaja Hari Singh's offer of accession to the Indian Union. It took him almost a year to sack Lockhart for this act of grave treachery. Unaware of this background information, Vallabhbhai Patel urged the Maharaja to proclaim a general amnesty and release the political prisoners on 2 October (Sheikh Abdullah, however, was released on 29 September). Meanwhile, Karachi was putting the finishing touches on its bold plan, code-named Operation Gulmarg, to seize Jammu and Kashmir by force.

Liaquat Ali Khan played a pivotal role in this venture which Jinnah approved.[29] On 12 September, the former finally okayed the plan for an 'Armed Revolt inside Kashmir', under which a clandestine invasion was to be launched by a force composed of Pathan tribesmen, ex-servicemen and soldiers 'on leave', who would put on the garb of disgruntled local tribesmen. The plan was prepared by Colonel Akbar Khan (1912–93), DSO, later

Major General, who adopted the alias General Jebel Tariq and established his headquarters in Rawalpindi.[30]

According to Khan's account, Brigadier Sher Khan, director of intelligence, Colonel Azam Khanzada of the Ordinance Corps, Lieutenant Colonel Masud of the Cavalry, and Air Commodore Janjua of the Royal Pakistan Air Force were involved in the planning and execution of the operation.[31] Personnel once belonging to the INA and members of the Muslim League National Guard were deployed for actual operations.[32]

General Frank Messervy, commander-in-chief of the Pakistan Army, knew about Operation Gulmarg and he kept his Indian counterpart, General Lockhart, informed about it. It was quite unlikely that Field Marshal Auchinleck, now Supreme Commander of military affairs in both India and Pakistan, and even Mountbatten, for that matter, were totally unaware of the goings-on.[33] But at no time before 24 October 1947 did Auchinleck direct the attention of the Indian government to any untoward development in Pakistan or in the vicinity of the Pakistan-Kashmir border. His report to the Indian government came after the tribal attack on Muzaffarabad.[34]

The operation first sought to exploit local grievances in the Poonch area of Jammu where landholders, joined by thousands of demobilized soldiers from World War II (Poonch was a major recruiting centre for the Raj), had been agitating against the excessive tax burden imposed on them and the general lack of employment opportunities in the area. The efforts of Pakistani agent-provocateurs met with only moderate success in the Jammu region and fizzled out by 29 September. Major General H.L. Scott, the chief of staff of the Jammu and Kashmir State Forces, resigned from his position the same day and the Maharaja replaced the acting chief of staff, Banbury, and the police chief, Richard Powell, with Hindu officers on 6 October.

After he was sacked, Powell left for Rawalpindi via Muzaffarabad and reportedly joined Pakistan security as an advisor.[35] Pakistan thereafter rapidly stepped up its cross-border infiltration activities and initiated a confrontation with the Maharaja's forces, which had the strength of a single infantry division and hardly any artillery or other supporting arms.[36]

On 1 October, the Maharaja's government appealed to the Indian government to send them military equipment and followed it up with a fervent request for stationing Indian troops near the border so that they could come to the state's rescue in case of an emergency.[37] Vallabhbhai Patel asked the Ministry of Defence to take care of these requirements immediately. In his letter to the defence minister, Baldev Singh, dated 7 October, he reiterated that there was no time to lose.[38] But the decision that the supply of arms to Kashmir should be a top priority was derailed by Lockhart, acting in collusion with Auchinleck, through various dilatory tactics.

On 15 October, the diwan, Mehr Chand Mahajan, approached the British prime minister and requested him to advise the Pakistani government to deal with Kashmir in a fair manner, but his appeal was ignored by Whitehall.[39] However, Pakistan's tactics did not succeed in other areas within the state because it lacked popular support. So much so that Pakistan decided to organize a massive invasion with the help of tribal irregulars along the main highway that linked Rawalpindi to Srinagar, via the towns of Domel and Muzaffarabad. The tribal hordes were expected to capture Srinagar in a matter of days. While the Kashmir government did not receive the arms or the army personnel that it needed from India, Pakistani tribal *laskar*s invaded the Jhelum Valley on 22 October.

On 21 October, Vallabhbhai Patel wrote to Mehr Chand Mahajan advising him to do something substantial as a symbolic gesture to win Sheikh Abdullah's support.[40] The Maharaja, accordingly, exchanged cordial messages with Sheikh Abdullah, but he was still reluctant to involve him in the governance of the state. Jawaharlal was annoyed with his attitude. Just hours before Pakistan launched a thrust towards Srinagar, he wrote to Mehr Chand Mahajan that Jammu and Kashmir's accession to India would be accepted only after a government under Sheikh

Abdullah was formed.[41] When the Maharaja finally signed the Instrument of Accession, a part of the state was already captured by Pakistan.

INDIA'S ARMED INTERVENTION

The Indian government first came to learn of the invasion on the evening of 24 October, a Friday, when it received a frantic call from the Kashmir state authorities asking for assistance. Jawaharlal was at a dinner party with Mountbatten at the Thai Embassy then. He took Mountbatten aside and told him about the crisis. Normally, the matter would have been discussed in the cabinet immediately, but on Mountbatten's suggestion, a meeting of the Cabinet Defence Committee to consider India's response was scheduled for the next morning.

This set a bad precedent for the future, as henceforth all such meetings concerning Kashmir and other states would be held under the auspices of the Defence Committee and they would all be chaired by Mountbatten. The next day, the Defence Committee met at 10 a.m. and Lockhart informed the members that he had received a telegram from the acting commander-in-chief of the Pakistan Army, Sir Douglas Gracey, the day before, which said that a force consisting of around 5,000 tribesmen had entered Kashmir and seized Muzaffarabad and Domel on 22 October and was about to attack Kohala.[42] Neither the Intelligence Bureau nor the Kashmir State Intelligence sources had reported on this likely attack.[43] Strangely enough, the army chief did not consider it necessary to inform the defence minister or the prime minister of the invasion sooner.

At the meeting, Nehru exhibited his prior knowledge—which he had not shared with his two colleagues in the cabinet—that large-scale raids had taken place in the Jammu area and that Pakistani authorities had lent support to the trucks carrying the attackers. He also disclosed that the invasion had been planned a fortnight ago at a conference in Rawalpindi.[44]

In Kashmir, no State Force units of any description existed between Domel and Srinagar at the time and the route to the Valley and Srinagar lay open to the tribal hordes.[45] If they had not wasted their time pillaging the villages and raping women en route, they could have covered a mere 110 miles on a good tarmac road to Srinagar in a matter of hours, as was originally planned. Besides, Brigadier Rajinder Singh, the newly appointed chief of the State Forces, had demolished the large steelgirder bridge at the eastern exit of Uri on his own initiative after receiving information about the imminent mayhem on 22 October, and this had helped delay the marauders.[46] If they could reach on time, the capture of the state capital and the decimation of the royal family would have been a fait accompli by the time Gracey's telegram reached Lockhart.

On 25 October, Vallabhbhai Patel raised the issue of weapons not being sent to Kashmir as ordered by the government at the Defence Committee meeting. Lockhart came up with the excuse that the Joint Council had decided earlier that they would not be sending arms in case of such an eventuality. In response, Patel pointed out that the said decision was supposed to apply only to Hyderabad. Mountbatten agreed with him. Accordingly, the army headquarters was instructed to depute officers to pick up arms from various depots and supply them to Kashmir in a chartered aircraft that very day.[47]

After this, once again Jawaharlal brought up his stipulation that the Maharaja must hand over power to Sheikh Abdullah before the question of Kashmir's accession to India could be considered. Jawaharlal's persistent emphasis on this point about Kashmir, which never figured in the case of any other princely state, made an impression that he was averse to granting the same privileges to Maharaja Hari Singh with regard to title, purse and property in the Indian Union as were granted to other princes. In fact, one major plank of the 'Quit Kashmir' agitation launched by his protégé, Sheikh Abdullah, was that the Maharaja's ancestor had acquired the kingdom through deceit. Thus, his descendant had no legal right over it and should quit the kingdom. There was a strong feeling in the state that if Sheikh Abdullah got the reins of the government, he would take legislative measures to deny the present Maharaja his title and privileges and then accede to India as the head of a democratic state. In that case, the Indian government would have no legal obligations to Hari Singh.

Mountbatten was aware of Jawaharlal's complicated feelings about Maharaja Hari Singh because of his own Kashmiri ancestry. He did not want to precipitate an inter-dominion war on the Kashmir issue and was therefore keen to see the state at least temporarily accede to India before it could be helped out on that front.[48] Thus, probably to accommodate Jawaharlal, Vallabhbhai Patel opined that he saw no reason why India should not respond to a request for assistance from a friendly state. Nehru agreed with him and stated that a final settlement on Kashmir's accession to India must be made after consulting the people.[49]

Mountbatten knew that even if Hari Singh opted to join India, they could always engineer a plebiscite later to decide which dominion Kashmir should accede to (he had said so in his personal report to the King on 7 November[50]). At the meeting on 25 October, it was decided that the chiefs of staff would 'examine and prepare plans' for (a) Indian troops to take over the Jammu front, (b) using the Royal India Air Force (RIAF) planes in Kashmir, particularly for reconnaissance and a show of strength, and (c) exploring the possibility of flying Indian troops into Srinagar. The service chiefs were asked to prepare contingency plans for sending Indian troops to Kashmir '...in case this should be necessary to stop the tribal invasion.'[51]

It was also decided that they would fly Vallabhbhai Patel and Mountbatten's trusted go-getter, V.P. Menon, to Srinagar the same afternoon (25 October) to discuss the question of accession with the Maharaja, assess the situation, and report to the committee the next day. Jawaharlal instructed V.P. Menon not to offer any assurance on the acceptance of the offer of accession.[52] Sam Manekshaw, then a daredevil colonel at the army headquarters, who was also Patel's favourite and was affectionately called

'Manekji' by Mountbatten, accompanied V.P. Menon in this trip. In Srinagar, Menon got the Instrument of Accession signed by the Maharaja and brought it straight to Vallabhbhai Patel's residence from the airstrip, presumably following a private instruction. The way V.P. Menon handled the matter saved the day for India as Mountbatten readily accepted the accession.

Subsequently, arranging the movement of the troops to Srinagar by air on such short notice proved to be a Herculean task, and all the more so because of the various excuses made by the service chiefs including the inadequacy of the forces, the difficulty of maintaining the supply line, and the lack of motor transportation for troop movements in Srinagar. Air Marshal Elmhirst delivered the final blow when he informed them that the RIAF could only provide four aircraft to transport the troops.[53] Undaunted, Vallabhbhai Patel requisitioned all the available civil aircraft, which were sizeable in number, by a radio broadcast.[54] His leadership forced the service chiefs to give up their hostility after sometime.

On 27 October, right at dawn, the first batch of the Sikh battalion emplaned at Safdarjung Airport. It was not known whether the Srinagar airfield was still untouched by the enemy. So, the commanding officer, Lieutenant Colonel Dewan Ranjit Rai, was instructed to make sure of this before landing, and fly to Jammu if necessary. At 10.30 a.m., a wireless message was received from the Srinagar airfield that Dewan Ranjit Rai and his troops had safely landed there.[55] Mountbatten, who had grave misgivings about the whole thing, was surprised by this smooth and efficient operation.[56]

The civilian pilots and their crews played a decisive role in saving Kashmir from the ravages of the marauders. Day after day, they flew flight after flight from New Delhi to the Valley, starting from first light till darkness fell, without a single accident.[57] The Indian military also exhibited extraordinary valour, initiative, planning, and acumen for combat in saving Baramulla, Uri, Poonch and even Ladakh, among others, from the clutches of Pakistani marauders. The Battle of Shalateng (7 November) and the tank expedition over the snowbound Zoji La Pass for protecting Srinagar and Ladakh were all the stuff of epics.[58]

The Indian forces were, however, greatly handicapped by the fact that the English generals systematically sabotaged their battle plans. On the other hand, Jawaharlal Nehru was indecisive about the strategy and tactics of war; Vallabhbhai Patel often had to put his foot down to allow the Indian commanders on ground to fight the enemy properly.[59] Jawaharlal thought that Pakistan would cease the hostilities after the accession, but he could not be more wrong.

On the other side of the border, Jinnah threw caution to the wind after the collapse of his scheme and ordered Gracey to march the regular army into Baramulla and Srinagar on 27 October, seize Banihal Pass, and occupy the Mirpur district of Jammu.[60] A jittery Gracey rang up Auchinleck at 1 a.m. that night and sought his guidance. The next morning, the Supreme Commander flew to Lahore, met Jinnah and told him that all the British officers would be withdrawn if Pakistan sent its regular army to Jammu and Kashmir, as this would effectively amount to an invasion of India. As Pakistan was heavily dependent on the services of the British officers (over 500 of them were in the army and just as many in the Civil Services[61]), Jinnah relented.[62]

Throughout October, the British generals of both dominions depended on the Supreme Commander for guidance. Vallabhbhai Patel felt that Auchinleck was '...throttling the initiatives of Headquarters Indian Army and acting as the advanced outpost of Pakistan.'[63] Mountbatten tried to defend his compatriot, but by late September, India moved a formal proposal in the Joint Defence Council to close down the Supreme Commander's Headquarters in New Delhi.[64]

On Mountbatten's advice, Auchinleck proposed the closure of the headquarters on 26 September, of his own accord.[65] Liaquat Ali Khan opposed this move in the Joint Defence Council, but Whitehall endorsed Auchinleck's proposal. Privately, Whitehall thought that Auchinleck was not handling the situation well enough and he was not given any assignments after his retirement on 1 December 1947. The Supreme Commander's Headquarters closed down on 30 November 1947, long before the scheduled date of 15 August 1948.[66]

BRITAIN'S PRO-PAK ACTIVITIES

On 25 October, Jawaharlal Nehru cabled Attlee to inform him that the Indian government was giving urgent consideration to Kashmir's appeal for help[67] and that the situation embodied a 'threat of international complications.'[68] Attlee had his own agenda tailored to Britain's strategic interests and he counselled both Jawaharlal and Liaquat Ali Khan to exercise the utmost restraint and hold bilateral discussions to solve the issue. In his message to Jawaharlal, he discouraged armed intervention in Kashmir, which might lead to an armed conflict with Pakistan. Simultaneously, he advised Liaquat Ali Khan to use his influence to bring back the members of the tribal militia who had already entered Kashmir.[69]

Before Attlee's message was delivered to Jawaharlal on 27 October, they had already begun airlifting the troops to Srinagar. Nevertheless, in deference to Attlee's request, Nehru proposed to Liaquat that they meet and discuss the Kashmir situation and meanwhile, the raiders should be prevented from entering Kashmir. He reiterated that the accession was subject to a referendum by the people of the state after it was cleared of the invaders.[70]

Contrary to Jawaharlal's hopes, Attlee had no intention of playing the role of an impartial judge because a group in Whitehall knew exactly what was happening in Kashmir and was closely monitoring the situation. Sir George Cunningham, an ex-captain of the Scottish national rugby team, a distinguished officer of the ICS and twice the governor of the NWFP, had played a key role in the tribal invasion plan.[71] He had a powerful hold over local tribal groups whose languages and culture he knew well. A few days ago, he had agreed to become the governor of the province for the third time at Jinnah's fervent request.

Cunningham had supported the idea of Pakistan since it was first mooted in 1940 and had a fair idea of how things were going to take shape in the future. Way back in 1944, he had arranged to withdraw the Hindu and Sikh troops of the Indian Army from the Razmak, Wana and Khyber Pass garrisons and replaced them with Muslim scouts and *khassadar*s (tribal levies).[72] This time too, he had helped organize the tribal groups from the border areas to prepare them for Operation Gulmarg. A few days before the incursion, he had sent a message to Abdul Ghaffar Khan that one way he could rehabilitate himself with Jinnah was to lead a tribal lashkar or militia into Kashmir.[73]

Pakistan's plan misfired and Jinnah's intrepid order to send the regular army into Jammu and Kashmir was about to expose the fact that there was a British hand in the matter. Whitehall was vastly relieved by the way Auchinleck handled the situation and officially congratulated him, but it disapproved of his stand that Jammu and Kashmir was now a part of Indian territory. Meanwhile, a powerful group in the Commonwealth Relations Office (CRO), London, headed by Philip Noel-Baker, secretary, and his principal staff officer, General Geoffry Scoones, was determined to help Pakistan have her way.

The CRO had an able source of support in Sir Laurence Grafftey-Smith, the British high commissioner in Pakistan. Attlee was unhappy about Mountbatten's acceptance of the Instrument of Accession. On 31 October, the British high commissioner in Delhi informed the viceroy that the CRO wanted Kashmir to go to Pakistan 'on agreed terms'.[74] A dedicated operative as he was, Mountbatten informed London that he could still underplay the accession part and put the matter on an even keel if Pakistan could establish locus standi in Kashmir with the help of international opinion, particularly American opinion.

Two days later, on 1 November, he met Jinnah in Lahore, accompanied by Lord Ismay, and discussed with him the prospect of holding a plebiscite in Kashmir at the earliest possible date under the supervision of the United Nations. A joint India-Pakistan force would be employed to ensure peace during this exercise. He wanted to use Jawaharlal to achieve this objective.

Meanwhile in Kashmir, Lieutenant General Kulwant Singh, GOC, Kashmir Operations, made a plan with the help of Brigadier L.P. Sen, the commander of 161 Brigade, in early November to oust the invaders from the border. However, General Roy Bucher, the acting army chief and Jawaharlal's old contact, opposed this plan calling it too risky. He had Mountbatten's support, although Jawaharlal and the other ministers pressed for the attack.[75] When Mountbatten left for London on 9 November to attend the wedding of Princess Elizabeth and Prince Philip, Kulwant Singh recovered the towns of Kotli, Jhangar and Naushera from Pakistani tribal occupation on his own within fifteen days. He simultaneously reinforced the besieged town of Poonch. When Mountbatten came back to India, he expressed his annoyance over this to Jawaharlal.[76]

On 3 December 1947, Bucher tried to make the Defence Committee agree to the proposed evacuation of Poonch, which, according to the British, had to be left with Pakistan. Mountbatten supported Bucher's proposal, but Jawaharlal was able to nullify it. Bucher, however, succeeded in postponing the planned push from Uri to Domel to clear the Jhelum Valley till the following spring.[77] The operation had to be discarded subsequently due to changed circumstances. Bucher also prevented the destruction of the bridges across the river Kishanganga, which would have cut Muzaffarabad off Pakistan and prevented Pakistani forces from advancing further into the area.[78]

In March, Lieutenant General K.M. Cariappa, the new General Officer Commanding-in-Chief, reoccupied Jhangar and beat back a powerful Pakistani attack on Naushera. In April 1948, Indian troops entered the town of Rajouri and restored the Jammu-Naushera line of communication. K.M. Cariappa had taken care not to inform the army headquarters about his operational plans. He was secretly in touch with Jawaharlal, whom he had met as a Brigadier in Peshawar before the Partition. K.M. Cariappa had to fight '...two enemies, Army Headquarters headed by Roy Bucher, and the Pakistan Army headed by Messervy.'[79]

Bucher admitted to Gracey, who succeeded Messervy as Pakistan's army chief, that he had no control over Cariappa. He, however, assured Gracey that he would not launch an offensive into what was now effectively Azad Kashmir, i.e., the Mirpur and Poonch area, and would try to get the Indian troops to withdraw from Poonch. Grafftey-Smith, the British ambassador, and Liaquat Ali Khan knew about this arrangement. This conspiracy was brought out into the open when Sardar Muhammad Ibrahim Khan, the leader of 'Azad Kashmir', issued a press statement on 31 March 1948 which said that the Indian Army had approached his government asking for a ceasefire. Consequently, the Indian government stalled Bucher's action, but it did not pull him up.[80] Now Mountbatten was also trying his best to scuttle India's military initiatives. He advised Gracey that after his departure from India, things should be done in such a way that both the governments would feel thoroughly impotent on the military front. This, according to him, would be the best way to reduce the risk of a war between the dominions.[81]

In fact, the regular Pakistan Army had entered Kashmir before the Indian Army could press ahead from Uri to Domel, which thwarted India's two-pronged attack to capture Domel and Muzaffarabad. The Indian troops captured Tithwal, to the north of Uri, but they could not advance on the Jhelum Road beyond ten kilometres west of Uri.[82] Soon afterwards, members of the United Nations Commission for India and Pakistan (UNCIP) arrived and India suspended operations for the duration of their stay in the subcontinent.

UN INTERVENTION

Mountbatten's secret mission succeeded when India lodged a complaint with the Security Council on 1 January 1948 about Pakistani incursion into the Indian state of Jammu and Kashmir.

Jawaharlal Nehru was convinced that India had an open-and-shut case and a favourable verdict was in the offing. They requested the Security Council to ask the Pakistani government to forbear from participating or assisting in the invasion of Indian territory in any manner whatsoever. Strangely enough, Jawaharlal ignored Britain's involvement in the matter, just as he ignored the existence of squabbles and politicking among the leading members of the Security Council.

From the very beginning, the British Foreign Secretary Ernest Bevin championed Pakistan's case at the Security Council so as not to alienate the Islamic world. The British Foreign Office felt that as a Muslim-majority state, Kashmir should have gone to Pakistan. Accordingly, Philip Noel-Baker, secretary of the CRO and recipient of the Nobel Prize for Peace in 1937, sought to form a lobby in Washington to prompt international agencies to ignore Kashmir's accession to India and consider Pakistan's incursion into Indian territory as a fait accompli. He lobbied for the establishment of a neutral administration under the auspices of the UN in Kashmir, superseding the Sheikh Abdullah government. He also advocated for a plebiscite to be held under the UN's supervision.

Attlee was reluctant to push India beyond a certain point, but he also recognized the need to appease the Islamic countries of the Middle East.[83] The US State Department was unwilling to ignore the accession, but it was prepared to accommodate Noel-Baker as regards (a) a truce declaration, (b) the establishment of a UN commission for implementing the truce and the peaceful settlement of the problem, and (c) an early plebiscite in an impartial and secure milieu.[84]

When the Security Council met on 15 January, N. Gopalaswami Ayyangar, a former prime minister of Kashmir (1937–43) and Jawaharlal's trusted associate, presented the case for India and asked the Security Council to persuade Pakistan to withdraw the invaders from the state. His presentation was overshadowed by the flamboyant appeal from Sir Muhammad Zafarullah Khan,

Pakistan's foreign minister and an eminent jurist, who was well connected in the USA and was involved in Noel-Baker's scheme.

Muhammad Zafarullah accused India of attempting to undo the Partition, carrying out genocide against Muslims in East Punjab, Delhi and other places, unlawfully occupying Junagadh, and securing the accession of Jammu and Kashmir through fraud and violence.[85] Noel-Baker coordinated his manoeuvres with his Western Allies in such a way that Britain, the United States, Canada and France supported Pakistan's stand that the raiders could not be induced to withdraw without a change of government in Jammu and Kashmir.[86] At Noel-Baker's behest, Senator Warren R. Austin from the United States even threatened N. Gopalaswami Ayyangar that without a settlement with Pakistan, India could not hope to have Indo-US political and economic relations of a permanent nature.[87]

Jawaharlal was so exasperated by these complex political manoeuvres that he told N. Gopalaswami Ayyangar to inform Austin that India sought no favours from any country in the form of bilateral relations and that conditions in India were quite stable.[88] On 3 February, he informed N. Gopalaswami Ayyangar that the majority of the members of the cabinet felt that India should get out of this UN entanglement as gracefully as she could unless the Security Council showed greater consideration for India's point of view.[89]

India's strong reaction to Noel-Baker's one-sided approach at the UN gave Whitehall cause for concern. Initially, Jawaharlal had suspected that the Western bias towards Pakistan was due to America's search for military and economic concessions in Pakistan. After N. Gopalaswami Ayyangar briefed him about the moves they had all pulled on him back in New York, he realized that Noel-Baker was the 'villain of the piece in spite of his pious professions.'[90] He angrily complained to Attlee that Noel-Baker had, in a conversation with Sheikh Abdullah, dismissed the charge that Pakistan had assisted the raiders as a lie.[91] Though Noel-Baker denied the charge, Attlee realized that his minister's initiatives in New York were casting a shadow on Indo-British relations. His view was reinforced by Mountbatten's strong plea for a more even-handed approach as regards the issue which would not permanently alienate either dominion.[92]

The British were afraid that if the Soviets supported India at this critical moment, there would be a powerful pro-Russian sentiment in India. So, the Commonwealth Affairs Committee of the British Cabinet met and discussed the Kashmir issue for the first time. As usual, Noel-Baker made light of India's objections. But he was vigorously opposed by Patrick Gordon Walker, the parliamentary under-secretary of his own ministry, who had just returned from a tour of the subcontinent and had firsthand knowledge of the situation. Finally, they decided to ask Pakistan to withdraw the raiders and put an end to Pakistani infiltration across the border, and also to explain to the American delegation why Britain was unable to support its proposals earlier.[93]

For Noel-Baker, this was a temporary setback. A few days later, when Pakistan sent its regular army into Jammu and Kashmir, he sought to help Pakistan once again by urging the UN Commission to proceed to the subcontinent urgently, curtailing its leisurely discussions in Geneva, and to be in position before 21 June 1948, the date of Mountbatten's departure from India.[94] Nevertheless, the five-member Commission, with representatives from Czechoslovakia (nominated by India), Argentina (nominated by Pakistan), Belgium and Colombia (selected by the Security Council), and the United States (nominated by the president of the Security Council), took their own time and left for Pakistan on 5 July, eleven weeks after its constitution.

The Commission delivered a series of proposals on 13 August. These, however, did not reflect any pro-Pakistan bias and accepted Jammu and Kashmir as a part of India. The Commission felt that Pakistan was more interested in a ceasefire and thus gave primacy to it, subject to the withdrawal of the invaders. The question of the plebiscite was to be taken up after both sides had accepted the truce agreement.

India maintained that she would have to retain a certain degree of military presence in the state to meet the threat of external aggression, as well as internal disorder. She also maintained that the sovereignty of the state extended to the entire territory and that it could not recognize the so-called 'Azad Kashmir Government'. Moreover, if a plebiscite were to be held in the future, it would be India's internal matter and Pakistan would have no say in it.

On the other hand, Pakistan demanded that the plebiscite be held on an equal footing, under the direct supervision of the UN, along with that of the joint Indo-Pakistani forces along the earlier guidelines. Also, the Azad Kashmir Government was to be treated as a separate party to any settlement and its militia was not to be disbanded. Likewise, all Indian troops were to be withdrawn from the state, as their presence, even if it was negligible, would be prejudicial to a fair plebiscite. In the resolution that it passed on 13 August, the Commission accommodated some of Pakistan's concerns, most notably the one about 'Azad Kashmir', although an immediate ceasefire was considered impossible under the circumstances.

The Commission did not condemn Pakistan publicly for violating international law in Jammu and Kashmir, but it did so privately and left the matter at that.[95] Britain's intention was to partition Jammu and Kashmir if it could not facilitate a wholesale transfer of the state to Pakistan. Her desire was, thus, fulfilled in some measure. The Commission left the subcontinent for Geneva on 21 September 1948. The departure of the Commission reduced the diplomatic constraints on India that stopped it from launching military offensives in the area. In the same month, Hyderabad was integrated into India successfully, under Vallabhbhai Patel's directions and more troops were freed up for launching an offensive in Jammu and Kashmir.

Meanwhile, General Roy Bucher, whom Jawaharlal still trusted, sent a telegram to London through the British High Commission, pressing for a ceasefire order from the United Nations which, he assured, India would obey.[96] This was an act of mischief on his part because Jawaharlal had asked him to prepare a military appreciation outlining an Indian offensive to rid Kashmir of regular and irregular troops from Pakistan before he left for London to attend the Commonwealth Prime Ministers' Conference in October 1948. When he returned in November, Bucher submitted his appreciation, stating that it was not possible to clear Kashmir of invaders during the winter and even afterwards,[97] whereas K.M. Cariappa had already prepared the outline plans to advance to Mirpur and Muzaffarabad.

Before his recommendations were discussed by the Indian cabinet, Bucher gave them to the new British high commissioner, Sir Archibald Nye, who had a good reputation in military circles for having been the deputy chief of the Imperial General Staff during World War II. On the basis of Bucher's recommendations, Nye reassured London that an all-out war was unlikely.[98] Bucher also informed Nye that Vallabhbhai Patel had agreed with him that Pakistani raiders could not be driven out of Kashmir without attacking their bases in Pakistan, which was not possible under the circumstances. On the contrary, at that time, Pakistan was apprehensive that Indian troops would advance up to the river Jhelum in the Mirpur area.

To meet this threat, Liaquat Ali Khan sought to have an immediate defence pact with Britain. He used the services of Major General Sir Walter Joseph Cawthorn, the deputy chief of the Pakistan Army, for this purpose.[99] He had worked with Peter Fleming and the ultra-secret double-agent network in Rangoon (now Yangon) during World War II.[100] This man was different from Major General Robert Cawthorn, who was also an intelligence officer and had set up the Inter-Services Intelligence (ISI) in Pakistan in January 1948.

Cawthorn met Noel-Baker in London on 18 September, and the latter arranged for him to meet Attlee. The British premier was agreeable to Liaquat Ali Khan's proposal, provided that India was kept informed about the developments.[101] Later, the CRO verbally informed Cawthorn that a formal proposal from Pakistan would be welcome. Liaquat Ali Khan followed up the matter during the Prime Ministers' Conference in October 1948. He met Jawaharlal Nehru in Attlee and Bevin's presence to explore options for a settlement, but their talks failed.

Unknown to Jawaharlal, Bevin and Noel-Baker met Liaquat separately afterwards and assured him that the Kashmir question would be raised in the Security Council once again.[102] They hinted that henceforth Britain would take a lenient view on the deployment of British officers in Jammu and Kashmir.[103] The Pakistan Army thereafter shifted the Seventh Division from West Punjab to Palandri in Jammu and Kashmir for covering Kotli, on the covert assurance that the UNO would impose sanctions on India if she attacked Pakistan.[104]

Strangely enough, Jawaharlal was unaware of these goings-on. He did not even sack Bucher when he had irrefutable proof of his duplicity and disloyalty. On 22 November, Nye reported to London that he was '...arranging to be fed into Jawaharlal that the morale of the Indian troops had begun to deteriorate...' He also commented: 'I hope by making these various representations to Nehru that it will be possible to bring home to him that there is no military solution to this [Kashmir] problem.'[105]

As for Bucher, he advised Jawaharlal that the army was running short of transport and vehicle spares, as well as a certain type of ammunition, and had no prospects of getting new supplies in the near future. Jawaharlal agreed with him that securing Muzaffarabad and Mirpur (K.M. Cariappa had already prepared a plan for capturing them) was out of the question, while efforts could still be made to recover Kotli, though not in the near future.[106]

Towards the end of the year, Bucher was able to calm Gracey's fears about the possibility of an all-out Indian drive to the Jhelum River. On 29 November, Grafftey-Smith informed the CRO in a telegram that he had no doubts about Bucher's dedication to curb Indian initiatives, but his worry was '...that Indian commanders on the spot may edge forward here and there in search of better position with dangerously provocative effect on the morale of

Azad Kashmir and Pak army.'[107] Grafftey-Smith was also '... less sure whether General Cariappa was "firmly under Bucher's control."'[108] Bucher had promised to alert Pakistan in case the Indian government tried to double-cross him.[109]

Nevertheless, the British failed to win American support for their plan to impose an unconditional ceasefire, circumventing the UNCIP.[110] John Foster Dulles, the new US delegate at the United Nations (Jawaharlal considered him 'dull' and shared Churchill's dislike of him for his directness[111]), complained to Washington that the British approach to the Kashmir problem was extremely pro-Pakistan. He urged the United States not to depart from its neutral path in seeking common ground with the British.[112]

On 25 December, the UNCIP's mediatory efforts led to a ceasefire agreement between India and Pakistan. Nye suggested to Air Marshal Elmhirst, the rotational chairman of the Chiefs of Staff Committee, that India should take the initiative to declare a ceasefire.[113] Accordingly, Jawaharlal authorized Bucher to announce a ceasefire proposal to his counterpart on 30 December. This dramatically came into effect one minute before midnight on 31 January 1948. Fifteen days later, K.M. Cariappa took charge as the first Indian chief of the army.

JAMMU AND KASHMIR ON THE EDGE

On the political front, a great many things were happening in Jammu and Kashmir during this period—all at the behest of Sheikh Abdullah. The terms of the ceasefire required Pakistan to withdraw all its forces from the state, including the Poonch-Muzaffarabad belt and the Gilgit Agency, and they allowed India to retain a slight military presence to maintain law and order. Only when they complied with all these conditions would a plebiscite be held to determine the future of the state. To Pakistan, the conditions for holding the plebiscite came as a shattering blow.

Meanwhile, Hari Singh had installed an emergency government in the state at the end of October 1947, with Mehr Chand Mahajan as the prime minister and Sheikh Abdullah as the head of the emergency administration, with a cabinet of his own choice. Jawaharlal Nehru's public assertions that Abdullah represented the true voice of the Kashmiri people bolstered his position in the eyes of the Indian public. Fortunately for Jawaharlal, the military situation in the state and the rhetoric of Indo-Pakistan arguments distracted public attention from Sheikh Abdullah's activities.

A highly egotistic and power-hungry man, Sheikh Abdullah also had a simulating nature, as assessed by Brigadier L.P. Sen[114] and B.N. Mullik, the director of the Intelligence Bureau (DIB).[115] Vallabhbhai Patel did not have any illusions about him from the very outset,[116] but Jawaharlal took his own sweet time to get to the truth. Soon after assuming office, Sheikh Abdullah arrested many officials from the Maharaja's old administration, including the governor of Jammu, and replaced them with his own men. Neither government offices nor the High Court could function properly at this time, while his party began to sell trade concessions and rent out state vehicles at will.

Members of the Muslim Conference, whom the Maharaja had also put in jail for opposing him, languished in captivity. Within six weeks of the installation of the emergency government, Mehr Chand Mahajan complained to Vallabhbhai Patel that it reminded him of Nazi Germany run by gangsters and that he wished to be no part of it.[117] When Mahajan resigned from his post on 5 March 1948, Sheikh Abdullah became the sole custodian of the interim government.

A few months later, T.G. Sanjeevi Pillai, who was the DIB then, informed Jawaharlal that the communists were conspiring to stage a coup in Kashmir with Sheikh Abdullah's support on 5 August 1948.[118] Although the coup did not take place, Sheikh Abdullah's 'socialist' inclination engaged the attention of the CIA, the ISI and the IB. In December 1950, the CIA prepared a note on the communist personalities in Kashmir, which included the name of Baba Pyare Lal Bedi, who had drafted the new constitution of Jammu and Kashmir at Sheikh Abdullah's request, his wife

Freda, G.M. Sadiq, Mirza Afzal Beg, Ghulam Mohiuddin Karra and Dhanwantri.[119] The US State Department was worried that Kashmir would be the site for the unfolding of the final scene of the political drama that began in Sinkiang.[120]

In 1950, Sheikh Abdullah secured a separate status for Jammu and Kashmir through Article 370 (originally 306A) of the Constitution of India, with Jawaharlal Nehru's implicit support. The Article, which has been recently abrogated, was drafted by N. Gopalaswami Ayyangar in consultation with Sheikh Abdullah[121] and granted special status to the state, circumscribing the power of the Indian Parliament to only three matters specified in the Instrument of Accession, viz. defence, external affairs and communication. Jawaharlal probably wanted the state to be a testing ground for implementing his socialist ideas or, perhaps, he gave enough rope to his protégé to keep him under control.

In the middle of 1949, Ghulam Mohiuddin Karra, who had masterminded the Quit Kashmir movement and could alone measure up to Sheikh Abdullah, quit the National Conference under Pakistan's inspiration and formed the Kashmir Political Conference, which supported Kashmir's accession to Pakistan.[122] Pakistan had now switched over to internal subversion and sabotage with the help of various anti-Indian groups and individuals in Jammu and Kashmir. The Inter-Services Intelligence (ISI) was financing several mushroom organizations, the Kashmir Political Conference being one of them.[123] When B.N. Mullik became the director of the Intelligence Bureau (IB) in July 1950, Jawaharlal instructed him to pay special attention to Kashmir.[124]

On 17 June 1952, Sheikh Abdullah sent a National Conference delegation to New Delhi. It comprised Mirza Afzal Beg, D.P. Dhar and Syed Mir Qasim—all of them communists or crypto-communists in his government—to hold talks with Jawaharlal Nehru about the future governance of the state. Sheikh Abdullah joined the group on 17 July. He was accompanied by Bakshi Ghulam Mohammad, G.M. Sadiq and Maulana Masoodi. D.P. Dhar and Bakshi Ghulam Mohammad were Jawaharlal's men in

Kashmir.[125] An agreement emerged between Sheikh Abdullah's group and Jawaharlal Nehru on 24 July. It came to be known as the Delhi Accord.

The Delhi Accord legitimized the following: (a) the exclusive right of Kashmiri citizens to own land in Kashmir, (b) recognition of the exceptional authority of the constituent assembly, (c) declaration of an emergency only at the request of or with the concurrence of the state government, (d) use of the state flag, alongside the national flag, (e) appointment of the sadr-e-riyasat (governor) on the recommendation of the constituent assembly, (f) no intervention by the President of India or the Chief Justice of the Supreme Court in matters relating to the state, except in certain circumstances, and (g) vesting of residuary constitutional powers in the state and not in the centre.[126] These provisions made Sheikh Abdullah a virtual dictator in Jammu and Kashmir.

Meanwhile, feelings of resentment were growing against Sheikh Abdullah's rule in Jammu and Kashmir. Ladakh, which was the largest district and was situated on an alternative route to Sinkiang that bypassed the Gilgit Agency, wanted to break away. By the end of 1948 when it became clear that Ladakh would remain in India, Ladakhis wanted to have a separate identity from Kashmir. In a 1949 memorandum, Chhewang Rigzin, president of the Ladakh Buddhist Association, requested Jawaharlal Nehru to integrate Ladakh either with Jammu in the form of a separate state, or with Punjab. He argued that the annulment of the Treaty of Amritsar (1846) had entitled Ladakh to a separate existence. In 1952, the demand was renewed by the abbot of the Spituk Monastery, Kushok Bakula, who was widely accepted as the Ladakhi equivalent of Sheikh Abdullah.

Kushok Bakula complained to Jawaharlal about the injustices of the Sheikh Abdullah regime and hinted that if matters did not improve, Ladakh might seek to secede from India and join Tibet. He made it clear that Ladakh was prepared to cohabit with the Hindus of Jammu and needed to be, in some way, separated from Srinagar. Ladakhi grievances against the Muslim domination of the region were communicated to Karan Singh, the sadr-e-riyasat, during his visit to Leh in the latter part of 1952. Singh also apprised Nehru of the deep-seated disappointment of the Ladakhi people for being completely ignored by the Kashmir government.[127]

Meanwhile, an opposition to Sheikh Abdullah's regime was developing in Jammu at the behest of the Jammu Praja Parishad, founded by Balraj Madhok (1920-2016) of the Rashtriya Swayamsevak Sangh (RSS) in November 1947. The organization had close links with Dr Syama Prasad Mookerjee (1901–53), president of the newly-formed Bharatiya Jan Sangh.[128] Syama Prasad Mookerjee was basically a secular politician, who had left the Hindu Mahasabha partly because it did not admit non-Hindus in the party.[129] Jawaharlal acknowledged his pioneering contribution to the development of modern science and technology in India as the first Minister of Commerce and Industries of independent India in 1947–50.[130]

The Delhi Accord alarmed the Praja Parishad, which considered the National Conference a communal party as well as a surrogate organization for spreading communism. Sheikh Abdullah's cabinet had several active communist party cardholders, including G.M Sadiq. The CIA was concerned about G.M. Sadiq's visit to Moscow, ostensibly for medical reasons, in November 1952.[131] It was rumoured to have been arranged by his Soviet handlers.[132] The Parishad sought the separation of Jammu from the Valley either as an independent state or as a part of Punjab, and demanded the abrogation of Article 370 and special status of Jammu and Kashmir.

In the midst of these developments, Sheikh Abdullah announced the end of the Dogra dynasty on 17 November 1952. The Maharaja was replaced by a constitutional head of state, the sadr-e-riyasat, to be elected for a five-year term by the legislative assembly, and in the absence of such an elected body, by the existing constituent assembly. At Jawaharlal Nehru's behest, the Maharaja's son, Karan Singh, was elected unopposed as the first sadr-e-riyasat of Jammu and Kashmir.

The same month, the Praja Parishad leader Prem Nath Dogra

and his close associate, Shyam Lal Sharma, were arrested. This created a volatile situation in Jammu. Simultaneously, the Jana Sangh launched an agitation in Delhi demanding Kashmir's complete integration with India.[133] Sheikh Abdullah bitterly called these developments Hindu revivalism.[134] Against this backdrop, Syama Prasad Mookerjee set out for Jammu to look into the situation and was arrested by the state police at the border in Lakhanpur in Kathua district of Jammu, on 11 May 1953. He was then taken to Srinagar, where he was placed under house arrest under appallingly shabby circumstances.

Across India, criticism was mounting against the Sheikh Abdullah regime following the arrest. And this, in turn, made him more defiant towards Delhi. Sheikh Abdullah's associates—Bakshi Ghulam Mohammad, G.M. Sadiq, Syed Mir Qasim and even Maulana Masoodi—did not support his anti-India line. Jawaharlal sent several hints to Sheikh Abdullah and even extended an open invitation to him to come to Delhi and talk the matter over, but all these went unheeded.[135] At Jawaharlal's request, Maulana Azad went to Srinagar in spite of his fragile health to talk sense to Sheikh Abdullah, but all of it was in vain.

From 23 to 25 May, Jawaharlal visited Srinagar to sort things out with Sheikh Abdullah, but he did not meet Syama Prasad Mookerjee, who died in police custody on 23 June. A week after his death, Jawaharlal sent his condolences to his mother, Jogamaya Devi, professing great affection for her son.[136] In reply, the lady simply asked Jawaharlal why he could not make some time to see her son during his visit to Srinagar, if he had so much affection for him.

Syama Prasad Mookerjee's death shocked the people of India and became a subject of stormy debates. It was widely believed that he was murdered. Jawaharlal disregarded Jogamaya Devi and many others' request to hold an official inquiry into the incident. On 31 July, he decided at a meeting with the intelligence chief, B.N. Mullik, to remove Sheikh Abdullah and install Bakshi Ghulam Mohammad in his place. B.N. Mullik was asked to make all the necessary arrangements to make this happen. On the same day, Jawaharlal instructed Brigadier B.M. Kaul to discreetly alert Lieutenant General Atal, the corps commander at Udhampur, and the divisional commander in Srinagar about the impending action.

Rafi Ahmed Kidwai (1894–1954), who was in charge of the political affairs of Kashmir, was taken into confidence. On his suggestion, Ajit Prasad Jain, who was the minister in charge of rehabilitation at that time, was sent to Srinagar to keep watch over the situation on Jawaharlal's behalf.[137]

Things now began to move faster in Srinagar. On 6 August, Sheikh Abdullah ordered Sham Lal Saraf, an old associate, to resign from the ministry under provocation. Sham Lal Saraf met the sadr-e-riyasat and refused to resign. Sheikh Abdullah had to swallow his pride and request Karan Singh to dismiss him. Meanwhile, a few other members of the cabinet—Bakshi Ghulam Mohammad, G.M. Sadiq, Prem Nath Dogra and D.P. Dhar—supported Sham Lal Saraf and constituted the majority in the cabinet. Even Maulana Masoodi, the general secretary of the National Conference, opposed the Sheikh for his anti-Indian attitude. Sheikh Abdullah consequently lost his majority in all the three bodies that counted, viz. the National Conference, the constituent assembly and the cabinet.

By this time, the Intelligence Bureau had received information that the pro-Pakistan leader Pir Maqbool Gilani had established contact with Pakistan and that a Pakistani emissary was on his way to Tanmarg, near Gulmarg, to meet Sheikh Abdullah. Their suspicion deepened when the Sheikh suddenly left for Tanmarg on the evening of 8 August.[138] Jawaharlal was at once informed of this development.[139] Shortly afterwards, the sadr-e-riyasat, Karan Singh, issued orders dismissing Sheikh Abdullah as prime minister of Jammu and Kashmir, and invited Bakshi Ghulam Mohammad to form a new ministry.[140]

Bakshi Ghulam Mohammad wanted to confirm the news of the Sheikh's arrest before he committed to anything. He was afraid of the repercussions if, by any chance, Sheikh Abdullah evaded arrest. At 11 p.m. B.N. Mullik met Jawaharlal and Rafi Ahmed Kidwai at a party at the Hyderabad House and informed them of this predicament. They all came back to the prime minister's house unobtrusively to discuss the situation. A.P. Jain, a minister, and D.W. Mehra, the deputy director of the IB in Srinagar, were advised to keep in constant touch with Bakshi Ghulam Mohammad and goad him to take over as soon as possible.[141]

At midnight, Karan Singh issued orders for the Sheikh's arrest. When Sheikh Abdullah was at his clandestine meeting with the Pakistani intelligence officer at Tanmarg, he was arrested by L.D. Thakur, DIG of Police, and taken forthwith to Udhampur. D.P. Dhar was the man who held the fort through the entirety of this crisis.[142]

THE AFTERMATH

Maulana Masoodi, who had opposed Sheikh Abdullah's anti-India stand, was unhappy about his arrest and tried, along with Mridula Sarabhai (now estranged from Jawaharlal[143]), to develop an anti-Bakshi and anti-Nehru lobby in the capital against this. Mridula Sarabhai had a soft spot in her heart for the Sheikh, although he often misbehaved with her.[144] Jawaharlal hated to be in a controversy and the lobby embarrassed him a great deal.

Bakshi Ghulam Mohammad reorganized the National Conference and under his leadership, Kashmir enjoyed a period of phenomenal progress in the economic and educational spheres. The roads linking the region with India were improved; a tunnel was cut through Banihal; trade with the rest of the country flourished. The Bakshi government integrated the state's higher administrative and police services with the all-India services. The Supreme Court's jurisdiction was also extended to Jammu and Kashmir. The process of integration with India progressed similarly in many other fields.[145]

About a month after Sheikh Abdullah's arrest, Pakistan's prime minister, Mohammad Ali Bogra (1909–63), decided with Jawaharlal in Delhi that the best way to ascertain the people's wishes with regard to Jammu and Kashmir would be to hold a plebiscite under an administrator from a small country and not from the USA or the UK, which had their own interests in the region. However, Mohammad Ali Bogra could not get his own cabinet to accept this proposal. The USA also put pressure on them to retain Admiral Chester W. Nimitz as the plebiscite administrator. Subsequently, Pakistan's Mutual Defence Assistance Agreement with the USA and a membership of the SEATO (South-East Asia Treaty Organization) in 1954, and then the Baghdad Pact (1955) with Britain, Turkey, Iran and Iraq changed the situation completely.

Khrushchev and Bulganin's visit in 1955 gave some respite to India. The Soviet dignitaries visited Srinagar and declared that Soviet Russia considered Jammu and Kashmir to be a part of India and that the Kashmiris had already made their final choice. Russia's attitude towards India also changed in the Security Council. The Soviet representative there declared that his country could not vote for any resolution that was unacceptable to India.[146]

However, shortly after the elections in March 1957, G.M. Sadiq left the Bakshi government along with Prem Nath Dogra, D.P. Dhar, Syed Mir Qasim and a few others, and formed the Democratic National Conference, which was soon joined by the Kashmir Communist Party. This alliance gave the miniscule Communist Party a new lease of life as well as some strength, and helped it build a firm footing in the Jammu region.

As a result of this rift, Bakshi Ghulam Mohammad became somewhat isolated, having only Sham Lal Saraf among his old associates. The acrimony and mud-slinging campaigns between the National Conference and the Democratic National Conference vitiated the political and administrative atmosphere and made Bakshi Ghulam Mohammad more and more autocratic in his ways. Some members of his family also began to indulge in corruption and mired his reputation.[147]

In the meantime, Sheikh Abdullah's followers maintained their contact with Pakistani intelligence agents who were led by one Major Asgar Ali. They formed an underground War Council, which had connection with Mirza Afzal Beg's Plebiscite Front.[148] It also came to their notice that Sheikh Abdullah was corresponding with the Pakistani intelligence officer, Niazi, under the following pseudonyms: Asad Saheb, Asadullah, Asadullahs, Aaid-i-Azam, Aaid-i-Aza, Aziz, and so on. Begum Abdullah was also accepting money and help from Pakistani sources. This group was using Mridula Sarabhai for organizing anti-India activities and her house had become a site for clandestine meetings between the Plebiscite Front and the Pakistan High Commission.[149]

By October 1957, sufficient evidence had been collected to start a conspiracy case against Mirza Afzal Beg, Pir Maqbool Gilani, Begum Abdullah, and a few others for plotting to overthrow the government. Sheikh Abdullah was not included in the first information report (FIR) initially as the evidence against him was not strong enough even at that point. However, by January 1958, the entire gamut of the conspiracy was unearthed and a case was made against all the above-mentioned people as well as Sheikh Abdullah. In March 1958, Jawaharlal desired to have the brief of the case presented to him within a week. As the matter was already ready, it was produced before him the very next day.

The proposed chargesheet consisted of sixteen hundred-odd pages. Since Jawaharlal was not in a position to scrutinize it, he passed it on to Govind Ballabh Pant, the union home minister, to take a decision.[150] The case was vetted by eminent lawyers such as A.K. Sen, M.C. Setalvad, J.P. Mitter and others before it was ready to be presented before the court.

At this stage, Bakshi Ghulam Mohammad declared that however strong the evidence might be against Begum Abdullah, he could not agree to her prosecution. Quite possibly, Jawaharlal was behind this move. It was argued by the case officers that if she was let off, the case would be substantially weakened. Nevertheless, Jawaharlal agreed with Bakshi Ghulam Mohammad, and it was decided to submit the chargesheet without mentioning her.[151] A couple of days later, Jawaharlal stated that Sheikh Abdullah should not be prosecuted either. The officials were in a quandary because Sheikh Abdullah could not be indefinitely detained without a trial and would have to be set free.[152] Finally, on 21 May 1958, a complaint was filed against twenty-five conspirators, including Mirza Afzal Beg, Pir Maqbool Gilani and Pir Maqbool Wilgami, in the court of the special magistrate of Jammu, for conspiracy and waging war against the state.[153] The case dragged on in court thanks to the dilatory tactics deployed by the lawyers of the accused.

Four years later, in April 1962, Jawaharlal wanted the case to be withdrawn when he fell ill. A petition was accordingly drafted by the senior counsel and sent to Bakshi Ghulam Mohammad for consideration. As B.N. Mullik and Krishna Menon, the then defence minister, counselled Jawaharlal against this step, he asked B.N. Mullik to visit Jammu to discuss the pros and cons of the matter with Bakshi Ghulam Mohammad. B.N. Mullik did so, and, together with Bakshi Ghulam Mohammad, he briefed Jawaharlal that no one favoured the withdrawal of the case, not even the sadr-e-riyasat or D.P. Dhar.[154] Jawaharlal accepted their suggestions.

However, in September 1963, Jawaharlal became impatient with the delay of the trial and suggested that the case be withdrawn. As many as forty-nine MPs and even Jayaprakash Narayan had written to him to withdraw the case, having been influenced by Mridula Sarabhai's propaganda.[155] Bakshi Ghulam Mohammad, G.M. Sadiq, D.P. Dhar, and other Kashmiri leaders opposed this step and the matter was set at rest for the time being.

In December 1963, serious disturbances took place in Srinagar over the disappearance of the Moi-e-Muqaddas (the hair of the Prophet), masterminded by pro-Pakistani elements. Some top Kashmiri leaders approached Jawaharlal to bring back Sheikh Abdullah into Kashmiri politics to calm the situation. Bakshi Ghulam Mohammad was no longer in the picture after relinquishing his office in compliance with the Kamaraj Plan. So Jawaharlal considered this a gamble worth taking and the Kashmir conspiracy case was withdrawn shortly before his death.

12
THE ORPHAN OF POLITICS: TIBET

A HISTORICAL PRELUDE

Tibet is a country with an area of approximately 500,000 square miles and is almost as vast as Europe. It is bounded on the north by the towering Kunlun Mountains separating it from the Chinese province of Xinjiang, and in the west by the mighty Karakoram Range on its border with Kashmir. The majestic Himalayas form a natural boundary with India in the south. Only to the east of the country is there a gap that connects it to the outside world. Through this gap flow the headwaters of three great rivers—the Yangtze, the Mekong, and the Salween—on their way to China and Southeast Asia.

The core of Tibet is in its eastern part, in the Yarlung region to the south of the Brahmaputra ('Yarlung Tsangpo' in Tibetan). From this region, in seventh century CE, Tibet's first historical character, Songtsen Gampo, ruled the whole region, including the present-day Yarlung and the Chongye Valley and the ancient trade routes into India and Bhutan. In 637 and 638, Gampo defeated the Chinese Emperor Taizong (598–649) of the Tang dynasty and married Princess Wencheng in 641.[1] The Tang dynasty ruled China from 618 to 907, with a break between 690 and 705, and is generally regarded as a high point in the Chinese civilization.

Gampo was a path-breaker in many ways. In 641, he was a king-maker in Nepal, and in 647, he married the Licchavi princess, Bhrikuti, and became a champion of Buddhism under Wencheng and her influence. He sent his minister, Thonmi Sambhota, to India to devise the Tibetan alphabet and begin the composition of the first literary works and translations in Tibetan, as well as court records and a constitution.[2] Many Buddhist temples, including Jokhang in Lhasa, his new capital, and the Tradruk temple in Nedong, were built during his reign and several Buddhist texts were translated from Sanskrit.[3] In 649, the Tang Emperor Gaozong (628-683) paid homage to him as the King of Xihai Jun,[4] a province of ancient China in the Qingzang Plateau.

By the late 660s, the Tibetans overran the Tuyuhuns in the Qilian Mountains and the upper Yellow River Valley in modern Qinghai in China, and the two empires fought sporadically over the following decades. Much of Northwestern China fell into Tibetan hands. Tibetans from Ngari settled in Songzhou ('Sharkok' in Tibetan). This area was identified in Tibetan geographical writings as part of Amdo or Kham in the expanding Tibetan Empire. Even now, the inhabitants of Sharkok and the neighbouring Khopokok ('Jiuzhaizou' in Chinese) speak a variation of Tibetan, known as Sharkhog Tibetan.[5]

Songtsen Gampo had even made an alliance with the Arabs.[6] Around 715 CE, Tibet and Arabia jointly established a king in the Fergana principality. He served as a link between the Tibetan king and the Arab caliphs.[7] Subsequently, Arab rulers like Harun al-Rashid (763-809), the Abbasid caliph of Baghdad, became more interested in their Western allies, but his son, al-Ma'mun (786-833), a scholar by nature, renewed their treaties with Tibet in 810 CE.[8]

Twelve years later, in 822, Gampo's spiritually inclined descendant, Ralpachen or Tritsuk Detsen (802-836), was tricked by his clever maternal uncle, Chinese Emperor Bun-Pu-He-u-Tig Hwang Te, into making a treaty for the mutual welfare of their two empires. The treaty underlined that Tibet and China would guard their land and frontier jointly. To the east of the frontier would be the territory of China and to the west that of Tibet. By this thoughtless act, Ralpachen, who was more interested in religious rituals, made his people vulnerable to Chinese overlordship in the future. The stele or monolith on which the ambiguous treaty was inscribed still exists in Potala Palace in Lhasa.[9]

During 1271–1354, Tibet came under the rule of the Yuan dynasty of China, which was established by Genghis Khan's grandson, Kublai Khan. Shortly after Genghis Khan's death in 1227, the Mongols embraced Buddhism. Kublai Khan, who conquered China in 1271 and ruled over present-day Mongolia, China, Korea and some adjacent areas, patronized the religion. In the past centuries, the Chinese emperors had only a tenuous political relationship with Tibet, but after the Mongol conquest of China, Tibet began to depend on the 'Middle Kingdom' politically.

Nevertheless, the Mongols honoured the Grand Lama of Tibet, Gedun Drupa (1391–1474), as their spiritual leader. In 1577, during the tenure of the third Grand Lama, Sonam Gyatso (1543–88), Lamaism was accepted as their official religion. The Mongol chief Altan Khan (1507–82) conferred on him the honorary title *ta-le* ('Dalai'), meaning 'ocean', starting the institution of the ta-le lama or the Dalai Lama. Two of Gyatso's predecessors received this title posthumously. When he died, the relationship between the Mongols and the Tibetans was further strengthened when it was discovered that he had been reborn in the Mongolian royal family.

The fourth Dalai Lama, Yonten Gyatso (1589–1617), was a great-grandson of Altan Khan. In 1602, he confirmed the existence of a Mongolian reincarnation of another Bodhisattva (enlightened beings) near Ugra. Later, in 1639, yet another Mongol was declared to be the reincarnation of the great Tibetan scholar Taranatha. This practice of finding incarnations in highborn Mongol families ceased when the Manchus or the Qing dynasty (1636–1912) began to rule China proper from 1644. It was then ordained by an imperial order that no man bearing the lineage of Genghis Khan could be 'discovered' to be a reincarnation or 'a cyclical Buddha', and that all such reincarnations must be found in Tibet.

During the reign of the Manchus, the sovereignty of China over Tibet, which Tibet had always felt to be nominal, no longer remained so. During the Mongol period in China, the fifth Dalai

Lama, Ngawang Lobsang Gyatso (1617–82), effectively wielded both temporal and spiritual power all over Tibet and was referred to as 'the Great Fifth'. Soon after coming to power, the Qing emperor invited him to Beijing. Together, they arrived at an unwritten concordat that the Chinese would govern Tibet and respect the Dalai Lama as politically the highest among the lamas, but that the latter must act only as a spiritual authority.[10] Tibet did not gain any political importance in the region ever again in its long history, until Russia and England began to take interest in the country much later.

BRITISH POLICY ON TIBET

The British began to show interest in the region in 1768 when the Court of Directors of the East India Company thought of seeking out possibilities for trade and commerce in Tibet and in Western China.[11] However, the matter lay dormant till 1792, when Nepal got involved in a war with China and hastily made a commercial treaty with the British in India. The Chinese commander-in-chief also sought Governor-General Lord Cornwallis's help against Nepal in his letter dated 31 March. He was supported by the Dalai Lama and the Panchen Lama.[12]

Yet, Tibet remained closed to Britain, even though individual Britons attempted to cross the Himalayas and reach the land. The sinologist Thomas Manning, 'friend M' in Charles Lamb's *Essays of Elia*, was the first Englishman to visit the court of Lhasa in 1811. He, however, painted a very dismal picture of the squalor and disorderliness of Lhasa in his travel account. And this became the standard British view of the country.

In 1842, the Treaty of Nanking opened five Chinese ports to the British, but it did not cater to any form of trade with Tibet. This continued till 1876, when the Sino-British Convention recognized the right of the British to negotiate for permission to send trade missions to Tibet.[13] After another two decades, in March 1890, the British managed to separate Sikkim from Tibet politically and make her a British protectorate through a treaty with the Chinese governor in Lhasa.[14]

The Tibetans, however, declared that they were not bound by this convention. In October 1900 and July 1901, the young and enterprising thirteenth Dalai Lama, Thubten Gyatso (1876–1933), asserted Tibet's independence from China and sent a resourceful Mongolian, Agran Doryiyev, to the court of Tsar Nicholas II with a proposition that he should declare himself the protector of Buddhism and the liberator of the 'Asiatic peoples'.[15]

Thubten's action drew sharp criticism from Britain. In August 1901, the British foreign minister Lord Lansdowne instructed the British ambassador in St. Petersburg to inform the Russian foreign minister, Count Lamsdorf, that his government would not remain indifferent if any attempt was made to change Tibet's present status.[16] The chronic Russophobe George Nathaniel Curzon, the viceroy of India, saw it as a revival of 'the Great Game' of the nineteenth century for the control of Central Asia. In 1904, he sent Lieutenant Colonel Francis Edward Younghusband to Tibet under the auspices of the Tibet Frontier Commission with a military posse of his own. Younghusband engaged in several gruesome skirmishes and forced his way into Lhasa.[17] The Dalai Lama fled to Mongolia and his government signed a convention with Great Britain, which gave the British the right to open markets at Gyantse and Gartok, in addition to the one already established at Yatung under the Anglo-Chinese Convention of 1890.[18] Although the 1904 convention was a direct transaction with Tibet, Britain continued to recognize Chinese suzerainty over Tibet. In the subsequent convention between Britain and China in 1906, this was formally confirmed.[19] In 1907, Britain signed another convention with Russia regarding Persia, Afghanistan and Tibet, which also recognized the 'suzerainty of China over Tibet'.[20]

The thirteenth Dalai Lama sought to correct the subordinate position of Tibet, which was more conventional than actual, by asserting himself more and more in temporal matters. The Manchus did not like this and in 1910, the Manchu emperor sent troops into Tibet to reinforce his rule. The Dalai Lama fled to Darjeeling this time. The Chinese emphasized that Nepal and Bhutan were the vassal states of China and Tibet. A year later, in October 1911, China lost its imperial and monarchic character and became a republic. Consequently, the Dalai Lama proclaimed the independence of Tibet, which lasted till 1950.[21]

In 1912, Tibet issued its first postage stamps, which continued to appear till 1950. Around 1933, after the death of the thirteenth Dalai Lama, some Tibetan leaders conspired to reunite Tibet with China, but the majority was against it. In January 1934, Ra-dreng Hutukhtu, the pro-Chinese abbot of the Radreng Monastery, became the regent of Tibet. But he was removed from power and imprisoned the very next month for his pro-Chinese activities. The political climate of Tibet remained in the doldrums for the next two decades.

JAWAHARLAL NEHRU'S PRO-CHINESE VIEWS

Jawaharlal Nehru had been a strong votary of Kuomintang China and Chinese leftwing politics since the Brussels Congress in February 1927. In his first broadcast to the nation on 7 September 1946, as the vice-president of the interim government, he lauded China as a 'mighty country with a mighty past, our neighbour' and 'our friend during the ages', and hoped that the friendship between the two nations '...will endure and grow.'[22]

On the other hand, he considered the theocratic Tibet to be a land of 'arid wastes'.[23] He had accepted the traditional British view as well as Chinese propaganda that Tibet was a subordinate country, although he held a different yardstick for the ethno-cultural and historical identities of Nepal, Bhutan and Sikkim, which were outside of Chinese interest.[24] He recognized the strategic importance of these three countries as they lay to the south of the Himalayan watershed, which fell within India's outer defence perimeter. He made treaties with them and declared Sikkim a protectorate,[25] but surprisingly, he did not recognize

Tibet's even greater geostrategic importance for India. This was probably because he felt safe that she was under Chinese control.

The outside world had almost forgotten about Tibet till an OSS (Overseas Secret Service) 'reconnaissance mission via India to Tibet' code-named 'FE-2' was approved by the US President in May 1942 with a view '...to move across Tibet and make its way to Chungking, China, observing the attitudes of the people of Tibet; to seek allies and discover enemies; locate strategic target and survey the territory as a possible field for future activity.'[26] Captain Ilya Tolstoy (1866–1933), grandson of the Russian novelist, was chosen for this mission.

When Tolstoy was en route to Tibet, a US naval attaché reported from Xining that around 10,000 Chinese troops had moved towards the Tibetan border following Chiang Kai-shek's orders.[27] Tolstoy submitted his report to General Stilwell in Chungking. This report, despite the OSS's dismissal of the significance of the mission, was the first detailed and well-documented report on Tibet available to the United States.[28] It was due to Ilya Tolstoy's efforts that five years from then, Lhasa would make a serious effort to build a relationship with Washington coming out of its isolation.

In October 1945, the *Kashag* (Tibetan governing council) and its clerical chiefs decided to send a mission to India and China on the pretext of congratulating the Allies' victory. The delegation came to New Delhi in March 1946 and proceeded to China in April. The delegation to China was attended by Gyalo Thondup, the elder brother of the present Dalai Lama, who later played a significant role in the fight for Tibetan independence. Once in China, the Tibetans were forced to sign an agreement by Chinese authorities, acknowledging Tibet's subordination to China, although they were not authorized to do so by the Dalai Lama. New Delhi also witnessed a show of Chinese might in August 1946 at the semi-official conference of Asian countries organized by the Indian Council of World Affairs (ICWA) at Jawaharlal's behest.[29] Tibet was invited at the conference but not allowed to discuss the country's border or its political status.[30] Phillips Talbot, then a correspondent for the *Chicago Daily News*, recalled that when China protested against a huge map displayed in the conference hall showing Tibet as a separate country, it was repainted overnight and the border between China and Tibet was blurred.[31]

During this time, the United States became interested in Tibet as a potential bulwark against the spread of communism from the USSR and China. In January 1947, the US chargé d'affaires in New Delhi, George R. Merrell, proposed to the State Department that Tibet could be used as a rocket base for the US, but the proposal was rejected because the place was too remote.[32] The Americans refrained from doing anything to help the Tibetans at this stage and deferred to India whenever they approached them for help. Whenever this happened, Jawaharlal Nehru deftly stood aside and let things take their course without intervening.

When the Chiang Kai-shek government fell in April 1949, Gyalo Thondup fled Nanking and came back to Delhi. For nine months, he pleaded for independence for Tibet and was contacted by Jawaharlal Nehru, the US ambassador Loy Henderson, and the Chinese communist commander, Zhu De, all of whom tried to use him as a conduit to Lhasa.[33]

The US State Department proposed that discussions with the Tibetans should be held in New Delhi and not in Washington. The proposal received a cool response from the Indian government. Jawaharlal, however, sent his trusted emissary, K.M. Panikkar, to Kalimpong to advise Gyalo Thondup to remove Tibet's historical and cultural treasures to India for safekeeping. Thondup was told that if the situation worsened, India could be used as a base and the Dalai Lama could be evacuated by a helicopter.[34]

Nevertheless, when North Korean forces invaded South Korea on 25 June 1950, the security scenario in Asia changed in its entirety. The CIA was instructed to initiate psychological warfare and paramilitary operations against communist China.[35] Two weeks later, Loy Henderson was asked to tell the Tibetan delegation, which was still in India, that the United States was ready to help Tibet in procuring and purchasing arms in their struggle for independence. Soon, reports came from Lhasa about the concentration of Chinese troops in various spots along Tibet's eastern border. In late July, General Liu Bocheng announced that his command would soon march to Tibet to '...bring that mountainous land of the lamas back into the Chinese family.'[36] On 14 August, Henderson contacted Jawaharlal's senior Foreign Office advisor, G.S. Bajpai, about sending military supplies to Tibet and asked if these could be transported through India.[37]

TRUST BETRAYED

When, on 24 October 1950, the Chinese formally announced the invasion which had started some weeks earlier, the Indian government reacted with a sense of outrage. This was more of a show for the public because New Delhi already knew what was happening in Tibet. Beijing was informed that Indian military and civilian personnel had been asked to stay at their posts in Lhasa.[38]

Henderson had earlier described Jawaharlal to Washington as 'a vain, sensitive, emotional and complicated person,' even though the latter had supported the US resolution at the UN that gave a stamp of international legitimacy to the American troops, enabling them to resist the North Korean attack on the south. Now, he reported that despite Jawaharlal's present irritation with the Chinese, there was no evidence that he would '...take such drastic steps as to terminate India's chosen role of best friend of Peking among the non-Communist powers.'[39] When Henderson met with Jawaharlal to discuss Chinese aggression in Tibet, he was advised that the US would achieve the most by doing nothing and should avoid lending credence to Beijing's charge that the great powers were scheming in Tibet. In public, he made light of the issue by saying that Mao might have acted on misinformation from Moscow about 'Anglo-American intrigues' to create an anti-communist Tibet.[40]

At this time, Jawaharlal was arguing for offering the People's Republic of China (PRC) a permanent seat in the Security Council as the real government of China, in lieu of Kuomintang China, the founder-member of the United Nations.[41] Indeed, he considered the communist takeover of China to be a major historical event. On 17 March 1950, he told the Indian Parliament: 'It is not a question of approving or disapproving; it is a question of recognizing a major event of history and of appreciating it and dealing with it.'[42]

On 13 November, the Tibetan cabinet and national assembly appealed to the United Nations to restrain China, telling Secretary-General Trygve Lie: 'Tibet will not go down without a fight, though there is little hope of a nation dedicated to peace resisting the brutal effort of men trained to war.'[43] The United States did not take any action on this appeal in the UN and waited to support India's diplomatic initiative, if any. Britain also deferred to New Delhi to initiate some action, but India looked the other way. In this predicament, Tibet found a surprise ally in El Salvador. On 15 November, this tiny nation demanded an immediate debate on the issue in the General Assembly. A loyal Catholic country, El Salvador had responded to the personal appeal by Pope Pius XII and the Vatican's behind-the-scenes move to get Tibet's case heard by the international community.[44]

Ernest Gross, who had shepherded the UN resolution on Korea five months ago, was now instructed by the US State Department to support this resolution. The Department's idea was that the debate might yield them an advantage on the propaganda front against the Chinese communists' aggressive action in the Far East. It would also help the cause of the United States in Korea. Gross, however, coaxed Sir Benegal Narsing Rau, ICS and India's ambassador in the UN, to take the initiative in the matter. But this seasoned bureaucrat, who had helped Dr B.R. Ambedkar draft the Indian Constitution, prevaricated on Jawaharlal's instructions.

Against the backdrop of this complex political milieu, on 24 November 1950, the UN General Committee, which sets the Assembly's agenda, voted unanimously to postpone the consideration of the Tibetan appeal on the basis of B.N. Rau's motivated assertion that Beijing's latest note pointed towards a peaceful settlement.[45] The United States supported the postponement, as Tibet was a smaller priority to Washington than Korea. A chapter in Tibet's history was thus closed.

On 23 May 1951, Beijing announced that a seventeen-point agreement had been signed by the Chinese and Tibetan representatives. This provided, inter alia, that China would deal with all external affairs relating to Tibet, but that Tibet's autonomy and its peculiar political system would not be interfered with. The Tibetan delegation was led by Ngabo, the governor of Chamdo in outer Tibet, whom the Chinese army had captured during its westward march towards Lhasa. Lhasa had no option but to accept the agreement;[46] India, thus, promptly got over the Tibetan controversy.

Meanwhile, Jawaharlal Nehru continued to plead for the PRC's admission to the United Nations because Western policy was forcing it towards complete dependence on the Soviet Union.[47] He never realized that it would be better for India to try to become a member of the Security Council herself instead of China, and that Beijing could pose a threat to Indian interests in the future.[48] In April 1954, he signed a new five-point Sino-Indian Agreement, which included a memorandum known as 'Panchsheel' or the five principles of good conduct, whereby it was agreed that India and China would, under no circumstances, interfere with one another's internal affairs. According to this treaty, Tibet was a part of China.[49]

There was some criticism of the treaty in Parliament on the grounds that Tibet was described as the 'Tibet region of China' in it. Jawaharlal's retort was that India had only repeated what was stated earlier by the British. He said during his speech: 'This Agreement is good not only for our country but for the whole of Asia and the rest of the world.'[50] According to him, the Government of India could not do anything other than give up, with grace, the rights which the British had acquired in Tibet by force, and not '...go like Don Quixote with lance in hand...merely getting into trouble.'[51] Later, in 1956, when the Dalai Lama met him for the first time in New Delhi and pointed out this anomaly in the treaty, he was dismissive about it.

Initially, after occupying Lhasa in 1951, the Chinese tried to win over Tibetan aristocrats by offering them gifts and money, even when the Tibetan Resistance was fighting the Red Army in the outlying areas. They also took some populist measures to woo the common man. Very soon, however, the Chinese curtailed the powers of the Dalai Lama and those who were close to him, to prevent them from functioning independently. In such a situation, Gyalo Thondup, who had returned to Lhasa to help his younger brother, fled to Darjeeling, where he formed an underground movement to oppose the Chinese occupation of Tibet.

In April 1954, India withdrew the military escort and training posts from southern Tibet following the Sino-Indian Agreement. In September, the Dalai Lama visited Beijing at the PRC's 'request'. He was felicitated with full ceremonial honours by Zhou Enlai and Zhu De and stayed in China for seven months. Back in Lhasa, he came to know about the bombardment of the Litang Monastery by the Chinese army, about the degrading abuse that the monks and nuns had to face in their hands, and finally, the torture and execution of the women and children whose husbands and fathers had joined the resistance movement.

In 1956, Gompo Tashi Andrugtsang (1905–64), a daredevil businessman from a highborn family, organized the common people of Kham and Amdo in guerrilla warfare against the Chinese. He heroically conducted a resistance movement almost entirely with the help of local resources, and as such, it can be easily compared with any other guerrilla movement in other parts of the world. Subsequently, the CIA came into the picture at the initiative of the Dalai Lama's brothers, Takster and Gyalo Thondup, for supplying funds and offering training to some Tibetan operatives in Camp Hale, Colorado. It also airdropped arms and ammunition inside Tibet. The CIA used an air base near Dhaka in East Pakistan, now Bangladesh, and thereafter another one at Charbatia, near Cuttack in India, for its airdropping operations. But without adequate planning and knowledge about the terrain, these were of little real use.[52]

Throughout 1957, the Khampas and the Amdowas fought the Chinese occupation forces. Their activities met with increasingly repressive measures, which, in turn, sent a flow of refugees to central Tibet and transformed the local uprising near the border into a national insurrection. In early 1958, Gompo secretly called a meeting of the resistance leaders in Lhasa and exhorted the chiefs of the two dozen Khampa and Amdowa groups, which constituted the Army of the National Defenders of the Faith, to unite in a nationwide resistance. His appeal succeeded and his effort got the support of Phala, the influential advisor of the Dalai Lama, who later organized the latter's escape from Lhasa with the help of the CIA's Special Activities Division.

On 3 April 1959, Jawaharlal informed a cheering Parliament that the Dalai Lama and a party of eighty officials, members of his family and bodyguards had crossed into Indian territory three days earlier and they had been granted asylum. P.N. Menon, the former Indian consul general in Lhasa, greeted the Dalai Lama at Bomdila in Arunachal Pradesh when he arrived there after a difficult ten-mile pony ride from the border. New Delhi had sent P.N. Menon to lay down the ground rules for the Tibetan ruler's political activities in India.

P.N. Menon conveyed to the Dalai Lama that Jawaharlal was of the opinion that Tibet's goal should be achieving internal autonomy and not independence. He also suggested that he only make a brief statement at his first press conference on Indian soil, mainly to give thanks to the Indian authorities for granting them asylum in India. Upon hearing this, the young pontiff summarily rejected his counsel and reminded him that he had come to grief by following Jawaharlal's advice in 1957. He made it clear that the Tibetans were fighting for complete independence and were determined to do so, regardless of the Indian government's attitude. He would seek asylum elsewhere if the Indian government found his presence embarrassing.[53]

When a shaken P.N. Menon cabled this to his ministry, he was told to let the Dalai Lama speak his mind with the exception of the issue of establishing a Tibetan government-in-exile that repudiated the seventeen-point agreement with the Chinese. He also could not mention the fact that he had sent three embarrassing letters to General Tan from the Norbulingka palace in Lhasa. After further negotiation, the Dalai Lama agreed to issue a full statement of the grievances plaguing the ongoing Tibetan resistance as well as his own flight, choosing not to refer to a free Tibetan government and the embarrassing letters, and he did not specifically denounce the seventeen-point agreement.[54] A week later, he issued a press statement in his name from Tezpur in Assam. It was on the Tibetan people's strong desire for independence, but it did not demand that India should support it.

Jawaharlal met him on 24 April in Mussoorie, where the Dalai Lama was staying as the guest of G.D. Birla. They talked for over four hours, during which the Dalai Lama said that he had originally intended not to seek India's hospitality but to establish his own government at Lhuntse Dzong in eastern Bhutan. Later, he wrote in his autobiography that Jawaharlal was often impatient and irritated during their talks and '...banged the table...However, I went on in spite of the growing evidence that he could be a bit of a bully.'[55] The two leaders were unable to reconcile their views. Jawaharlal's policy was to work towards restoring Tibet's autonomy, while the Dalai Lama remained adamant about independence.

Subsequently, the CIA launched a few half-hearted operations for some time, assisted by the Indian intelligence, and then stopped. According to a CIA official,

> These missions caused almost more harm to the Tibetans than to the Chinese forces. Because the Americans did not want their assistance to be attributable, they took care not to supply US-manufactured equipment. Instead, they dropped only a few badly made bazookas and some ancient British rifles which had once been in general service throughout

India and Pakistan and thus could not be traced to source in the event of capture. But the mishandling they received whilst being air-dropped rendered them almost useless.[56]

In the days that followed, China sought to transform Tibet culturally and ethnically. Chinese men and women were forced to stay in Tibet and marry Tibetans so that their progeny became ethnically and culturally Chinese. Likewise, planned efforts were made to change or influence Tibet's various social, cultural and political institutions surreptitiously. In his travelogue, *From Heaven Lake,* Vikram Seth has drawn on his own experiences in Tibet to poignantly describe the flagrant violation of human rights there. He has also described the horrendous demographic and cultural miscegenation, systematically engineered by the Chinese government to obliterate the ancient nation.

JAWAHARLAL NEHRU'S STAND ON TIBET

When the situation in Tibet was worsening, on 27 April 1959, Jawaharlal declared at the Parliament that India's policy would be governed by the following principles: the preservation of the security and integrity of India, the maintenance of friendly relations with China, and the expression of deep sympathy for the people of Tibet.[57] It would be a tragedy, he said, 'if the two countries in Asia—India and China—which had been peaceful neighbours for ages past should develop feelings of hostility against each other...nothing should be said or done which would endanger the friendly relations of the two countries, which are so important from a wider point of view of peace in Asia and the world.'[58]

On his part, the Dalai Lama announced his intention to refer the Tibetan issue to the United Nations towards the end of August 1959. He came to Delhi in the first week of September to implore Jawaharlal to lend his support to the cause. Jawaharlal strongly advised him against taking such a step.[59] A non-official resolution was, however, moved in the Parliament urging that the Indian government should take up the Tibetan issue in the United Nations.

During the discussion, Jawaharlal made a long speech reaffirming the Indian government's policy on the Tibetan question. He expressed his doubts about the constitutional or legal validity of referring the issue to the U.N. This was because the PRC was still not represented in the U.N. and Tibet was not an independent state. He also doubted if the Chinese could be accused of either violating the U.N. charter or committing aggression in Tibet, as Tibet was officially under Chinese suzerainty.[60] Rather, referring the case to the U.N. might raise the matter to the level of a cold war and provoke global action against the Chinese government. That, in turn, might be more adverse to Tibet and the Tibetan people than the way things were at the moment.[61]

Nevertheless, on 9 September 1959, the Dalai Lama sent a long cable to the U.N. headquarters, appealing to it for immediate intervention and requesting the General Assembly to consider the Tibetan issue on its own initiative. This was an issue which had been adjourned nearly nine years earlier, on 24 November 1950.

Contrary to Jawaharlal's expectations, the United Nations adopted a joint Malaya-Ireland resolution on 29 October 1959. Here, the General Assembly expressed grave concern about reports of the forcible denial of fundamental human rights and freedom to the people of Tibet. The resolution called for a recognition of the fundamental human rights of the Tibetan people and for their distinctive culture, religion and way of life. Forty-five nations supported the resolution and nine opposed it. Twenty-six nations, including India, abstained.[62] China had probably expected India to play a more positive role in the U.N. and fight for its cause there. As a result, from that point onwards, it relentlessly pursued all its territorial claims against the traditional frontier.[63] In fact, from April 1959 the Chinese began to blame India for the Tibet issue, although Jawaharlal had informed Zhou Enlai during his visit to Beijing in October 1956 about the possibility of India granting political asylum to the Dalai Lama.[64]

These Chinese misgivings primarily stemmed from their suspicion that the Indian intelligence was secretly supporting Tibetan insurgents in Kham, Amdo, and other disturbed areas in conjunction with the CIA. In July 1958, China officially protested to India that '...subversive and disruptive activities against China's Tibet region were being carried out by the United States with fugitive reactionaries from Tibet.'[65]

This protest suggested that the Chinese assumed some degree of Indian complicity in the CIA operation. The Chinese were apparently unaware of the role played by Pakistan because they did not lodge a complaint in Karachi.[66]

13

THE CHINESE EPISODE

FORWARD POLICY

India shares a vast and historically undefined border with Tibet, which is now a Chinese territory. The borders run in both the North-East Frontier Agency (NEFA) and the Aksai Chin region. When India became independent, it was only natural that the issues surrounding the border should be settled with the People's Republic of China (PRC), which was then on good terms with India. Beijing took some initiative in the matter and wrote to New Delhi on 26 December 1959: '...an overall settlement of the boundary question between the two countries should be sought by the Chinese and the Indian sides, taking into account the historical background and present actual position.'[1]

According to Durga Das, the then editor of the *Hindustan Times*, Zhou Enlai proposed a 'reciprocal acceptance of present actualities in both sectors and constitution of a boundary commission' when he visited India in April 1960.[2] This implied that the Chinese were ready to accept the validity of the McMahon Line in the east, in exchange for India's acceptance of China's actual line of control in the western region. Considering the vast, uninhabited and mostly snowbound landmass of the Aksai Chin that provided strategic advantages to both countries, this was seen as a viable solution.

Zhou Enlai reiterated during a press conference in Delhi: 'We have asked the Indian Government to adopt an attitude towards this western area similar to the attitude of the Chinese government towards the area of the eastern sector; that is, it may keep its own stand, while agreeing to conduct negotiations and not to cross the line of China's administrative jurisdiction as shown on Chinese maps.'[3] This was the closest the two sides ever came to an agreement. However, the proposal was not acceptable to the Indian government.

The CIA was keeping a close eye on the Sino-Indian border situation. In 1960, it noted in its National Intelligence Estimate (NIE) on 'Sino-Indian Relations' that although Beijing was suspicious that the revolt in Tibet was instigated and sustained by India, it was still possible for China and India to settle their border disputes. But they were unlikely to return to the warm relations of the early 1950s.[4] The estimate said that India might look to the Soviet Union for help with China and that the USSR was also perturbed about the situation.

Against this backdrop, Jawaharlal decided to pursue a policy of quietly exerting control in the area by setting up advanced intelligence and army posts and patrol in both the NEFA and the western sector. In this, he was probably acting on the advice of his new defence minister, Krishna Menon, and his intelligence chief, B.N. Mullik. Another person who influenced him in the matter was Lieutenant General Brij Mohan 'Bijji' Kaul, a distant kinsman and great favourite, who had acted as a troubleshooter in Kashmir when he was a colonel. This group of officials believed that the disputed border could be legitimately brought under India's control in this manner without any backlash from the Chinese. In this close official circle, this was known as Jawaharlal's 'Forward Policy.'

At this time, Krishna Menon was beginning to have differences with the brilliant but outspoken army chief, General K.S. Thimayya, whom he also personally disliked. When K.S. Thimayya objected to inaugurating these posts in the disputed territories without adequate logistical support, B.N. Mullik volunteered to perform the task with his own resources. Jawaharlal was always distrustful of the army and had little patience in military matters. Publicly, he openly expressed his fondness for 'Timmy', but privately he viewed K.S. Thimayya's popularity as an army general with suspicion[5] (indeed, the IB discreetly kept tabs on his activities). Jawaharlal often displayed favouritism and interfered with the discipline observed by the higher echelons of the army.[6]

By 1958, B.N. Mullik opened up over sixty posts in Ladakh, twenty-two in the NEFA, and about thirty along the borders of Uttar Pradesh, Sikkim and Himachal Pradesh.[7] Also, he set up an effective pattern of sending long-range summer patrols into the extremities of the northwest territories where permanent posts were logistically impossible to maintain.[8]

Earlier, in 1951, the Himmatsingji Committee had recommended that the responsibility for gathering internal and external intelligence should be taken away from the Directorate of Military Intelligence (DMI) and assigned to the IB.[9] Once this was formalized, the director of the Intelligence Bureau (DIB) became the de facto DMO (Director of Military Operation) for the northern border, establishing checkpoints along the whole length of the watershed and sending reconnaissance patrols into the disputed territory, independent of the army headquarters and the Ministry of Defence.[10] B.N. Mullik's intimacy with Jawaharlal Nehru gave him a pre-eminent position in the ad hoc decision-making cell of the government.

In the NEFA, the Forward Policy did not elicit an antagonistic response from China, as India was already in occupation of the disputed territory.[11] But things were different in Aksai Chin, where the Chinese occupied the disputed territory, parts of which had never been inhabited, administered, or even properly surveyed by either country. The Chinese had realized the area's strategic value as a route from Sinkiang (now Xinjiang) to Lhasa only after their invasion of Tibet. They surreptitiously constructed a road through it and moved well inside the Aksai Chin region by 1959.[12]

When everything was quiet on the political front, two incidents took place in the NEFA that seriously embarrassed Jawaharlal. On 7 August 1959, approximately 200 armed Chinese soldiers appeared in Khinzemane and pushed a dozen or so Assam Rifles patrolmen almost a kilometre inside the territory and then withdrew. Thereafter, the Indian side put up a picket line there and raised the tricolour. The Chinese came back once again, but the Assam Rifles held firm to their position. There was no firing, though there was a very heated exchange and lots of jostling.

The second incident was more serious and known as the Longju incident. It took place on 25 August 1959 when a powerful Chinese detachment crossed into the Indian territory south of Migyitun on the NEFA border and fired on a twelve-man Indian forward picket. They then tried to nab the entire picket. Eight Indian soldiers escaped. The incident grabbed the headlines on 28 August and created such public furore that for the first time in twelve years, Jawaharlal was unsure about himself in Parliament. He had to admit that serious disputes existed between China and India over the Indo-Tibet border and that an area of several thousand square kilometres within the Indian territory in Ladakh was under Chinese control. He also had to disclose that the Chinese had built a highway across Aksai Chin.

Then, as a face-saving measure, he declared in an off-the-cuff manner, as was typical of him, that the government had already placed the border area of the NEFA directly under the military and that henceforth the Assam Rifles and other forces would function under directions from army headquarters.[13] He did this without any prior consultation with K.S. Thimayya. When the army chief learned about this development from the Director of Military Intelligence (DMI), Brigadier Prem Bhagat, he sought an appointment with the prime minister and met him at his residence the same evening (28 August). The war hero was aware of Jawaharlal's deep-seated paranoia about the army and his reluctance to strengthen and improve it. He explained during the meeting that handing over the border to the army without providing additional resources that they desperately needed was a meaningless gesture. Moreover, this step would give the Chinese an opportunity to claim that it was the Indians who were the aggressors, as they described their own troops as border guards and not soldiers.

He told Jawaharlal to find a way out of the mess in the next couple of weeks. After K.S. Thimayya left, a shaken Jawaharlal summoned Krishna Menon and asked him to suggest a way out.[14] Krishna Menon took his time and sent for K.S. Thimayya after three days. He was extremely agitated and vented his anger at the army chief for having approached the prime minister instead of resolving the matter with him first. He warned K.S. Thimayya of the 'possible political repercussions if the matter became public.'[15] K.S. Thimayya returned to his office and, after a brief conversation with his wife, sent in his resignation.

The resignation letter, the contents of which still remain a closely guarded secret, was received in Teen Murti Bhavan the same afternoon and was handed to Jawaharlal, who sent for K.S. Thimayya at once. This time he found a different version of the prime minister. He was composed in his manners and exuded charm and authority. In the course of a long conversation, he persuaded the army chief to withdraw his resignation in the larger interest of the nation.[16]

On 2 September, Jawaharlal made a statement in Parliament that he had persuaded the army chief to withdraw his resignation. He dilated on the essential superiority of civilian authority compared to the military, as well as the duties of the army in the nation's interest; then he added in an offhand manner that the issues that led to the army chief's resignation were 'rather trivial and of no consequence' and that they had arisen '...from temperamental differences.'[17]

Vague stories were circulated that K.S. Thimayya had resigned out of annoyance since Krishna Menon had taken him to task. The need of the hour—building resources for the Indian Army and logistical preparations for meeting the Chinese challenge—was excruciatingly underplayed. This myopia landed the nation in big trouble and ruined Jawaharlal Nehru's reputation and Krishna Menon's political career within three years of Thimayya's retirement.

HEAD IN THE SAND

On 20 October 1959, the focus shifted dramatically from the NEFA to Ladakh when two members of an Indian police party went out on a patrol in the Kongka Pass area and did not return to the post. When a search party was sent the next day, a Chinese picket fired at it from a hilltop, killing seventeen Indian soldiers, including the officer-in-charge, and capturing a few others.[18] India alleged that the Chinese had used mortars in this incident; China denied the allegation.

On 14 November, the Chinese returned the dead bodies and the prisoners of their own accord near Kongka Pass. Around the same time, Zhou Enlai claimed in an interview that a freed Indian soldier had admitted that the Chinese border guards did not use mortars in the clash as India had alleged.[19] In the meantime, Jawaharlal had declared on 1 November that henceforth the Indian Army would take over from the border police in the western sector as well. He realized that he needed to project a tough image of himself to ensure his own political survival, as well as that of Krishna Menon.

K.S. Thimayya decided to give these politicians the real picture of India's defence preparedness, to make them understand how it would be reasonably possible to counter the Chinese on the military front. Accordingly, he had a defence plan prepared by Lieutenant General S.P.P. Thorat, who had a brilliant combat record during World War II. The plan, known as the Thorat Plan in defence circles, recommended a three-tier defence strategy for the eastern sector, especially the NEFA, which could also be applied, mutatis mutandis, to the western sector.

According to the plan, small outposts were to be established as close to the McMahon Line as possible, with the intention of keeping watch and giving early warnings, if necessary. Under no circumstances were these outposts supposed to get drawn into battle. They were expected to fall back before the Chinese could advance. The second tier would consist of strong delaying positions, which would force the enemy to halt, deploy and fight. It was planned in such a way that the Chinese would have to regroup and bring their supply bases ahead before attempting to move forward. The third tier would be the tactical ground of their own choosing where the Indian troops would take up positions and fight, having terrain advantages and maintainable supply lines.

However, as Brigadier D.K. Palit, who saw the whole thing from the inside as DMO, said, Jawaharlal's border policy was just an act of crisis management.[20] The Thorat Plan, therefore, became just a file in the defence ministry that was never made public. Jawaharlal was now convinced that China posed no serious threat to India due to the economic crisis it was facing, as well as the PLA's own internal problems. The IB also did not report any hostile intentions or unusual military concentration on the border.[21] The mood of the opposition leaders in Parliament was rather anti-Chinese after the failure of the Zhou-Nehru talks in April 1960. This encouraged the government to adopt a tough posture on the border issue.

The army was now directed to send out patrols into the disputed but unoccupied areas of Aksai Chin. But they were asked not to engage in clashes if they were accosted by a Chinese post or patrol.[22] Still lacking resources, K.S. Thimayya toned down the operational instructions to the Western Command. He directed the personnel '...to maintain [their] positions firmly *on [their] side* of the international border' (italics added) and to 'prevent any further infiltration into our territory...[by] establishing additional posts ahead of our present defensive positions.'[23] The actual task that he had given to the Western Command was '...to deny the main approaches to Ladakh and to defend Leh.'[24] The instructions made no mention of patrols in the Aksai Chin region.[25]

Even for this limited defensive role, India's troops and logistical resources proved to be hopelessly inadequate. Against an estimated threat of more than a brigade, the Indian Army could deploy only one battalion, which it later increased to two. Without a road linking it with the rest of India, it was impossible to send regular troops to Ladakh at short notice, considering the inhospitable terrain and the shortage of aircraft and paradropping equipment. It was estimated that a brigade of five regular battalions supported by artillery would be required, besides the two militia battalions already in position there. To cope with the increasing pressure from the government to send patrols to the forward territory, the army headquarters left the matter to the discretion of the local commander,[26] a decision which was far from fair and fraught with risks.

After K.S. Thimayya's retirement in May 1961, the not-so-bright Prem Nath Thapar was appointed as the army chief, superseding S.P.P. Thorat, who resigned in protest. Soon, B.M. Kaul began to call the shots as Chief of the General Staff (CGS). He convinced Jawaharlal that India must demonstrate her presence in the empty areas of Ladakh which were not officially under Indian occupation as 'claimed' territory, just as in the NEFA. He overlooked the fact that whereas the Indians were the first to arrive in the NEFA, it was the opposite in Aksai Chin. China had apparently accepted the Indian position in the NEFA for strategic reasons, but she might now consider India's presence in Aksai Chin as an act of aggression.[27]

In February 1962, the Chinese government protested against the increase in India's military presence in Aksai Chin in spite of the restraint it had shown in the NEFA. It gave India enough indications that it might respond with aggression in the NEFA if India did not restrain herself in Aksai Chin. The Ministry of External Affairs (MEA), which received this note of protest, and the Ministry of Defence (MOD) as well as the army headquarters, to which a copy of the note was sent, ignored the warning.[28]

By the end of June, the Western Command set up a number of posts well past the border claimed by the Chinese in 1960, and occupied both the shores of Pangong Lake, which had no military significance whatsoever. The MEA claimed that India had '...brought under physical control more than 2,000 square miles of Chinese claimed area,' and an article in a leading daily eulogized

Jawaharlal Nehru's Forward Policy as 'Napoleonic planning'.[29] The Chinese set up a chain of strong-points facing the Indian posts and forestalled Indians in the previously unoccupied areas.

During the summer of 1962, India pursued the Forward Policy in both the NEFA and Aksai Chin. In the army headquarters, B.M. Kaul undertook to handle the NEFA as Chief of the General Staff (CGS) and left the DMO to deal with Ladakh. He had no previous combat experience, which was a major drawback for an army commander, and he was desperate to prove his prowess in these operations. Fortunately, these political tensions softened a little at this time. On 21 July, the Chinese government said in a note to the MEA that China was not interested in fighting with India and that the Sino-Indian border dispute could only be settled though negotiations.

As usual, Jawaharlal construed this as a sign of weakness. The Government of India, however, responded with a proposal to initiate negotiations on the basis of the talks of 1960. After a few more notes were exchanged between the two powers, the Chinese government suggested that the talks should start in Beijing in mid-October. At this point, members of the opposition in Parliament and the leading newspapers vehemently criticized India's 'accommodation' of the Chinese. Jawaharlal was sensitive to public opinion, so the matter was shelved.[30]

CHINESE BACKLASH

By June 1962, Assam Rifles had set up a post in Tsedong in the disputed Thagla Ridge area and renamed it Dhola in spite of objections from the NEFA political officer's representative accompanying the army patrol. Thagla Ridge was a watershed border, overlooking the Chinese forward base at a village called Le and was therefore tactically significant for them.[31] According to Brigadier J.P. Dalvi, the commander of the 7th Infantry Brigade in Tawang who was overall in charge of the area, the Dhola post was tactically unsound for India in the event of a serious clash of arms.³² There was, however, no objection from him or from other senior formations, or even from the Chinese for that matter, when they actually set up a post there.³³

On Saturday, 8 September, at 6.30 p.m., J.P. Dalvi, who was then on leave in Tezpur and en route to his leave station, had just finished playing a round of golf with Major General Niranjan Prasad, GOC, at the newly laid course. This was when he got a phone call from the headquarters that about 600 Chinese soldiers had crossed Thagla Ridge at 8 a.m., had come down to Dhola Post after having destroyed a log bridge on the post's supply route, and were about to disrupt the water supply.³⁴ The message had to travel for six hours through the Assam Rifles network to reach Dalvi's headquarters in Tawang, and another four and a half hours to reach him in Tezpur.

In Delhi, DMO D.K. Palit got the news from the ops room at dinnertime.³⁵ The Chinese had intentionally selected a Saturday for launching the assault, knowing full well that the army headquarters and the government would be unable to address the situation promptly on the weekend. A week later, it was decided at the defence minister's meeting that India would mount a retaliatory attack on the Chinese at Thagla ridge,³⁶ although by this time the IB had informed them that the Chinese had massed nearly two brigades near Thagla and that they were well stocked with ration and ammunition.³⁷ B.M. Kaul was on leave at that time. He was holidaying in Kashmir, having had a tiff with the defence minister a few days ago. He came back promptly and was assigned the task of chasing the Chinese out of Indian territory. Accordingly, he took charge of the NEFA operations from Lieutenant General Umrao Singh, commander of the XXXIII Corps in Tezpur. He re-designated his corps as IV Corps, after the famous corps that had fought the Japanese and the INA in Imphal during World War II.

The Chinese backlash and the veritable spree of conquests that followed this, as well as the debacle faced by the Indian Army have been described in many accounts. The debacle began on 8 September with a confrontation in Thagla and ended in a massive

Chinese attack on Northeastern India on 20 October. In the first phase of the war, from 8 September to 20 September, there was an exchange of fire between the regular battalions belonging to India and China. During the second phase, which stretched from 20 September to 3 October, the Indian Army hurriedly collected a posse of infrantrymen in Lumpu, about fifteen miles from Thagla, with instructions to evict the Chinese intruders regardless of the consequences. During the third phase, from 3 October to 10 October, B.M. Kaul personally took command of the operation to speed it up. There was a major skirmish in Tseng Jong, in which the Indians were worsted. In the fourth and final phase, from 10 to 20 October, Brigadier Dalvi's 7 Brigade was completely decimated.[38] B.M. Kaul fell seriously ill and was evacuated to Delhi in a special plane.

In the next stage the Chinese forces captured Tawang, Se-La, Dirang Dzong, Bomdila, Tenga, Rupa, Chaku, Walong and Kameng one by one by the evening of 19 November, and came down heavily on the Assam plains. Kaul, who had resumed his command, assessed that India would have to call for military help from the United States.[39] Jawaharlal pleaded with Kennedy for the 'active participation of the US Air Force' for the defence of India, and for sending 'twelve squadrons of F-104 fighters and two squadrons of B-57 bombers' for the purpose immediately.[40] Meanwhile, General Thapar, the army chief, accompanied by the DMO, visited Tezpur to review the situation and boost B.M. Kaul's morale.

On 19 November, General Thapar took responsibility for the army's failures and resigned. Two days later, on 21 November 1962, China unilaterally declared a ceasefire. A month later, Chinese troops were duly withdrawn twenty kilometres from the Line of Actual Control (LAC) that had existed between the two countries since 7 November 1959.

On 24 November, two high-level foreign military delegations, one led by General Sir Richard Hull, Britain's top soldier, and the other by General Paul Adams, the commander of the US Strike

Command, visited the army headquarters in New Delhi and arranged a reconnaissance mission to Siliguri, Gangtok, Tezpur and Ladakh. The Chinese 'betrayal' of 1962 came to Jawaharlal as perhaps the greatest shock of his political life.

14
THE MAKING OF A DYNAST

FAMILY, FRIENDS AND ASSOCIATES

As a socialist in the early 1930s, Jawaharlal Nehru was critical of the leaders of the Second International for usurping power and heading governments while giving up on the principle of collective leadership. But towards the end of the decade, when he became more and more powerful in the Congress Party, he began to change. As prime minister, he often acted as a purposeful benefactor for those who, he believed, had earned the right to reap the benefits of Independence. He often used his office and his political powers to this effect. He ran his own departments, particularly the Foreign Office, as if it were his own household, doling out favours as he pleased without caring for rules and regulations. If rules stood in the way, he used to say, something must be wrong with them.[1]

Jawaharlal once had a tiff with Girija Shankar Bajpai, his principal advisor on Foreign and Commonwealth Affairs, on the issue of the appointment of professional Foreign Service officers as ambassadors in foreign countries. Jawaharlal was of the opinion that these top jobs must go to politicians instead of bureaucrats of the ICS or IFS who enjoyed a cushy life. When Girija Shankar Bajpai pointed out that in that case, the government would not be able to recruit the best people in the service and that he would himself have to resign, Jawaharlal relented.[2] He set up a Committee of Secretaries with Girija Shankar Bajpai as its chairman, and K.P.S. Menon, foreign secretary, and C.C. Desai, commerce secretary, as members, to interview the Public Service Commission's nominees, but he freely continued to have his own nominees appointed to the Foreign Office with the help of this committee.[3]

Foremost among them was his own favourite sister and emotional prop, Vijaya Lakshmi. In 1947–49, she became the first Indian ambassador to the Soviet Union, a country Jawaharlal was eager to woo. However, the fact that Stalin refused to receive her personally and did not even allow her to tour the Soviet Union and the Asian republics was a different matter altogether.[4] Between 1946 and 1968, Vijaya Lakshmi headed the Indian delegation to the United Nations in addition to this charge, although there were many more accomplished and deserving candidates for the job. Her tenure in Moscow was followed by ambassadorships in the USA and Mexico in 1949–51; in the United Kingdom and Ireland in 1955–61; and in Spain in 1958–61. From 1962 to 1964, she served as the governor of Maharashtra. Jawaharlal was even contemplating making her the Vice-President of India, but he had to reconsider because of the pressure that was being put on him by external forces and people who were dead against this appointment.[5] She fell out of favour with him after the media reported a charge of grave financial irregularities against her. Besides, Indira had come of age by this time and Jawaharlal did not want her as a rival for his daughter.[6]

Jawaharlal's other emotional prop and 'dear friend', Padmaja Naidu, was appointed as the governor of West Bengal. She lived in Teen Murti Bhavan, his official residence, whenever she was in New Delhi and was considered a part of the Nehru family. Although Vijaya Lakshmi was intensely jealous of Kamala, she did not resent Padmaja. They met for the first time when they were both fifteen, and '...from that time until her sad death in 1975 she [Padmaja] was the closest woman friend...' she ever had.[7] After Kamala's death, the family circle believed that Jawaharlal would marry her someday.[8] But the marriage did not take place for reasons of political expediency,[9] or perhaps because Jawaharlal did not want to hurt his daughter's feelings.[10]

Indeed, everything was secondary to him where his daughter's welfare or interest was concerned. He was very fond of his niece Nayantara, a pretty and bright girl who knew Russian and who also went on to become an award-winning author later. In December 1946, he promised to take her with him to Russia the next time he went on a visit.[11] But when he visited the Soviet Union a few months after Stalin's death in 1953, he took Indira with him instead of Nayantara, with a desire to introduce his daughter to Soviet leaders.

Indira had her first brush with the KGB (she was code-named 'VANO') during this visit.[12] She was accorded a lavish welcome and lodged in posh, seaside bungalows, surrounded by handsome and attentive male admirers. But all the while, she was under the discreet round-the-clock surveillance of the KGB.[13] Indira was so overwhelmed by the attention lavished on her that she wrote to her father: 'Everybody—the Russians—have been so sweet to me[...] I am being treated like everybody's daughter—I shall be horribly spoilt by the time I leave. Nobody has ever been so nice to me.'[14] She did not, of course, mention her male admirers. Jawaharlal took Indira to Russia again in June 1955. He was somehow secretive about this visit and quietly ensured that his watchful security officer, K.F. Rustamji, IP, did not accompany him during this trip.[15]

Jawaharlal's rather plain-looking sister, Krishna Hutheesing (1907–67), was not as lucky as her elder sister before or after Independence, even though she earnestly took part in Congress activities along with her sister-in-law Kamala, whom she liked. She attended various government functions, met foreign dignitaries, and regularly visited her brother. As the title of her memoir, *We Nehrus* (1967), indicates, she too was fiercely proud of being a Nehru.

Her husband, Gunottam (Raja) Hutheesing, was a barrister and belonged to a well-known industrialist family from Ahmedabad.[16] Jawaharlal took him along as his secretary on his trip to Malaya in February 1946[17] and sponsored his posting as the commissioner to Malaya, but Gunottam did not accept this favour.[18] Later, he became a vocal critic of Jawaharlal and helped Chakravarti Rajagopalachari form the Swatantra Party in 1959.[19] Indira liked Krishna and her family, but hated her eldest aunt.[20] Her son, Rajiv, stayed with the Hutheesings for some time in Bombay.

One of Jawaharlal's early choices for the Foreign Office was Niranjan Singh Gill, who had betrayed the INA's secrets to the British and was jailed by the Japanese in December 1942.[21] Jawaharlal appointed this smooth-talking ex-Lieutenant Colonel of the British army as ambassador to Ethiopia in 1955, Thailand in 1962, and Mexico in 1964, knowing full well that Gill's betrayal of the revolutionary cause during World War II was well known in Thailand. He did not, however, show such commiseration for Mohan Singh, the chief of the first INA, who became a homeless refugee and settled in the village of Jugiana, near Ludhiana.

Another controversial INA bigwig whom Jawaharlal favoured was Nedyam Raghavan, a lawyer by profession, who swore allegiance to him after Independence. During World War II, Raghavan had joined the Indian Independence League (IIL), and then left it due to personal differences towards the end of 1942, then rejoined the movement in 1943 and functioned as a minister in the Provisional Government of Free India established by Subhas Chandra Bose. Jawaharlal made him the ambassador to Czechoslovakia, Belgium and Luxembourg in 1948–51, with accreditation to the Holy See and the Allied Commission for Austria in 1951–52. Thereafter, he became ambassador to China in 1952–55, Argentina in 1956–59, with accreditation to the government of Chile, and finally to France in 1959–62. His colleagues thought him conceited and cantankerous.[22]

According to Ram Manohar Lohia, Jawaharlal's personal and political relationships were guided by 'a mutuality of interest'.[23] He could be exceedingly charming when he so desired[24] and could also discard an inconvenient person or idea at the drop of a hat. K.F. Rustamji, who was his security officer for over six years from December 1951 to May 1958, also mentioned that

Jawaharlal's charm was 'positively diabolic' and that he '...knew it and shamelessly used the "elbow huddle" to make friends and win over his worst adversary.'[25]

He did not meet his friend and benefactress Madame Chiang Kai-shek during his visit to the United States in 1949, when she was lying ill in a hospital, as this could create a misunderstanding with the new PRC leadership.[26] Interestingly, during her visit to India in the summer of 1942, he had fastidiously selected gifts for her from a heap of Benaras brocades, South Indian silks and regional handicrafts with the help of Aruna Asaf Ali (née Ganguly) and others.[27] Aruna Asaf Ali recollected later: 'Not knowing the bond between her and Jawaharlal, some of us whom he had asked to assemble gift items for the lady from China were amused by the fastidiousness with which he selected some items and rejected other.'[28]

He similarly avoided meeting Agnes Smedley when she desperately sought his help to exonerate herself from the FBI's charge of espionage for the Soviet Union.[29] When she died a year later in London, Jawaharlal merely sent a cable which was read at her funeral.[30] Edgar Snow was mortified by the indifference of Smedley's friends when she needed them the most.[31] In stark contrast to this, Jawaharlal purchased orchids for Lady Mountbatten during his tour to Shillong and made sure they reached her in London safely.[32] A decade later, he sent a frigate, all decked out with flowers and guns, to attend her funeral at sea, a gesture that pleased the British government as well as his admirers.

Among his many relatives who prospered under his patronage was Braj Kumar Nehru, ICS, MBE, Padma Bhusan. He was Brijlal Nehru's son and Nand Lal Nehru's grandson. 'B.K.' moved like a colossus in the corridors of South Block due to his uncle's influence and became executive director of the World Bank in 1949, secretary of economic affairs in 1957, and commissioner general of economic affairs of India (external financial relations) in 1958.[33] During Indira's premiership, he became governor in seven states: Assam (1968–73), Nagaland (1968–73), Meghalaya

(1970–73), Manipur (1972–73), Tripura (1972–73), Jammu and Kashmir (1981–84), and Gujarat (1984–86).

There were others. Vijaya Lakshmi's daughter Chandralekha Pandit's husband Ashok Mehta and his brother-in-law Jagat S. Mehta got posts in the Foreign Office. Jagat Mehta's wife Rama, who was Ashok's sister, was 'persuaded' by K.P.S. Menon (senior), the then foreign secretary, '...to apply for the overage recruitment to the FS [foreign service], which was then underway.'[34]

Rama and Jagat developed a close friendship with Carol Laise, a suspected CIA operative at the US Embassy, New Delhi. They did not believe that she was an operative in spite of several warnings, and were quite frank with her.[35] According to Jagat, Laise was on good terms with many eminent personalities, including Indira Gandhi, Khushwant Singh, General Thimayya, B.K. Nehru, Inder Malhotra, Ms Mukherjee of the AICC, and many others from most political parties in the Delhi VIP circuit.[36] No wonder then that India's foreign office was as porous as a sieve during Jawaharlal's premiership.

Jawaharlal's bias for those that he liked can be gauged from his treatment of A.C.N. Nambiar and V.K. Krishna Menon. A.C.N. Nambiar was a leftwing journalist and a covert Soviet agent when Jawaharlal first met him in Berlin in November 1927. He became his Man Friday in Europe. After Independence, he was appointed as a counsellor in the Indian Embassy in Berne in 1948 and then the ambassador to Sweden, with accreditation to Denmark and Finland, in 1954. A year later, he became ambassador to West Germany. When Nanu retired voluntarily in 1957 on the grounds of ill health, Jawaharlal ensured that his financial needs were met.

Jawaharlal's weakness for Krishna Menon was also well known. He had grown close to Krishna Menon in England, in 1935–36 when the latter took charge of the publication of his autobiography. Jawaharlal thought highly of his intellect and included him as a minister without a portfolio in the Foreign Affairs Committee (FAC) in 1956. It decided all important policy matters.[37] Krishna Menon had the extraordinary ability to reconcile different and sometimes opposing points of view.[38] When he became the defence minister in 1957, the KGB began to maintain a close connection with him.[39] The organization even tried to resuscitate his political career after the 1962 debacle by secretly sending funds to a newspaper.

From the mid-fifties, Krishna Menon led the Indian delegation at the annual sessions of the General Assembly.[40] In his memoir, *Witness to an Era,* Frank Moraes wrote:

> I met Nehru in New Delhi on my return to India...I thought it a good opportunity to tell him frankly of the damage done to India's image by Krishna Menon's partisan performance at the UN. Nehru's mobile face, until then relaxed and genial, slowly turned wooden. But he let me talk on without interruption, and I talked somewhat self-consciously in what seemed a vast, oppressive silence. From wood, Nehru's face turned to lead, and then to iron.
>
> He suddenly banged his fist on the table. 'You talk with a great deal of assurance,' he said icily. 'How long have you known Krishna Menon?' I had the perfect come-back. 'Longer than you have, sir,' I said politely. It was true. I had met Krishna Menon in London before Nehru did. I gave him some of the details. He said nothing, but it was obvious that he regarded the interview as closed. Our relations, never close but always cordial, were never quite the same again.[41]

Only after the 1962 debacle did Jawaharlal grow disillusioned with Menon. Then he put the entirety of the blame on him and made him resign from his office to save his own position.

Jawaharlal's other surprise confidant was M.O. Mathai from central Travancore, now part of Kerala. He had written to him offering his services in the summer of 1945. When they met, he told Jawaharlal that he was a bachelor, looking for a purpose in life and '...was prepared to live dangerously.' At first, M.O. Mathai merely dealt with Jawaharlal's correspondence and typed for him. Then his responsibilities became more and more complicated and extensive. He began to look after Jawaharlal's financial affairs, including the publishing arrangements that Indira used to handle earlier.[42] After Independence, he became Jawaharlal's personal private secretary and everything that came to Jawharlal passed through him.[43]

In the process, M.O. Mathai built up his own power, which Jawaharlal's family members, such as Indira, Vijaya Lakshmi and her daughters, and their close friends like Padmaja Naidu resented. However, they were careful enough to remain on good terms with him because of his omnipresence and proximity to Jawaharlal.[44] Even eminent politicians and senior bureaucrats, including B.N. Mullik, kept him in good spirits. Everyone, however, agreed that 'Mac' was efficient, tireless and clever. He was the first person in the office in the morning and the last one out at night. He was on call to Jawaharlal all twenty-four hours of the day, travelling with him and virtually overseeing all his activities—political and personal. Even though he humoured and chaperoned Indira Gandhi,[45] she often resented his presence. Krishna Menon and M.O. Mathai, both of whom depended on Jawaharlal's favours, hated each other, but they took care to maintain an outward show of friendliness. However, according to A.C.N. Nambiar's account, it appears that Mathai was genuinely loyal to Jawaharlal.[46]

In spite of his cunning and efficiency, serious allegations of corruption were brought against Mathai in Parliament in the winter of 1958; he tendered his resignation in January 1959. At a press conference on 7 February, Jawaharlal clarified his own position and dissociated himself from his minion's activities.[47] Mathai had expected to bag an important position in the government after the storm passed,[48] but this did not happen.

INDIRA'S INITIATION

From the very beginning, Jawaharlal wanted Indira to grow up as a down-to-earth woman. For this reason, he sent her to Rabindranath Tagore's Visva-Bharati in Santiniketan instead of a Western-style university after her matriculation from Bombay University. On 27 April 1934, he wrote to Anil K. Chanda, the then secretary to Rabindranth Tagore, from Alipore Central Jail: 'I dislike the education which prepares a girl to play a part in the drawing room and nowhere else. Personally, if I had a chance I would like to have my daughter work in a factory for a year, just as any other worker, as part of her education.'[49]

Tagore's informal, nature-oriented boarding school was the next best option for his only child.[50] He did not arrange a separate accommodation for her and made her live like the other boarders at the hostel. He kept track of her academic progress and was particularly insistent on her physical fitness.[51] Even when she joined Somerville College in Oxford after her mother's death, Jawaharlal was concerned about her education. He was particularly anxious that she did not lose her cultural roots and that she entered public life after graduating from university.

So, when Indira informed him during a jail interview on 8 July 1941 that she wanted to marry Feroze Ghandy (later Gandhi), he was quite upset. The next day, he wrote her a long letter, beseeching her to reconsider the matter. He told her that he had thought about her future ever since she was a child. He wanted her to complete her formal education at the university, specialize in two or three languages, and visit various countries, especially Russia, to see things for herself. This academic training and intellectual experience, and the knowledge that she would gain would be a just foundation on which she would be able to build her future life and career.[52] He assured her that he would personally train and guide her and look after her career and public life.

Jawaharlal was disappointed when his daughter disregarded his advice and married Feroze, but he took the matter in his stride. Indira's marriage was a stormy affair, which ended with Feroze's untimely death in September 1960. Long before this, Indira lived separately from her husband and led her own life. As prime minister, Jawaharlal took her on most of his foreign trips and she became the official hostess at his residence. In this way, she came to be on personal terms with many important leaders at home and abroad.

Meanwhile, Feroze, who had taken part in Congress politics off and on from 1930, became a member of the provisional parliament in 1950–52 and won independent India's first general election from Raebareli in 1952. For more than two years, he remained an unprepossessing backbencher. Then, quite dramatically, in early 1955, he made his maiden speech at the Lok Sabha, the lower house of Parliament, attacking the nexus between insurance companies and the business community. He exposed the shady deals of Bharat Insurance Company run by a wealthy Indian businessman, Ram Krishna Dalmia. A commission of enquiry was formed and Ram Krishna Dalmia was convicted. Feroze's effort led to the nationalization of the life insurance business in India. This established his reputation as a radical and an enemy of corruption. It was further enhanced by the fact that he sponsored the Parliamentary Proceedings Act of 1956, which gave the Indian press the hitherto absent right to publish parliamentary proceedings without running the risk of prosecution or being held up for contempt of parliament.

Against this backdrop, Indira was made a member of the Working Committee in early 1955 at the initiative of the party president, U.N. Dhebar, and Lal Bahadur Shastri—Jawaharlal's trusted men. Up until this time, Indira was perceived as merely a conduit to the prime minister and as a potentially useful tool. Now, her election to the Working Committee changed her status completely. Earlier, even Feroze used to publicly criticize her presence at meetings and functions where he was denied ingress despite being an MP. Now she became a politician in her own right.

Shortly afterwards, in April 1955, she accompanied her father to the Bandung Conference in Indonesia and met a throng of important leaders, including Gamal Abdul Nasser from Egypt and Chou Enlai. Around this time, she took control of the Nehru household. When M.O. Mathai resigned following allegations that he had abused his connection with Jawaharlal, Indira advised her father to accept his resignation.[53] Mathai was cleared of the charge, but he was never called back to office.

The cold indifference with which Mathai was treated revealed the ruthless side of both father and daughter and lent credence to the belief that the Nehrus never carried excess baggage. Around this time, people began to ask: 'After Nehru, who?' When Durga Das wrote in his weekly 'Diary' in the *Hindustan Times* on 18 June 1957 that it was his daughter whom the prime minister was grooming as his successor, and not Krishna Menon or anyone else, Jawaharlal was furious and sent for the journalist. They parted smiling as Durga Das told Jawaharlal that the publicity Indira had received through his column would stand her in good stead in the future.[54]

Two months after the Bandung Conference, Jawaharlal and Indira toured the Soviet Union. As in 1953, Indira was greatly impressed with the Soviet system and the trip initiated an important and protracted period of Indo-Soviet collaboration.

Indira was now clearly taking control of her life and becoming more and more like her father, albeit more assertive and with a clearer goal. In April 1956, she cautioned Jawaharlal that he should not rely too heavily on Morarji Desai, the chief minister of Maharashtra, and the South Indian Congress leader Kumaraswami Kamaraj, because it '...creates dissatisfaction in many and cuts at [his] contacts with all those who hold different views.'[55]

In 1957, Indira was elected to the party's Central Election Committee, a powerful body that selected parliamentary candidates. There was also talk of her joining the Congress Parliamentary Board, but she waited till the following year to become a member thereof. However, she did not contest the election in 1957. She told Padmaja that U.N. Dhebar and 'other mischievous people' were still hoping that they could persuade her to accept a seat.[56] Instead, she canvassed more for her father than her husband and also campaigned for the Congress candidates in Gujarat and Punjab during the election. Thus, she created a niche for herself in the political field just as her father had wanted.

In October 1958, Jawaharlal published a collection of letters he had written before Independence, *A Bunch of Old Letters*, which adequately highlighted his and his family's importance in the freedom struggle. The very first letter in the volume was from Sarojini Naidu, dated 17 December 1917, affectionately hailing the newborn Indira as 'the new Soul of India'.[57] The publication coincided with Indira's emergence in the political scene of India.

Jawaharlal's health was failing now. Just before the Nagpur session in 1959, U.N. Dhebar resigned and Indira succeeded him as party president. This was a surprising turn of events because the veteran South Indian leader S. Nijalingappa (1902-2000) was earmarked for the presidency and was on his way to Nagpur via Madras to attend the AICC.[58] Kumaraswami Kamaraj informed S. Nijalingappa of the new arrangement in Madras. Durga Das gave an interesting behind-the-scenes account of the incident, which showed how the party functioned. What happened was that the evening S. Nijalingappa left Bangalore for Nagpur, U.N. Dhebar had disclosed at a hurriedly convened meeting of the Working Committee that he wanted to retire. Lal Bahadur Shastri had then proposed that Indira should be asked to accept the office in his stead. Unaware of these manoeuvres in the background, Govind Ballabh Pant had remarked that Indira was not healthy enough for the job. At this, an agitated Jawaharlal had rebutted that there was nothing wrong with Indira's health and she would in fact feel better if she had some work to keep herself busy. He had then asked Govind Ballabh Pant to broach the matter delicately with S. Nijalingappa, but he requested Kumaraswami Kamaraj to do it. It was then decided on Kumaraswami Kamaraj's suggestion that a joint statement would be issued by Kumaraswami Kamaraj, S. Nijalingappa and Sanjiva Reddy which would propose Indira's name as the next president.[59]

According to Indira, it was Govind Ballabh Pant who broached the subject of presidency with her and when her instinctive response was that she could not handle it, he insisted that it was her duty to accept the party's final decision. When she spoke to her father about it, he merely said that he would not interfere with it as it was her decision.[60] On 2 February 1959, Indira was elected as president of the Congress for the first time.

Jawaharlal used to plan his daughter's tours after she became president. She visited Kerala in April, where the Congress had aligned with non-secular forces including the Muslim League, and launched a scathing attack on the communist government. In Delhi, Feroze Gandhi agitated against the party's action, denouncing his wife's leadership. Jawaharlal put Kerala under central rule in July 1959 and it was the first instance of its kind in independent India. Indira was re-elected to the Working Committee and became a member of the Central Election Committee once again. Indira, Lal Bahadur Shastri and Jawaharlal approved the candidates for the 1962 elections.

The Chinese incursion in 1962 rattled Jawaharlal badly. This was followed by his party's defeat in three parliamentary by-elections, in which his staunch critics—J.B. Kripalani, Ram Manohar Lohia and Minoo Masani—won. Against this backdrop, Jawaharlal quickly rearranged the power structure of the party by implementing what was known as the Kamaraj Plan. This plan mandated that the senior leaders of the party leave their offices voluntarily and devote their time to working at the grassroots level in order to rejuvenate the party. This would allow the party bosses to make new appointments to vacant posts. Biju Patnaik discussed the idea, which was mooted by Kumaraswami Kamaraj, with Jawaharlal in Pahalgam,[61] and it intrigued him. Shortly afterwards, during his tour of Hyderabad in August 1963, Jawaharlal had a detailed discussion about it with Kumaraswami Kamaraj himself, disregarding his disclaimer that this was only meant for his own state.[62]

The widely acclaimed Kamaraj Plan was introduced on 24 August 1963. Under the plan, Jawaharlal chose six cabinet ministers—including Morarji Desai and Lal Bahadur Shastri, who were being discussed as his likely successors—and six chief ministers, including Kumaraswami Kamaraj (soon to be Congress president) and Biju Patnaik, to resign. Lal Bahadur Shastri, a Nehru loyalist, was later called back to the cabinet as a minister without a portfolio. Morarji Desai's view was that the Kamaraj Plan was Jawaharlal's plot to install Indira Gandhi as his successor.[63]

EPILOGUE

On 8 January 1964, Jawaharlal Nehru had a severe heart attack during the annual Congress session in Bhubaneswar, the capital of Odisha, and was left partially paralyzed on the left side. Some Congress leaders like Biju Patnaik urged Indira to take over as deputy prime minister, although she was not an MP. Indira did not agree to their request.

The next few days, Indira was at her father's bedside at Raj Bhavan in Bhubaneswar. At that time, she told Marie Seton, an actress and film critic who later wrote a biography of Jawaharlal, that she tried to persuade her father to name a successor from among the other aspirants, but her father had not listened to her.[1] She gave the impression to whoever she met then that her father was strongly against the idea of her joining the government, let alone becoming his successor.

When Jawaharlal recovered sufficiently by the end of the month, rumours began to make the rounds that Indira would enter the cabinet shortly as the minister of foreign affairs. There was also some gossip in Delhi that she was running the show behind the scenes.[2] The Indian Institute of Public Opinion (IIPO) carried out a survey at this time about Jawaharlal's likely successor. It placed Lal Bahadur Shastri first, Kumaraswami Kamaraj second, Indira third, and Morarji Desai fourth in its estimates.

On 22 May 1964, Jawaharlal held his first press conference in seven months. It was attended by more than two hundred correspondents, and it lasted over forty minutes. The question, 'After Nehru, Who?' was raised in one form or another repeatedly, and finally, an exasperated Jawaharlal said, 'My life is not ending so very soon!' His response was received with a standing ovation.[3] Five days later, on 27 May, he died.

Three days after his death, Lal Bahadur Shastri called on Indira at Teen Murti Bhavan and requested her to assume leadership of the party.[4] A few other Congress leaders also approached Indira with the same request, but she remained steadfast in her refusal. Her public refusal to assume office set into motion a real conflict for succession to the Congress throne between Lal Bahadur Shastri and Morarji Desai. Kumaraswami Kamaraj and the Syndicate, consisting of Atulya Ghosh, S. Nijalingappa and Sanjiva Reddy, among others, backed Lal Bahadur Shastri. After a good deal of manoeuvring, Morarji Desai reluctantly withdrew.[5] On 2 June, Gulzarilal Nanda proposed Lal Bahadur Shastri's name as the leader of the party at a Working Committee meeting. Morarji Desai seconded the motion and it was carried. On 9 June, Lal Bahadur Shastri became the prime minister of India.

Indira was made minister for information and broadcasting in the new cabinet, apparently by her own choice. As she was unwilling to contest a parliamentary election, she was made a member of the Rajya Sabha, the upper house of parliament. In October 1964, Lal Bahadur Shastri deputed her to represent India at the Commonwealth Prime Ministers' Conference. While she was in London, Sardar Swaran Singh was appointed as the minister for foreign affairs. According to the journalist Inder Malhotra, who had some access to Indira at that time, Swaran Singh's appointment annoyed her, as she was expecting to be persuaded to accept the position.[6]

Indeed, from that moment, there was a visible change in her attitude and tactics vis-à-vis the Shastri government. She used this tour to renew her father's assets and contacts abroad to bolster her own political position. After attending the Prime Ministers' Conference in London, she visited Belgrade and met Marshal Tito, who was widely known in India and was a friend of the family. From there she went to Moscow and met the new premier, Alexei Kosygin, in a rather cosy and intimate setting and this made headlines in India. Subsequently, she visited France, the United States, Canada, Mongolia, Burma, and once again, the

USSR, representing the Indian government. It was quite obvious at home that no other Indian leader enjoyed such easy camaraderie with global leaders as she did.

In India too, she amassed more power for herself by helping pacify agitators against the forcible imposition of Hindi as the national language in Tamil Nadu. In August 1965, she visited Kashmir in the thick of a volatile situation caused by the infiltration of Pakistani troops in the guise of civilian volunteers. Thanks to her intrepid ventures, she was soon hailed by the press as 'the only man in the cabinet of old women.'

As her popularity soared, she made a conscious effort to consolidate her influence in the Congress Party and among the intelligentsia, deftly using her father's existing support base for the purpose. Gradually, she became a master of backroom politics—much more secretive, decisive, determined and ruthless than her father.

Lal Bahadur Shastri was annoyed at the way she had 'jumped over his head,'[7] but he could do little to change it. Yet, as late as December 1965, Indira professed to have no political ambition. When Vijaya Lakshmi Pandit heard that her niece wanted to contest the parliamentary election from her father's old constituency in Phulpur that she represented now, she offered to relinquish the seat (6 December), but Indira replied by return of post that she had no such political ambition.[8] Later events, however, proved otherwise.

On 3 January 1966, Lal Bahadur Shastri flew to Tashkent in Soviet Central Asia to hold peace talks with Ayub Khan from Pakistan, which would be mediated by Alexei Kosygin. By this time, he had attained a gigantic stature and a lot of fame in India as an honest, well-meaning and courageous politician. Late in the evening on 10 January, a settlement was finally reached between the two leaders. In the early hours of 11 January, Lal Bahadur Shastri had a fatal heart attack.

At 3.15 a.m. that day, before the city was awake, Gulzarilal Nanda took oath as the acting prime minister for a second time, at the President's House in New Delhi. Indira Gandhi was the only leader, apart from the finance minister T.T. Krishnamachari, who attended the ceremony.

Thirteen days later, on 24 January, after a great deal of hectic closed-door confabulations, in which D.P. Mishra, the powerful chief minister of Madhya Pradesh (Indira had called him to Delhi), and Kumaraswami Kamaraj played a crucial role, Indira Gandhi was sworn in as the fifth prime minister of India. Jawaharlal Nehru's fondest wish was thus fulfilled and a dynasty was born.

ACKNOWLEDGEMENTS

Many have helped me write this book and I am grateful to all of them. The main idea behind it took shape when a young enthusiast from Raiganj, Mr Kaushik Banerjee, convinced me that I should assemble my findings on Jawaharlal Nehru in a book rather than in the occasional seminar paper. Already, I had with me a bulk of documents on India's freedom movement collected during the course of my earlier research, some of which I had used in my two other books on the freedom movement. All these came in handy now. When I started, I had, of course, no idea that the present research would open so many new vistas for me and take me so much time and so much travelling to complete. I am glad that I have been able to finish it at last and as best as I could.

First of all, I am grateful to the officials of The British Library, London, for documents on the last phase of British rule in India. Research in England and the United States is always a pleasure on account of the systemic help a researcher gets from the archives and libraries there. The officials and staff of the National Archives of India, the Nehru Memorial Museum and Library, and the JNU Archives in New Delhi, the Swaraj Bhavan and the state archives in Allahabad, and the National Library, the West Bengal State Archives and the Ramakrishna Mission Institute of Culture Library in Kolkata have also been very helpful.

In Allahabad, Mr Girija Shankar Tiwari took great personal initiative in taking me around and arranging for me to meet people. Similarly, the good offices of Mr Debtaru Chattopadhyay and Mr Suman Chatterjee helped me in my hour of need. I do not know how to thank them enough for their help.

I take this opportunity to acknowledge my perennial indebtedness to my dear friends and erstwhile colleagues,

Mr Ranjit K. Das and Mr Prodyot C. Halder, who have done so greatly in their professional lives, for always standing by me. At this hour, I deeply miss my other two friends, the late Dhondup Tshering and the late Anjan Ghosh, who were so avidly interested in the subject. My earnest thanks are, moreover, due to Prof. (Dr) Ranjan Chakrabarti, Prof. Mary Joseph, Prof. (Dr) Dorothy Scouler, Prof. Nirmal Kumar Sarkar, Brig. Prodipto Goswami, Ms Modhumita Goswami, Dr Swarbhanu Chatterjee and Aryan for their help and encouragement. I also recall here the affection and goodwill of Mr Shyamal Banerjee, my friend of many years.

My wife Jaya has been, as always, a loving source of inspiration to me. Without her, this research and the writing of this book would not have been possible.

END NOTES

Chapter 1: The Rise of the Nehrus

1. Brecher, Michael, *Nehru: A Political Biography*, Oxford University Press, Oxford, 2014, pp. 2, 5, 9. This has been mentioned in several places in this book and Brecher has quoted Nehru describing himself as an aristocrat.
2. Kumar, Ravinder, and D.N. Panigarhi, eds., *Selected Works of Motilal Nehru, Volume One (1899–1918)*, Vikas Publishing House, New Delhi, 1982, pp. 79-80. Motilal wrote this to Jawaharlal from Marseilles, 20 October 1905.
3. Pandit, Vijaya Lakshmi, *The Scope of Happiness: A Personal Memoir*, Speaking Tiger Publishing, New Delhi, 2018, p. 38.
4. Nehru, Jawaharlal, *An Autobiography*, Penguin Books India, New Delhi, 2003, p. 216.
5. Pandit, *Scope of Happiness*, p. 63.
6. Gopal, Sarvepalli, *Jawaharlal Nehru: A Biography*, Oxford University Press, New Delhi, 2015, p. 28. The government was keen that leadership of the movement should be with Gandhi and Jawaharlal.
7. Quoted in Limaye, Madhu, *Mahatma Gandhi and Jawaharlal Nehru: A Historic Partnership 1916–1948*, B.R. Publishing Corporation, Delhi, 2013, p. 228.
8. Hasan, Mushirul, *The Nehrus: Personal Histories*, Mercury Books, London, 2006, p. 15.
9. Ibid.
10. Ibid.
11. Ibid., 18.
12. Pandit, *Scope of Happiness*, p. 32.
13. Hasan, *The Nehrus*, p. 39.
14. Nehru, *An Autobiography*, p. 1.
15. Gopal, *Jawaharlal Nehru*, p. 5.
16. Nehru, *An Autobiography*, p. 2.
17. Ibid., 5.
18. Pandit, *Scope of Happiness*, p 32.
19. Metcalfe, Charles Theophilus, Mainodin Munshi Khan and Munshi

Jeewan Lal, *Two Native Narratives of the Mutiny in Delhi*, Archibald Constable, Westminster, 1898, p. 50. Also, *Mutiny Papers*, National Archives, New Delhi.
20. The name of Mirza Abdulla figures as deputy kotwal in the deposition of Mohammed Ihsan ul Haque, dated 5 July 1857, in the court of Prince Mirza Mughal in connection with the disturbances created by Prince Mirza Abu Bakr and others at his residence on the night of 4 July 1857, which were quelled at the intervention of the deputy kotwal. See *Besieged: Voice from Delhi-1857*, Mahmood Farooqui (trans), Penguin Books, New Delhi, 2012, pp. 182–183.
21. Metcalfe, Munshi and Lal, *Two Native Narratives*, p. 50. Also, *Mutiny Papers*, National Archives, New Delhi. For orders issued by Syed Mubarak Shah during this period, see Farooqui, *Besieged*, pp. 48, 109, 110, 120–130.
22. Ibid., 110, 120, 122, 128.
23. *Delhi Urdu Akhbar*, 31 May 1957, *Mutiny Papers*, National Archives, New Delhi. In one communication, the commander-in-chief of the rebel army addressed Syed Mubarak Shah as 'the valiant kotwal'. See Farooqui, *Besieged*, p. 130.
24. In the Mughal Court, the chaprasi was an important attendant or messenger. See Hasan, *The Nehrus*, p. 19.
25. Nehru, *An Autobiography*, p. 2.
26. Ibid.
27. Dalrymple, William, *The Last Mughal*, Penguin India Books, New Delhi, 2006, p. 204. Also, regarding Zinat Mahal's communication with the British, see Farooqui, *Besieged*, p. 273.
28. Dalrymple, *The Last Mughal*, p. 204.
29. Nehru, *An Autobiography*, pp. 2-3.
30. Pandit, *Scope of Happiness*, p. 34. However, she has erroneously mentioned Bansi Dhar as Motilal's second-eldest brother.
31. Motilal Nehru was not a barrister. Even his granddaughter, Nayantara Sahgal, has erroneously called him a 'barrister'. See Sahgal, Nayantara, *Jawaharlal Nehru: Civilizing a Savage World*, Penguin, New Delhi, 2010, p. 1.
32. See Rashid, Omar, 'Mirganj's Stigma Hangs Heavy over Nehru's Birthplace', *The Hindu*, 16 November 2013. https://tinyurl.com/4e3w7c7r. Records of the rented house are available in the Nehru Museum, New Delhi.
33. Nehru, *An Autobiography*, pp. 9-10. Vijaya Lakshmi Pandit has also mentioned him in her memoir. See Pandit, *Scope of Happiness*, p. 51.

34. Lelyveld, David, 'The Mystery Mansion: Swaraj Bhawan and the Myths of Patriotic Nationalism,' *The Little Magazine*, Vol. IV, No. 4, 2004, p. 11.
35. Hasan, *The Nehrus*, p. 49.
36. Moraes, Frank, *Jawaharlal Nehru: A Biography*, Jaico, Mumbai, 2013, p. 28.
37. Nehru, *An Autobiography*, p. 9.
38. Hasan, *The Nehrus*, p. 48.
39. Nehru, *An Autobiography*, p. 9.
40. Rashid, 'Mirganj's Stigma.'
41. Lelyveld, 'The Mystery Mansion,' p. 9.
42. Ibid.
43. Nehru, *An Autobiography*, p. 13.
44. Ibid., 5.
45. Ibid.
46. Ibid.
47. Ibid.
48. This was in a letter from Motilal to Jawaharlal, dated 22 October 1905: Kumar and Panigarhi, eds., *Selected Works of Motilal Nehru*, p. 81.

Chapter 2: Boyhood Days

1. Rashid, Omar, 'Mirganj's Stigma Hangs Heavy over Nehru's Birthplace,' *The Hindu*, 16 November 2013. https://tinyurl.com/4e3w7c7r. According to some researchers, the family lived in Mirganj for a much longer time. There is also some difference of opinion about the location of the house. Some say it was near Chaddha Gali, while some others opine that it was a place near Badshahi Mandi. Both the places are in Mirganj. The majority of scholars hold that it was at 77 Mirganj where there is a blue building now, near a small red-coloured temple.
2. Ibid.
3. Moraes, Frank, *Jawaharlal Nehru: A Biography*, Jaico, Mumbai, 2013, p. 21.
4. The author gathered this information during an enquiry at Mirganj Chowk, Allahabad, in October 2017.
5. Nehru, Jawaharlal, *An Autobiography*, Penguin Books India, New Delhi, 2003, p. 216.
6. Ibid., 5.
7. Pandit, Vijaya Lakshmi, *The Scope of Happiness: A Personal Memoir*, Speaking Tiger Publishing, New Delhi, 2018, p. 50.
8. Ibid., 51.
9. Ibid., 52.
10. Nehru has mentioned it more than once in his autobiography. See Nehru, *An Autobiography*, pp. 249, 253.

11. Ibid., 362.
12. Ibid., 12.
13. Ibid., 9.
14. Ibid., 7.
15. Ibid., 11.
16. M.O. Mathai, Nehru's personal assistant, has mentioned this in his book. See Mathai, M.O., *Reminiscences of the Nehru Age*, Vikas Publishing House, New Delhi, 2015. See also, Brecher, Michael, *Nehru: A Political Biography*, Oxford University Press, Oxford, 2014, p. 35.
17. Moraes, *Jawaharlal Nehru*, p. 27.
18. Nehru, *An Autobiography*, p. 8.
19. Gopal, Sarvepalli, *Jawaharlal Nehru: A Biography*, Oxford University Press, New Delhi, 2015, p. 106.
20. Singh, K. Natwar, *One Life is Not Enough*, Rupa, New Delhi, 2014, p. 40.
21. Azad, Maulana Abul Kalam, *India Wins Freedom: The Complete Version*, Orient Blackswan, New Delhi, 2014, pp. 16–17.
22. Tunzelmann, Alex Von, *Indian Summer: The Secret History of the End of an Empire*, Pocket Books, London, 2007, p. 243.
23. Ibid.
24. Moraes, *Jawaharlal Nehru*, p. 76.
25. Nehru, *An Autobiography*, p. 8.
26. Ibid., 9.
27. Ibid., 10.
28. Ibid., 8.
29. Ibid.
30. Ibid., 13.
31. Hasan, Mushirul, *The Nehrus: Personal Histories*, Mercury Books, London, 2006, p. 40.
32. Nehru, *An Autobiography*, p. 13.
33. Gopal, *Jawaharlal Nehru*, pp. 5–6.
34. Nehru, *An Autobiography*, 15.
35. Ibid.
36. Ibid., 15–16.
37. Ibid., 114, 116, 124.
38. Ibid., 17.
39. Ibid., 18.
40. Ibid., 16.
41. Ibid.
42. Freud, Sigmund, *The Interpretation of Dreams*, A.A. Brill (trans), The Macmillan Company, New York, 1913, p. 160.
43. Ibid.

Chapter 3: A Passage to England

1. Letter from Motilal to Brijlal Nehru, dated 6 April 1905. See Kumar, Ravinder, and Panigarhi, D.N., eds., *Selected Works of Motilal Nehru, Volume One (1899–1918)*, Vikas Publishing House, New Delhi, 1982, pp. 63–64.
2. Ibid.
3. Motilal relied mainly on three doctors—M. A. Ansari, Bidhan Chandra Roy and Jivraj Mehta. During this tour, he had also had himself medically examined. See Nehru, Jawaharlal, *An Autobiography*, Penguin Books India, New Delhi, 2003, p. 259.
4. Moraes, Frank, *Jawaharlal Nehru: A Biography*, Jaico, Mumbai, 2013, p. 32.
5. Letter from Motilal to Jawaharlal, dated 20 October 1905. See Kumar and Panigrahi, *Selected works of Motilal Nehru*, pp. 79–80.
6. Ibid.
7. Ibid., 81.
8. Ibid.
9. Ibid., 82.
10. Ibid., 78.
11. Ibid., 67.
12. Nehru, *An Autobiography*, p. 20.
13. Letter from Motilal to Jawaharlal, dated 4 December 1905. See Kumar and Panigrahi, *Selected Works of Motilal Nehru*, p. 95.
14. Ibid., 110. Letter from Motilal to Jawaharlal, dated 27 October 1906.
15. Ibid., 113–114. Letter from Motilal to Jawaharlal, dated 20 December 1906.
16. Ibid., 129. Letter from Motilal to Jawaharlal, dated 26 July 1907.
17. Moraes, *Jawaharlal Nehru*, p. 33.
18. Letter from Motilal to Jawaharlal, dated, 18 January 1906. See Kumar and Panigrahi, *Selected works of Motilal Nehru*, pp. 100–101.
19. Nehru, *An Autobiography*, p. 21.
20. Gopal, Sarvepalli, *Jawaharlal Nehru: A Biography*, Oxford University Press, New Delhi, 2015, p. 7.
21. Nehru, *An Autobiography*, p. 27.
22. Ibid., 315–316.
23. Charles Tegart's address at the Royal Empire Society, London, on 'Terrorism in India' on 1 November 1932, as published in the *United Empire*, the journal of the Society, with a foreword by the secretary, reproduced in *Terrorism in Bengal: A Collection of Documents, Volume III*, 1995, pp. xxxii–lxxii. See also, Chattopadhyay, Tapan, *Kolkata and Its Police: A History of City Police from Charnock's to Present Day*, Naya Udyog, Kolkata, 2013, pp. 277–379.
24. Nehru, *An Autobiography*, p. 22.
25. Limaye, Madhu, *Mahatma Gandhi and Jawaharlal Nehru: A Historic Partnership*, B.R. Publishing Corporation, Delhi, 2013, p. 225.
26. Nehru, *An Autobiography*, p. 219.
27. Ibid., 22.

28. Ibid., 24.
29. Ibid.
30. Ibid.
31. Gopal, *Jawaharlal Nehru*, p. 8.
32. Nehru, *An Autobiography*, p. 27.
33. Moraes, *Jawaharlal Nehru*, p. 47.
34. Ali, Aruna Asaf, *Private Face of a Public Person: A Study of Jawaharlal Nehru*, Radiant Publishers, New Delhi, 1989, p. 9.
35. Ibid., 10.
36. Gopal, *Jawaharlal Nehru*, p. 10.
37. Ibid.
38. Nehru, *An Autobiography*, pp. 29, 31.
39. Gopal, *Jawaharlal Nehru*, p. 10.

Chapter 4: Tryst with Politics

1. Letter from Motilal to Jawaharlal, 3 June 2010, in Kumar, Ravinder, and Panigarhi, D.N., eds., *Selected Works of Motilal Nehru, Volume One (1899–1918)*, Vikas Publishing House, New Delhi, 1982, p. 148.
2. Ibid., 175. Letter from Motilal to Jawaharlal, dated 29 August 1912.
3. Nehru, Jawaharlal, *An Autobiography*, Penguin Books India, New Delhi, 2003, p. 31.
4. Ibid., 31–32.
5. Ibid., 33.
6. Ibid.
7. Gopal Krishna Gokhale (1866–1915) advocated self-rule through constitutional and social reform and played a leading role in the Morley-Minto Reforms. He was a member of the Public Services Commission and was awarded the CIE (Commander of the Indian Empire). Jawaharlal Nehru mentions in his autobiography that during a dinner, Ganesh Srikrishna Khaparde (1854–1938), a lawyer and Tilakite, accused Gokhale of being a British spy.
8. Nehru, *An Autobiography*, p. 33.
9. Ibid.
10. Ibid., 35.
11. Ibid. Also, Moraes, Frank, *Jawaharlal Nehru: A Biography*, Jaico Publishing House, Mumbai, 2013, p. 53.
12. Nehru, *An Autobiography*, pp. 35-36.
13. Ibid., 37.
14. Ibid.
15. Ibid., 15.
16. Ibid.
17. Ali, Aruna Asaf, *Private Face of a Public Person: A Study of Jawaharlal Nehru*, Radiant Publishers, New Delhi, 1989, p. 18.

18. Moraes, *Jawaharlal Nehru*, p. 55.
19. Nehru, *An Autobiography*, p. 36.
20. Gandhi, M.K., *An Autobiography or The Story of My Experiments with Truth*, Navajivan Publishing House, Ahmedabad, 2002, p. 449.
21. Home Department, *Report on the political and economic situation in the Punjab for the fortnight ending on 15 September 1919*, October 1919, Political Deposit, Proceeding 59.
22. Home Department, *Note of the UP Criminal Investigation Department dated 18 December 1919*, June 1921, Pol. A Proceedings, 248–262.
23. Nehru, *An Autobiography*, p. 55.
24. Ibid.
25. Ibid.
26. Nehru, Jawaharlal, *A Bunch of Old Letters*, Asia Publishing House, New Delhi, 1960, pp. 10–11.
27. Ibid., 13–14.
28. Nehru, *An Autobiography*, p. 56.
29. Siddiqi, M.H., 'The Peasant Movement in Pratapgarh, 1920,' *The Indian Economic and Social History Review*, Vol. 9, No. 3, 1972, pp. 316–317.
30. Ibid.
31. Siddiqi, M.H., *Agrarian Unrest in North India 1918–1922*, Vikas Publishing House, New Delhi, 1978, p. 180.
32. Gopal, Sarvepalli, *Jawaharlal Nehru: A Biography*, Oxford University Press, New Delhi, 2015, p. 22.
33. Nehru, *An Autobiography*, p. 55.
34. Gopal, *Jawaharlal Nehru*, p. 23.
35. Bayly, C.A., 'The Development of Political Organisations in Allahabad Locality 1880–1925,' University of Oxford, D. Phil. Thesis, 1970, pp. 369–370.
36. Gopal, *Jawaharlal Nehru*, p. 22.
37. Ibid., 26.
38. Ibid., 22.
39. Ibid., 23.
40. Nehru, *An Autobiography*, p. 62.
41. Ibid., 84.
42. Gopal, *Jawaharlal Nehru*, p. 22.
43. Ibid., 28.
44. Ibid.
45. Ibid., 28–29.
46. Ibid., 29.
47. Ibid.
48. Nehru, *An Autobiography*, p. 62.
49. Moraes, *Jawaharlal Nehru*, p. 75.

Chapter 5: Father, Son, and the Holy Ghost

1. Nehru, Jawaharlal, *An Autobiography,* Penguin Books India, New Delhi, 2003, p. 38.
2. Ibid.
3. Nehru, *An Autobiography,* p. 38.
4. Moraes, Frank, *Jawaharlal Nehru: A Biography,* Jaico, Mumbai, 2013, p. 55.
5. Nehru, *An Autobiography,* p. 29.
6. Limaye, Madhu, *Mahatma Gandhi and Jawaharlal Nehru: A Historic Partnership,* B.R. Publishing Corporation, Delhi, 2013, p. 19.
7. Ibid., 24.
8. Pandit, Vijaya Lakshmi, *The Scope of Happiness: A Personal Memoir,* Speaking Tiger Publishing, New Delhi, 2018, p. 72.
9. Edwards, Michael, *British India 1772–1947,* Rupa Publications, Calcutta, 1976, p. 281.
10. Ibid.
11. Ibid., 282.
12. Ibid., 288.
13. According to the Central Intelligence report, Tilak met Dr M. A. Ansari in Calcutta in February 1918 and told him that mass agitation was very important but it was only possible if one mixed politics and religion. See: Brown, Judith M., *Gandhi's Rise to Power: Indian Politics 1915–1922,* Cambridge University Press, London, 1972, p. 198.
14. Limaye, *Mahatma Gandhi and Jawaharlal Nehru,* p. 141.
15. Gandhi, M.K., *An Autobiography or The Story of My Experiments with Truth,* Navajivan Publishing House, Ahmedabad, 2002, p. 352.
16. Kripalani, J.B., *Gandhi: His Life and Thought,* Publications Division. Ministry of Information and Broadcasting, New Delhi, 1975, p. 56.
17. Ibid.
18. Gandhi, *An Autobiography,* p. 350.
19. Ibid., 351.
20. Kripalani, *Gandhi,* p. 54.
21. The bungalow was rented from the barrister Jivanlal Desai, an acquaintance of Gandhi. Gandhi, *An Autobiography,* p. 363. Also, Chattopadhyay, Rudrapratap, *Mohandas Karamchand Gandhi: Ekti Akapat Jibani,* Amrita Sharan Prakashan, Kolkata, 2004, p. 89.
22. Nehru, *An Autobiography,* p. 38.
23. Ibid., 39.
24. Ibid., 38.
25. Limaye, *Mahatma Gandhi,* p. 83.
26. Nehru, *An Autobiography,* p. 38.
27. Ibid., 33.
28. Ibid., 33–34.
29. Ibid., 33.

30. Ibid., 33–34.
31. Ibid., 33.
32. His junior party colleague and ministers. See Hati, Jaysukhlal, *As It Happened*, Bharatiya Vidya Bhavan, Mumbai, 2002, pp. 448–449.
33. Ali, Aruna Asaf, *Private Face of a Public Person: A Study of Jawaharlal Nehru*, Radiant Publishers, New Delhi, 1989, p. 18.
34. Pandit, *Scope of Happiness*, p. 81.
35. Kamala's daughter, Indira Gandhi, recalled in an interview in 1972, Swarup Rani (Kamala's mother-in-law) '...felt that my mother need not have encouraged my father in some of his ideas... Even when people were against what my father was doing and saying, they did not blame it on him, but it was taken out on her in a way...' See, Ali, *Public Face of a Public Person*, p. 18.
36. Pandit, *Scope of Happiness*, p. 81.
37. Ibid., 82.
38. Moraes, *Jawaharlal Nehru*, p. 7. Also, Nehru, *An Autobiography*, p. 37.
39. Nehru, *An Autobiography*, p. 116.
40. Charles Augustus Tegart, the commissioner of the Calcutta Police, helped Justice Rowlatt prepare the report as a member of the committee.
41. Nehru, *An Autobiography*, p. 45.
42. Gandhi, *An Autobiography*, p. 423.
43. Limaye, *Mahatma Gandhi*, p. 85.
44. Gandhi, *An Autobiography*, p. 449.
45. Bose, Subhas Chandra, *The Indian Struggle: 1920–1942*, Sisir K. Bose and Sugata Bose (eds.), Oxford University Press, New Delhi, 1997, p. 63.
46. Gandhi, *An Autobiography*, p. 449.
47. Ibid., 459.
48. Ibid., 449.
49. Ibid., 445, 446, 447.
50. Khaliquzzaman, Chaudhry, *Pathway to Pakistan*, Longman, Karachi, 1961, p. 54.
51. Bose, *Indian Struggle*, p. 60.
52. Gandhi, *An Autobiography*, p. 459.
53. Limaye, *Mahatma Gandhi and Jawaharlal Nehru*, pp. 81–82.
54. Ibid., 136. Gandhi once referred to him as a 'destructive genius'.
55. Ibid., 82.
56. Mukherjee, Tapan K., *Life and Letters of a Revolutionary Exile*, National Council of Bengal, Jadavpur University, Kolkata, 1998, pp. 27–32.
57. Gandhi, *An Autobiography*, p. 320.
58. Ibid., 321.
59. Nehru, Jawaharlal. *Selected Works of Jawaharlal Nehru, Volume 1*, B.R. Publishing Corporation, Delhi, 1988, pp. 143–144.
60. Limaye, *Mahatma Gandhi and Jawaharlal Nehru*, p. 86.

61. Gopal, Sarvepalli, *Jawaharlal Nehru: A Biography*, Oxford University Press, New Delhi, 2015, p. 34.
62. Chaudhry Khaliquzzaman, who was a prisoner with Motilal and his son in the Allahabad Jail at that relevant time, has mentioned this incident in his *Pathway to Pakistan*, p. 63.
63. Das, Sitanshu, *Subhas: A Political Biography*, Rupa Publications, New Delhi, 2006, pp. 95–99.
64. Nehru, *An Autobiography*, p. 136.
65. Saraswati, Swami Sahajanand, *My Life Struggle*, Walter Hauser and Kailash Chandra Jha (trans.), Manohar, New Delhi, 2018, p. 179.
66. Ibid.
67. Ibid., 180–181.
68. *The Communist International 1923*, Ted Crawford (trans.), No. 24, Marxist International Archive, 2007, pp. 69–81.
69. Nehru, *An Autobiography*, p. 107.
70. Ibid., 108.
71. Moraes, *Jawaharlal Nehru*, p. 113.
72. Nehru, *An Autobiography*, p. 108.
73. Ibid., 116.
74. Ibid., 125.
75. Limaye, *Mahatma Gandhi and Jawaharlal Nehru*, p. 101.
76. Gandhi, M.K., *Collected Works of Mahatma Gandhi, Volume 38*, The Publications Division, Ministry of Information and Broadcasting, New Delhi, 1970, p. 290.
77. Moraes, *Jawaharlal Nehru*, p. 4. See also Limaye, *Mahatma Gandhi and Jawaharlal Nehru*, p. 211.
78. Ibid., 4.
79. Jayakar, M.R., *The Story of My Life 1922–1925, Volume II*, Asia Publishing House, Bombay, 1959, p. 334.
80. Gandhi, M.K., *Collected Works of Mahatma Gandhi, Volume 24*, The Publications Division, Ministry of Information and Broadcasting, New Delhi, 1967, p. 350.
81. Jayakar, *Story of My Life*, p. 334.
82. Ibid., 332–336.
83. Ravinder Kumar and Parigrahi, D.N., eds., *Selected Works of Motilal Nehru, Volume Four*, Vikas Publishing House, New Delhi, 1986, p. 73.
84. Nehru, *An Autobiography*, pp. 112–113.
85. Chittaranjan Das was an established poet in Bengali and was known for his books of poetry, *Malancha, Sagarsangeet* and *Antarjami*. He founded the literary magazine *Narayan* in 1915. The dramatic version of his short story *Dalim* was very successfully staged at Minerva Theatre in Calcutta, on 15 July 1924.
86. Maulana Azad being close to all three—C.R. Das, Motilal Nehru and Mohandas Gandhi—assessed Das in his memoir, *India Wins Freedom: The*

Complete Version, as '...one of the most powerful men in the history of our national awakening' (p. 18). He wrote: 'After 1923, Congress activities remained mainly in the hands of the Swaraj Party' (p. 12). One of the major objections of the no-changers had been that Gandhiji's leadership would be weakened by the council entry programme. Subsequent events proved that they were wrong (p. 23). 'Mr. Das was able to overcome the fears and apprehensions of the Muslims of Bengal and was acclaimed their leader. The way he solved the communal problem of Bengal is memorable and should serve as an example even today (p. 23)... I am convinced that if he had not died a premature death, he would have created a new atmosphere in the country (p. 24).' Maulana Azad, *India Wins Freedom: The Complete Version*, Orient Blackswan, New Delhi, 2014, pp. 18, 12, 23, 24.
87. Jayakar, *Story of my Life*, p. 197.
88. Limaye, *Mahatma Gandhi and Jawaharlal Nehru*, p. 132.
89. Ibid., 133.
90. Ibid.
91. Namboodiripad, E.M.S., *A History of Indian Freedom Struggle*, Social Scientist Press, Trivandrum, 1986, p. 345.
92. Ibid.
93. Ibid.
94. Ibid.
95. Ibid., 346.
96. Ibid.
97. Ibid.
98. Kumar and Parigrahi, *Selected Works of Motilal Nehru, Volume Four*, pp. 43–44.
99. *Complete Works of Mahatma Gandhi, Volume XXIV*, Ministry of Information and Broadcasting, Government of India, New Delhi, 1967, pp. 536–578.
100. Ibid.
101. Limaye, *Mahatma Gandhi and Jawaharlal Nehru*, p. 108.
102. Letter from Motilal to Jawaharlal, dated 2 December 1926. See Nehru, Jawaharlal, *A Bunch of Old Letters*, Asia Publishing House, New Delhi, 1960, pp. 51–52.

Chapter 6: Presidency for Jawaharlal

1. This has been mentioned in Jawaharlal's letter to Gandhi dated 22 April 1927.
2. Limaye, Madhu, *Mahatma Gandhi and Jawaharlal Nehru: A Historic Partnership*, B.R. Publishing Corporation, Delhi, 2013, pp. 191–192.
3. Dr. M.A. Ansari, MD and MS (London, 1905), Ch. M. (Edinburgh), was a brilliant medical practitioner and a non-communal and acceptable nationalist leader.
4. Limaye, *Mahatma Gandhi and Jawaharlal Nehru*, p. 191–192.

5. Letter from Gandhi to Jawaharlal, dated 25 May 1927. See Nehru, Jawaharlal, *A Bunch of Old Letters*, Asia Publishing House, New Delhi, 1960, p. 57.
6. Limaye, *Mahatma Gandhi and Jawaharlal Nehru*, pp. 113–114.
7. The statement of Purshottam Tricumdas, a socialist leader, in the *Oral History Interview*, Nehru Memorial Museum and Library, New Delhi, p. 32.
8. Limaye, *Mahatma Gandhi and Jawaharlal Nehru*, p. 193.
9. Ibid., 148.
10. Ibid., 194.
11. Nehru, Jawaharlal, *An Autobiography*, Penguin Books India, New Delhi, 2003, p. 161.
12. This was revealed in recently declassified MI5 documents. See also, Balachandran, Vappala, *A Life in Shadow: The Secret Story of ACN Nambiar*, Roli Books, New Delhi, 2016.
13. Malhotra, Iqbal, 'Red Shadow Behind Subhas Chandra Bose,' *OPEN*, 6 April 2018. https://tinyurl.com/48bfduj5. Accessed on 14 October 2024.
14. McKinty, F.P., 'Terrorist Conspiracy in Bengal From 1st July to 31st December 1927,' *Terrorism in Bengal: A Collection of Documents on Terrorist Activities from 1905 to 1939*, Volume 1, Amiya K. Samanta (ed.), Government of West Bengal, Calcutta, 1995, p. 590. McKinty was the special superintendent, Intelligence Branch, C.I.D., Bengal. This report was dated October 1928.
15. Letter from Gandhi to Jawaharlal, Sabarmati, dated 4 January 1928. See Nehru, *Bunch of Old Letters*, p. 58.
16. Nehru, *An Autobiography*, p. 177.
17. Kripalani, J.B. *My Times: An Autobiography*, Rupa Publications, New Delhi: 2004, pp. 157–158.
18. Ibid., 158.
19. Letter from Gandhi to Jawaharlal, Sabarmati, dated 4 January 1928. See Nehru, *Bunch of Old Letters*, p. 58.
20. Gandhi, M.K., 'Independence v Swaraj,' in *Collected Works of Mahatma Gandhi, Volume 35*, 1969, p. 456. This was originally published in *Young India*, on 12 January 1928.
21. Nehru, Jawaharlal, 'On the Resolution on Independence,' *Selected Works of Jawaharlal Nehru, Volume 3*, B.R. Publishing Corporation, Delhi, 1948, pp. 3–4.
22. Letter from Gandhi to Jawaharlal, Sabarmati, dated 17 January 1928, in Nehru, *Bunch of Old Letters*, p. 59.
23. Letter from Jawaharlal to Gandhi, dated 23 January 1928, Nehru, Jawaharlal, *Selected Works of Jawaharlal Nehru, Volume 3*, p. 19.
24. Nehru, *An Autobiography*, pp. 176–177.
25. Kripalani, *My Times*, p. 172. And, Bose, *Indian Struggle*, p. 187.
26. Namboodiripad, E.M.S., *A History of Indian Freedom Struggle*, Social Scientist Press, Trivandrum, 1986, p. 350.
27. Ibid., 336.
28. Ibid., 350.

29. Kripalani, *My Times*, p. 172.
30. Nehru, *An Autobiography*, p. 181.
31. Lahiri, Tarapada, 'Eventful Decade: 1920–1929', *Freedom Struggle and Anushilan Samiti*, Buddhadeva Bhattacharyya (ed.), Anushilan Samiti, Kolkata, 1979, p. 236.
32. Nehru, *An Autobiography*, p. 181.
33. Bose, *Indian Struggle*, p. 196.
34. Ibid.
35. Nehru, *An Autobiography*, pp. 182–183.
36. Ibid., 183.
37. Ibid.
38. Letter from Virendranath to Jawaharlal, dated 29 August 1928: Nehru, *Selected Works*, p. 70.
39. Das, Sitanshu, *Subhas: A Political Biography*, Rupa, New Delhi, 2006, pp. 188.
40. Bose, *The Indian Struggle*, p. 162. Jawaharlal has indicated as if he was the one to handle the whole situation, making no mention of the Nationalists or the initiative taken by Subhas Bose. Nehru, *An Autobiography*, pp. 182–183.
41. Ibid., 161.
42. Namboodiripad has discussed the matter elaborately in his book: *A History of Indian Freedom Struggle*, pp. 357–363.
43. Letter from Motilal to Gandhi, dated 11 July 1928: Nehru, *Bunch of Old Letters*, pp. 60–61.
44. Saraswati, Swami Sahajanand, *My Life Struggle*, Walter Hauser and Kailash Chandra Jha (trans.), Mahohar, New Delhi, 2018, p. 378.
45. Ibid., 379.
46. Ibid.
47. Jatindra Mohan Sengupta mentioned his correspondence with Gandhi about the advisability of Motilal's presidency in his letter to Motilal dated 17 July 1928, in Nehru, *Bunch of Old Letters*, p. 61.
48. Letter from Sengupta to Motilal, dated 17 July 1928: Nehru, *Bunch of Old Letters*, p. 62.
49. Ibid., 61–62.
50. Letter from Bose to Motilal, dated 18 July 1928: Nehru, *Bunch of Old Letters*, p. 62.
51. Letter from Motilal to Sengupta, dated 19 July 1928: Nehru, *Bunch of Old Letters*, p. 63.
52. Ibid.
53. Ibid.
54. Ibid.
55. Ibid.
56. Nehru, *An Autobiography*, p. 183.
57. Bose, *The Indian Struggle*, p. 197.
58. Ibid.

59. Ibid.
60. Ibid.
61. Ibid.
62. Louro, Michele L., *Comrades Against Imperialism: Nehru, India, and Interwar Internationalism*, Cambridge University Press, Cambridge, 2018, p. 126.
63. Bose, *The Indian Struggle*, p. 198.
64. Louro, *Comrades Against Imperialism*, p. 127.
65. Ibid.
66. Ibid., 126.
67. Nehru, *An Autobiography*, p. 196.
68. Louro, *Comrades Against Imperialism*, p. 126.
69. Ibid., 128.
70. Ibid., 126.
71. Ibid., 127.
72. Limaye, *Mahatma Gandhi and Jawaharlal Nehru*, p. 221.
73. Louro, *Comrades Against Imperialism*, p. 127.
74. Nehru, *An Autobiography*, p. 196.
75. Ibid.
76. Ibid.
77. Ibid., 197.
78. Ibid.
79. Ibid. And, Louro, *Comrades Against Imperialism*, p. 128.
80. Ibid., 127–128.
81. Letter from Chatto to Jawaharlal, dated 1 October 1928, File No. 11, 'League against Imperialism,' P.C. Joshi Archives, Jawaharlal Nehru University, New Delhi.
82. Ibid.
83. Letter from Jhabvala to Virendranath, dated 19 April 1928. File No. 11, 'League against Imperialism,' P.C. Joshi Archives, Jawaharlal Nehru University, New Delhi.
84. Louro, *Comrades Against Imperialism*, p. 129.
85. Ibid.
86. Bose, *The Indian Struggle*, p. 198.
87. Ibid.
88. Ibid., 199.
89. Gandhi, Rajmohan, *Patel: A Life*, Navjivan, Ahmedabad, 2017, p. 172.
90. Chatterjee, Malini, *Do and Die: The Chittagong Uprising, 1930–34*, Picador, London, 2010, p. 39.
91. Ibid., 41.
92. Chaudhuri, Nirad C., *The Continent of Circe*, Chatto & Windus, London, 1965, pp. 103–104. Also, Gordon, Leonard A., *The Brothers Against the Raj: A Biography of Sarat and Subhas Chandra Bose*, Viking, New Delhi, 1989, p. 190.

93. Kripalani, *My Times*, p. 174.
94. Gandhi, *Patel: A Life*, p. 171.
95. Ibid.
96. Limaye, *Mahatma Gandhi and Jawaharlal Nehru*, p. 207.
97. Ibid.
98. Kripalani, *My Times*, p. 175.
99. Limaye, *Mahatma Gandhi and Jawaharlal Nehru*, p. 208.
100. Ibid.
101. Gandhi, M.K., *The Complete Works of Mahatma Gandhi*, Vol. XXXVIII, Publications Division, Ministry of Information and Broadcasting, Government of India, New Delhi, 1970, p. 309.
102. Document No. 36, National Archives, New Delhi, Confidential notes of the Intelligence Bureau concerning the Youth Conference organized by N.V. Gadgil in Pune on 12 and 13 December 1928 and Express Telegram to the Government of Bombay dated 19 December 1928 concerning the activities of Nehru, Bose, Gadgil and others, in Home Political 1929.
103. Gandhi, *Patel: A Life*, p. 185. The assassination attempt on Irwin took place on 23 December 1929 when a special train carrying him was derailed by bombs immediately outside Delhi. Two bogies were detached from the train as a result of the explosion. The viceroy escaped unhurt. Some members of the Hindustan Socialist Republican Association were involved in this act.
104. Ibid.
105. Ibid.
106. Balachandran, *Life in Shadow*, p. 76.
107. Ibid.
108. Letter from Gandhi to Vallabhbhai Patel, dated 17 August 1934: Tendulkar, D.G., *Mahatma, Volume 3*, Publication Department, Ministry of Information and Broadcasting, New Delhi, 1951, p. 386.
109. Gandhi, M.K., *The Collected Works of Mahatma Gandhi*, Volume 75, Publication Division, Ministry of Information and Broadcasting, New Delhi, 1979, p. 224.

Chapter 7: A Fellow Traveller

1. In 1924, the Dawes Plan, proposed by the Dawes Committee chaired by Charles G. Dawes, resolved the issue of the World War I reparations that Germany had to pay, and as such, it marked the end of Allied occupation and facilitated a staggered mode of payment for Germany's war reparations.
2. Smedley, Agnes, *China Correspondent*, Pandora Press, London, 1984, p. 21.
3. Schrader, Barbel, *The Golden Twenties' Art and Literature in the Weimar Republic*, Yale University Press, New Haven, 1988, pp. 25–27.
4. Balachandran, Vappala, *A Life in Shadow: The Secret Story of ACN Nambiar*, Roli Books, New Delhi, 2016., p. 34.
5. Ibid., 76.

6. Ibid.
7. Ibid.
8. Bose, Arun Coomer, *Indian Revolutionaries Abroad, 1905–1922: In the Background of International Developments*, Bharat Bhavan, Patna, 1971, pp. 84–85. See also, Price, Ruth, *The Lives of Agnes Smedley*, Oxford University Press, Oxford, 2005, p. 68.
9. Nehru, Jawaharlal, *An Autobiography*, Penguin Books India, New Delhi, 2003, p. 162.
10. Ibid., 77.
11. Smedley, *China Correspondent*, pp. 15–16.
12. Ibid., 16.
13. Balachandran, *Life in Shadow*, p. 45.
14. Barooah, Nirode K., *Chatto: The Life and Times of an Anti-Imperialist in Europe*, Oxford University Press, New Delhi, 2015, p. 275.
15. Ibid., 274.
16. Ibid., 275.
17. Ibid. Also, Price, *Lives of Agnes Smedley*, p. 61.
18. Smedley, *China Correspondent*, p. 16.
19. Ibid., 17.
20. Ibid.
21. Price, *Lives of Agnes Smedley*, p. 92.
22. Ibid.
23. Ibid., 60. Nambiar has also spoken about this. See Balachandran, *Life in Shadow*, pp. 54–55.
24. Agnes Smedley has described her disastrous sexual encounter with M.N. Roy and the subsequent animosity between them in her autobiographical novel, *Daughter of Earth*. See Smedley, Agnes, *Daughter of Earth*, Coward-McCann, New York, 1929, pp. 246, 250.
25. Narendranath Bhattacharya, or M.N. Roy, was a police informer during his revolutionary days in Bengal. See Daly, F.C., 'Note on the Growth of the Revolutionary Movement in Bengal,' *Terrorism in Bengal*, Vol. I, Amiya K. Samanta (ed.), Government of West Bengal, Calcutta, 1995, p. 27.
26. Price, *Lives of Agnes Smedley*, p. 90.
27. Ibid., 98.
28. Andrew, Christopher, and Vasili Mitrokhin, *The World Was Going Our Way: The KGB and the Battle for the Third World*, Basic Books, New York, 2005, p. 2.
29. Gross, Babette, *Willi Munzenberg: A Political Biography*, Michigan State University Press, East Lansing, 1974, pp. 130, 263.
30. Price, *Lives of Agnes Smedley*, p. 102.
31. Louro, Michele L., Comrades Against Imperialism: Nehru, India, and Interwar Internationalism, Cambridge University Press, Cambridge, 2018, p. 30.
32. Balachandran, *Life in Shadow*, p. 39.

33. Ibid., 58.
34. Louro, *Comrades against Imperialism*, p. 2.
35. Balachandran, *A Life in Shadow*, p. 58.
36. Smedley, *China Correspondent*, p. 23.
37. Smedley's espionage activities have been painstakingly recorded in Ruth Price's *The Lives of Agnes Smedley*. The FBI, under Director J. Edgar Hoover, had tried its best to indict Smedley, but was unable to prove her involvement with the Russian Intelligence convincingly.
38. Nambiar, A.C.N., *Oral History Transcript*, NMML. Willi Muenzenburg floated front organizations such as 'Friends of the Soviet Union,' 'World League against Imperialism' and 'International Workers Relief Fund.' After 1937, Muenzenburg fell out of favour with Stalin and was expelled from the Comintern. In June 1940, he fled from Paris and was imprisoned by the Daladier government in a camp in the Chambaran Forest in southeastern France. There he was befriended by a suspected NKVD agent. Subsequently, he went missing and his partially decomposed corpse was discovered by French hunters at the foot of an oak tree near Saint Marcellin on 17 October 1940.
39. Price, *Lives of Agnes Smedley*, pp. 7, 153, 160, 189–190, 246, 419–420.
40. Ibid., 155, 167.
41. Louro, *Comrades against Imperialism*, p. 1.
42. Balachandran, *Life in Shadow*, p. 67.
43. Ibid., 66.
44. Nehru, *An Autobiography*, p. 171.
45. Shindler, Colin, *Israel and European Left*, Bloomsbury Publishing, New Delhi, 2011, p. 86.
46. Hen-Tov, Jacob, *Communism and Zionism in Palestine: The Comintern and the Political Unrest in the 1920s*, Transaction Publishers, New Jersey, 1974, p. 48.
47. Letter from Jawaharlal to Vijaya Lakshmi, 12 November 1927: Nehru, Jawaharlal, *Selected Works of Jawaharlal Nehru*, Vol. 2, Orient Longman, New Delhi, 1972, p. 371.
48. Ibid.
49. Louro, *Comrades against Imperialism*, p. 81.
50. Ibid., 73.
51. Ibid., 78.
52. Ibid.
53. Nehru, *An Autobiography*, pp. 171–172.
54. Ibid., 172.
55. Louro, *Comrades against Imperialism*, p. 78.
56. Ibid.
57. Nehru, Jawaharlal, 'Note to the Working Committee,' 4 April 1927, *Selected Works of Jawaharlal Nehru, Volume 2*, B.R. Publishing Corporation, Delhi, 1929, pp. 316–323.

58. Ibid.
59. Nehru, *An Autobiography*, p. 194.
60. Ibid.
61. Ibid.
62. Ibid., 173.
63. Louro, *Comrades against Imperialism*, p. 169.
64. Ibid.
65. Ibid.
66. Ibid., 170.
67. Ibid., 171.
68. Ibid.
69. Ibid., 172.
70. Ibid.
71. Nehru has written 1931 in his autobiography. See Nehru, *An Autobiography*, p. 173. But the expulsion took place in 1930. See Louro, *Comrades against Imperialism*, p. 173.
72. Letter from Jawaharlal to the Secretary of the LAI, dated 9 April 1930. File No. 10, 'League against Imperialism,' Jawaharlal Nehru University, New Delhi.
73. Louro, *Comrades against Imperialism*, p. 94.
74. Mohanty, Arun, 'Remembering Nehru's first ever visit to the USSR,' *Russia Beyond*, 29 November 2012, https://tinyurl.com/2bs4tabx.
75. Letter from Chatto to M.N. Roy, dated 26 August 1927. Quoted in Roy, Purabi, Sobhanlal Das Gupta, and Hari Vasudevan, (eds.), *Indo-Russian Relations, 1917–1947*, The Asiatic Society, Calcutta, 2012, p. 73.
76. Balachandran, *Life in Shadow*, p. 76.
77. Mohanty, 'Remembering Nehru's first ever visit to the USSR.'
78. Nehru, Jawaharlal, *Soviet Russia: Some Random Sketches and Impressions*, Allahabad Law Journal Press, Allahabad, 1928, pp. 7–8.
79. Ibid.
80. Ibid.
81. Ibid., 6–7.
82. Ibid.
83. Smedley, *China Correspondent*, p. 25.
84. Nehru, *An Autobiography*, p. 162.
85. Mohanty, 'Remembering Nehru's first ever visit to the USSR.'
86. Kashin, Valeriy, 'What Stalin thought of Gandhi and Nehru,' *Russia Beyond*, 3 May 2012, https://tinyurl.com/y5xk9jnj. Accessed on 14 October 2024.
87. Mohanty, 'Remembering Nehru's first ever visit to the USSR.'
88. Ibid.
89. Nehru, *An Autobiography*, p. 174.

Chapter 8: Consolidation and Compromise

1. Louro, Michele L., *Comrades Against Imperialism: Nehru, India, and Interwar Internationalism*, Cambridge University Press, Cambridge, 2018, p. 124.
2. Nehru, Jawaharlal, *An Autobiography*, Penguin Books India, New Delhi, 2003, p. 194.
3. Bose, Subhas Chandra, *The Indian Struggle: 1920–1942*, Rathin Chakraborty (ed.), Oxford University Press, New Delhi, 1997, p. 217.
4. Low, D.A., *Britain and Indian Nationalism: The Imprint of Ambiguity 1929–1942*, Cambridge University Press, Cambridge, 1999, p. 51.
5. Ibid.
6. Bose, *The Indian Struggle*, pp. 219. Also, Sarila, Narendra Singh, *The Shadow of the Great Game: The Untold Story of India's Partition*, HarperCollins Publishers, Noida, 2009, p. 86.
7. Ibid.
8. 'The Delhi Manifesto,' November 1929, in Nehru, Jawaharlal, *Selected Works of Jawaharlal Nehru, Volume 4*, B.R. Publishing Corporation, Delhi, 1973, pp. 165–166.
9. Bose, *The Indian Struggle*, p. 220.
10. Pratt, Frederick G., 'The Indian Round Table Conference: Second Session,' *Pacific Affairs*, Vol. 5, No. 2, February 1932, University of British Columbia, Vancouver, pp. 151–167.
11. Bose, Subhas Chandra, *Netaji Collected Works, Volume 2*, ed. Sisir K. Bose, Netaji Research Bureau, Calcutta, 1981, p. 263.
12. Ibid.
13. Gordon, Leonard A., *The Brothers Against the Raj: A Biography of Sarat and Subhas Chandra Bose*, Viking, New Delhi, 1989, p. 254.
14. *Netaji Collected Works, Volume 2*, Netaji Research Bureau, Calcutta, 1981, p. 266.
15. Bose, Mihir, *The Lost Hero: A Biography of Subhas Bose*, Quartet Books, London, 1982, p. 174.
16. Frank, Katherine, *Indira: The Life of Indira Nehru Gandhi*, HarperCollins Publishers, London, 2001, p. 101.
17. Gopal, Sarvepalli, *Jawaharlal Nehru: A Biography*, Oxford University Press, New Delhi, 2015, p. 108.
18. Nehru, *An Autobiography*, p. 621.
19. Balachandran, Vappala, *A Life in Shadow: The Secret Story of ACN Nambiar*, Roli Books, New Delhi, 2016, p. 122.
20. Ibid.
21. Ibid.
22. Kripalani, J.B., *My Times: An Autobiography*, Rupa Publications, New Delhi, 2004, p. 292.
23. Ibid.

24. Gandhi, Rajmohan, *Patel: A Life*, Navjivan, Ahmedabad, 2017, pp. 181.
25. Kripalani, *My Times*, pp. 292–293.
26. Nehru, Jawaharlal, *A Bunch of Old Letters*, Asia Publishing House, New Delhi, 1960, pp. 128–130, 133, 140, 223, 231 and 287.
27. Ibid., 222, 316, 395 and 478 (Stafford Cripps) and 155, 208–210, 213, 217, 233, 275, 290, 295, 301, 310, 408, 420, 437, 438 and 441 (Edward Thompson).
28. Louro, *Comrades Against Imperialism*, p. 192.
29. Ibid. 193.
30. Balachandran, *Life in Shadow*, p. 122.
31. Ibid.
32. Louro, *Comrades Against Imperialism*, p. 204.
33. *Netaji Collected Works (India's Spokesman Abroad–Letters, Articles, Speeches and Statements 1933–1937)*, Volume VIII, Netaji Research Bureau and Permanent Black, Ranikhet, 1994, 109–110.
34. Bose, *The Lost Hero*, p. 182.
35. Letter from Bose to Nehru, sent from Badgastein (Austriche), dated 4 March 1936, in *Netaji Collected Works*, p. 144.
36. Ibid., 226–227. Letter from Bose to Nehru, dated 17 October 1937.
37. Namboodiripad, E.M.S., *A History of Indian Freedom Struggle*, Social Scientist Press, Trivandrum, 1986, p. 397.
38. Kripalani, *My Times*, pp. 274–275.
39. Ibid., 276–277.
40. Ibid., 282–285.
41. Nehru, *An Autobiography*, pp. 622–623.
42. Namboodiripad, *History of Indian Freedom Struggle*, pp. 598–599.
43. Andrew, Christopher, and Vasili Mitrokhin, *The World Was Going Our Way: The KGB and the Battle for the Third World*, Basic Books, New York, 2005, pp. 312–313.
44. Calcutta Police Headquarters, *Annual Report on the Police Administration of the Town of Calcutta and its Suburbs—For the year 1955*, Calcutta, p. 1.
45. Andrew and Mitrokhin, *The World Was Going Our Way*, p. 314.
46. Nehru, *An Autobiography*, p. 609.
47. Nehru, *Bunch of Old Letters*, p. 244.
48. Letter from Gandhi to Amrit Kaur, dated 27 September 1937: Gandhi, M.K., *Complete Works of Mahatma Gandhi*, Volume LXV, Publication Division, Ministry of Information and Broadcasting, Government of India, New Delhi, 1976, pp. 174–175.
49. Prasad, Rajendra, *Autobiography*, Penguin Books, Gurgaon, 2010, p. 446.
50. Nehru, *An Autobiography*, p. 628.
51. Balachandran, *Life in Shadow*, p. 126.
52. Ibid., 127.
53. Ibid., 128.
54. This is evident from Maisky's letter to Jawaharlal, dated 10 October 1938.

See Nehru, *Bunch of Old Letters*, p. 199.
55. Balachandran, *Life in Shadow*, p. 130.
56. Ibid.
57. Ibid., 131–132.
58. Ibid.
59. Gopal, *Jawaharlal Nehru*, p. 122.
60. Ibid.
61. Balachandran, *Life in Shadow*, pp. 131–132.
62. Gopal, *Jawaharlal Nehru*, p. 122.
63. The words of Maisky's letter to Nehru make it obvious. See Nehru, *Bunch of Old Letters*, p. 199.
64. Gopal, *Jawaharlal Nehru*, pp. 123–124.
65. Letter from Bose to Nehru, dated 19 October 1938: Bose, Subhas Chandra, *Subhas Chandra Bose—Congress President: Speeches, Articles, and Letters, January 1938–May 1939*, Netaji Research Bureau and Permanent Black, Kolkata and Ranikhet, 2016, p. 193.
66. Letter from Smedley to Nehru, dated 23 November 1937: Nehru, *Bunch of Old Letters*, p. 260.
67. Letter from Chu Teh to Nehru, dated 26 November 1937: Nehru, *Bunch of Old Letters*, p. 261.
68. Amalendu Dey's article in Chakraborty, Rathin (ed.), *The Man in the Long March: A Centenary Tribute to Dr D.S. Kotnis*, Lokmath Prakashan, Kolkata, 2010, p. 11. Ibid., 115–116. See also, Bose's public statements quoted in Rathin Chakraborty's article in the same volume.
69. Ibid., 11.
70. Smedley, Agnes, *China Correspondent*, Pandora Press, London, 1984, pp. 162–163.
71. Majumdar, A.K., *Advent of Independence*, Bharatiya Vidya Bhavan, Bombay, 1963, pp. 155, 409.
72. Bose, *The Lost Hero*, pp. 219–220.
73. Ibid., 223.
74. Ibid.
75. Ibid.
76. Ibid., 224.
77. Kripalani, *My Times*, p. 347.
78. Ibid.
79. Ibid.
80. Gordon, *Brothers Against the Raj*, p. 372.
81. Ibid.
82. Ibid.
83. Ibid.
84. Letter from Bose to Nehru, dated 28 March 1939. Quoted in Gordon, *Brothers Against the Raj*, p. 194.
85. Ibid.

86. Letter from Bose to Gandhi, dated 13 April 1939. Quoted in Gordon, *Brothers Against the Raj*, p. 171.
87. Ibid.
88. The matter has been discussed in detail in Tapan Chattopadhyay's book. See Chattopadhyay, Tapan, *Rivalry That Cost India: Jawaharlal Nehru, Subhas Bose, and Congress Politics 1921–1941*, H.P. Hamilton, London, 2023, pp. 192–193.
89. Bose, *The Lost Hero*, pp. 235–236.

Chapter 9: Jinnah and Congress Politics

1. Gandhi, Rajmohan, *Gandhi: The Man, His People, and the Empire*, University of California Press, Berkeley, 2007, pp. 178–179.
2. Matthews, Roderick, *Jinnah Vs. Gandhi*, Hachette India, Gurgaon, 2016, p. 78.
3. Wilson, Charles McMoran, *Jinnah of Pakistan*, Oxford University Press, Karachi, 1993, p. 38.
4. Matthews, *Jinnah Vs. Gandhi*, p. 84.
5. Ibid. Gandhi has also written about his recruitment drive and how people responded to it in his autobiography, see, Gandhi, M.K., *An Autobiography or The Story of My Experiments with Truth*, Navajivan Publishing House, Ahmedabad, 2002, pp. 410–415.
6. Stanley Wolpert, *Jinnah of Pakistan*, p. 59.
7. Gandhi, M.K., Appendix 1, *Collected Works of Mahatma Gandhi*, Vol. 17, Publication Division, Ministry of Information and Broadcasting, New Delhi, 1965, pp. 464–465.
8. Sarila, Narendra Singh, *The Shadow of the Great Game: The Untold Story of India's Partition*, HarperCollins Publishers, Noida, 2009, p. 80.
9. Ibid.
10. Matthews, *Jinnah Vs. Gandhi*, p. 103.
11. Limaye, Madhu, *Mahatma Gandhi and Jawaharlal Nehru: A Historic Partnership 1916–1948*, B.R. Publishing Corporation, Delhi, 2013, p. 170.
12. Ibid.
13. Reddy, Sheela, *Mr. and Mrs Jinnah: The Marriage That Shook India*, Penguin, Gurgaon, 2017, p. 324.
14. Limaye, *Mahatma Gandhi and Jawaharlal Nehru*, p. 172.
15. Ibid.
16. Reddy, *Mr and Mrs Jinnah*, p. 348.
17. Wilson, *Jinnah of Pakistan*, p. 97.
18. Reddy, *Mr. and Mrs Jinnah*, p. 354–355.
19. Ibid., 183.
20. Ibid.
21. Ibid.

22. Matthews, *Jinnah Vs. Gandhi*, 114.
23. Ibid.
24. Nehru, Jawaharlal, *An Autobiography*, Penguin Books India, New Delhi, 2003, p. 74.
25. Sarila, *The Shadow of the Great Game*, p. 86.
26. Ibid.
27. Ibid.
28. Matthews, *Jinnah Vs. Gandhi*, p. 115.
29. Wolpert, *Jinnah of Pakistan*, p. 120.
30. Matthews, *Jinnah Vs. Gandhi*, p. 121.
31. Ibid., 122.
32. Prasad, Rajendra. *Autobiography*, Penguin Books, Gurgaon, 2010, pp. 384–387. Jinnah has also mentioned this in his letter to Bose, dated 2 August 1938, quoted in *Subhas Chandra Bose—Congress President: Speeches, Articles, and Letters January 1938–May 1939*, Netaji Research Bureau and Permanent Black, Kolkata and Ranikhet, 2016, p. 117. Rajendra Prasad has stated that he and Jinnah had come to like each other.
33. Evidence of Jawaharlal's deep antipathy against Jinnah and the Muslim League can be found in his autobiography. See, Nehru, *An Autobiography*, p. 629. Also, Chagla, M.C., *Roses in December: An Autobiography*, Bharatiya Vidya Bhavan, Mumbai, 2019, pp. 81–82.
34. Prasad, *Autobiography*, p. 387.
35. Matthews, *Jinnah Vs. Gandhi*, pp. 138–139.
36. Jalal, Ayesha, *The Sole Spokesman*, Cambridge University Press, Cambridge, 1985, p. 42.
37. ibid.
38. Sarila, *Shadow of the Great Game*, p. 91.
39. Ibid.
40. Ibid.
41. Ahmed, Akbar S., *Jinnah, Pakistan, and Islamic Identity: The Search for Saladin*, Routledge, London, 2005, p. 1.
42. Letter from Jinnah to Nehru, dated 17 March 1938, in Nehru, Jawaharlal, *A Bunch of Old Letters*, Asia Publishing House, New Delhi, 1960, pp. 277–279.
43. Bose, Subhas Chandra, *Subhas Chandra Bose—Congress President*, p. 111.
44. Ibid., 117–118.
45. Matthews, *Jinnah Vs. Gandhi*, p. 144.
46. Ibid.

Chapter 10: The Politics of Partition

1. Sarila, Narendra Singh, *The Shadow of the Great Game: The Untold Story of India's Partition*, HarperCollins Publishers, Noida, 2009, p. 39.
2. Ibid.

END NOTES ■ 279

3. Herman, Arthur, *Gandhi and Churchill: The Epic Rivalry That Destroyed an Empire and Forged Our Age*, Arrow Books, London, 2008, p. 451.
4. Ibid., 450.
5. Ibid.
6. Sarila, p. 41.
7. Ibid., 42.
8. Khaliquzzaman, Chaudhry, *Pathway to Pakistan*, Longman, Karachi, 1961, p. 206.
9. Sarila, *Shadow of the Great Game*, p. 43.
10. Ibid., 36.
11. Ibid., 43.
12. Prasad, Rajendra, *Autobiography*, Penguin Books, Gurgaon, 2010, p. 474.
13. MSS/EUR 125/8, Vol. IV, OIC, British Library, London, pp. 169(a) to (e).
14. Ibid., 169(e), 170.
15. Sarila, *Shadow of the Great Game*, p. 45.
16. Ibid., 46.
17. Ibid., 38.
18. Ibid.
19. Ibid., 45.
20. Ibid.
21. MSS/EUR 125/9, Vol. V, OIC, British Library, London, pp. 45–49. Note on the viceroy's interview with Jinnah, 13 January 1940.
22. MSS/EUR 125/9, Vol. V, OIC, British Library, London, pp. 45–49. The viceroy's telegram (Paragraph 6) to the secretary of state, 6 February 1940, on his talk with Gandhi and Jinnah on the previous day.
23. Ibid.
24. Matthews, Roderick, *Jinnah Vs. Gandhi*, Hachette India, Gurgaon, 2016, p. 151.
25. Ibid.
26. *The Lahore Resolution: Resolved at the Lahore Session of the All India Muslim League held on 22nd-24th March, 1940*, Brian McMorrow, PBase internet archives.
27. MSS/EUR 125/8, Vol. V. Note on Jinnah's interview with the viceroy, 13 March 1940, OIC, British Library, London, pp. 191–195.
28. Ibid.
29. Elst, Koenraad, *The Saffron Swastika: The Notion of 'Hindu Fascism,'* Volume I, Voice of India, New Delhi, 2001, p. 532.
30. Sarila, *Shadow of the Great Game*, 53.
31. Ibid., 54.
32. Ibid., 55.
33. Maulana Azad has related the incident in his *India Wins Freedom: The Complete Version*, p. 35. It was Linlithgow's practice to ring the bell for an ADC to escort Gandhi to his car. On this occasion, he was so taken aback

that he neither rang the bell nor said goodbye to Gandhi. Gandhi had to find his own way to his car.
34. Nehru, Jawaharlal, *An Autobiography,* Penguin Books India, New Delhi, 2003, p. 635.
35. Sarila, *Shadow of the Great Game,* p. 56.
36. Ibid.
37. File No. L/P&J//8/507, containing Jinnah's interview with Linlithgow, dated 27 June 1940 at Simla, OIC, British Library, London.
38. Sarila, *Shadow of the Great Game,* p. 54.
39. Intelligence Bureau, *The Report of the Director,* New Delhi, 21 May 1940, OIC, British Library, London.
40. Sarila, *Shadow of the Great Game,* p. 59.
41. Ibid.
42. Ibid., 60. Ghulam Sarwar, local MLA, was oppressing and exploiting the Hindus of Noakhali (East Bengal) with the help of this organization. The Muslim National Guards indulged in looting and arson during the Noakhali riots in 1946. See also, Kripalani, J.B., *My Times: An Autobiography,* Rupa Publications, New Delhi, 2004, pp. 572–573.
43. Sarila, *Shadow of the Great Game,* p. 61.
44. Churchill, Winston, *Memories of the Second World War, Volume 6: War Comes to America,* Cassell & Co, London, 1950, pp. 209–210.
45. Ibid., 188.
46. Ibid., 286–287.
47. Ibid., 188.
48. War Cabinet Paper, 42/43, pp. 104–105, from the viceroy to the Secretary of State, *Transfer of Power,* Vol. I, S. No. 60, Para 10.
49. *Transfer of Power,* Vol. I, Para 10.
50. Pandit, Vijaya Lakshmi, *The Scope of Happiness: A Personal Memoir,* Speaking Tiger Publishing, New Delhi, 2018, p. 182.
51. Wilson, Charles McMoran, *Winston Churchill: The Struggle for Survival,* Constable, London, 1966, p. 74.
52. Maulana Azad, *India Wins Freedom: The Complete Version,* p. 39.
53. Ibid.
54. Sarila, *Shadow of the Great Game,* p. 105.
55. Ibid.
56. Ibid., 103.
57. Ibid., 105.
58. Ibid., 106–107.
59. Ibid.
60. Ibid., 107.
61. Azad, *India Wins Freedom,* p. 60.
62. Ibid., 57–58, 65–66.
63. Ibid., 40.
64. Pandit, *Scope of Happiness,* p. 182.

65. Ibid.
66. Ibid., 182. Maulana Azad's personal involvement with the Cripps Mission is mentioned in *India Wins Freedom* in Chapter 5: The Cripps Mission, pp. 46–69.
67. Sarila, *Shadow of the Great Game*, p. 113.
68. Ibid.
69. Ibid., 114.
70. Ibid.
71. Hallet's telegram to the viceroy in *The Transfer of Power 1942–7*, Vo. II (30 April – 21 September 1942), Nicholas Mansergh (ed.), Her Majesty's Stationery Office, London, 1971, S. No. 695.
72. Ibid.
73. Matthews, *Jinnah Vs. Gandhi*, p. 171.
74. Kamat, Jyotna K., *Socialism of Jawaharlal Nehru*, Abhinav Publications, New Delhi, 1980, p. 155.
75. Sarila, *Shadow of the Great Game*, pp. 146–147.
76. Ibid., 148.
77. Ibid.
78. Ibid., 149.
79. Matthews, *Jinnah Vs. Gandhi*, p. 172.
80. This is the view most historians endorse today. Clement Attlee, one of the architects of India's freedom, was himself of the same view.
81. Lohia, Ram Manohar, *Guilty Men of India's Partition*, Rupa Publications, New Delhi, 2008, p. 26.
82. Azad, *India Wins Freedom*, p. 164.
83. Ibid., 165.
84. Ibid.
85. Ibid., 166.
86. The Calcutta Disturbances Commission of Enquiry, *Calcutta Disturbances Commission of Enquiry—Record of Proceedings—Minutes of Evidence*, Volume III, Government Printing, Bengal, Calcutta, 1947, pp. 143–146.
87. Ibid.
88. Azad, *India Wins Freedom*, p. 197. Kripalani has also mentioned this in *My Times*, p. 607.
89. Ibid.
90. Ibid.
91. Ibid.
92. Tunzelmann, Alex Von., *Indian Summer: The Secret History of the End of an Empire*, Pocket Books, London, 2007, p. 163.
93. Matthews, *Jinnah Vs. Gandhi*, p. 200.
94. Krishna Menon's letter to Mountbatten, dated 14 June 1947, MBI/104, Hartley, University of Southampton, quoted in Sarila, *Shadow of the Great Game*, p. 275.
95. Azad, *India wins Freedom*, p. 200.

96. Report on 'The Last Viceroyalty', Part B, p. 123, OIC, British Library, London.
97. Matthews, *Jinnah Vs. Gandhi*, 200.
98. Tunzelmann, *Indian Summer*, p. 168.
99. Ibid.
100. Ibid., 164.
101. Ibid.
102. Ibid., 170. See also, Kripalani, *My Times*, p. 658.
103. Mathai, M.O., *Reminiscences of the Nehru Age*, Vikas Publishing House, Delhi, 2015, p. 205.
104. Louis Mountbatten's notes on the meeting on 24 March 1947, *The Transfer of Power 1942–47*, Vol. X (22 March–30 May 1947), Nicholas Mansergh (ed.), British Stationery Office, London, 1981, pp. 11–13.
105. Wolpert, Stanley, *Gandhi's Passion*, Oxford University Press, Oxford, 2001, p. 232.
106. Azad, *India Wins Freedom*, p. 197.
107. Ibid.
108. Ibid., 198.
109. Matthews, *Jinnah Vs. Gandhi*, p. 201. Also, Kripalani, *My Times*, pp. 659–660, for a detailed outline of Gandhi's proposal.
110. *The Transfer of Power 1942–47*, Vol. X (22 March–30 May 1947), p. 54.
111. Lohia, *Guilty Men of Partition*, p. 30.
112. Matthews, *Jinnah Vs. Gandhi*, p. 202.
113. Ibid.
114. Ibid.
115. Ibid., 203.
116. Ibid.
117. Sarila, *Shadow of the Great Game*, p. 286.
118. Ibid., 288.
119. Ibid.
120. Tunzelmann, *Indian Summer*, p. 190.
121. Collins, Larry, and Dominique Lapierre, *Mountbatten and Partition of India: Vol. I, March 22–August 15, 1947*, Vikas Publishing House, New Delhi, 1982, p. 57.
122. Menon, V.P., *The Transfer of Power of India*, Orient Longman, Mumbai, 1999, p. 426.
123. Sarila, *Shadow of the Great Game*, p. 306.
124. Ibid.
125. Kripalani, *My Times*, pp. 681–682.
126. Ibid., 682.
127. Lohia, *Guilty Men of Partition*, pp. 21–26.
128. Ibid.
129. Ibid.
130. Kripalani, *My Times*, p. 683.

131. Ibid., 684.
132. Ibid.
133. Letter from Edwina Mountbatten to Marchioness of Reading, dated 27 July 1947, quoted in Tunzelmann, *Indian Summer*, p. 214.
134. Ibid., 218.
135. Ibid.
136. Krishna, B., *Sardar Vallabhbhai Patel: India's Iron Man*, HarperCollins, New Delhi, 1996, p. 322.
137. Letter from Nehru to Mountbatten, dated 27 July 1947: Nehru, Jawaharlal, *Selected Works of Jawaharlal Nehru*, Vol. 3, B.R. Publishing Corporation, Delhi, 1948, p. 264.

Chapter 11: The Kashmir Imbroglio

1. Report on 'The Last Viceroyalty', March-August 1947, Part C, Para 87, OIC, British Library, London.
2. Ibid., Para 71.
3. Dasgupta, C., *War and Diplomacy in Kashmir 1947–1948*, Sage, New Delhi, 2002, pp. 12–15.
4. Ibid.
5. Ibid., 15.
6. Ibid.
7. Sarila, Narendra Singh, *The Shadow of the Great Game: The Untold Story of India's Partition*, HarperCollins Publishers, Noida, 2009, pp. 240–241.
8. Report on 'The Last Viceroyalty', March-August 1947, Part E, Para 69.
9. Sarila, *Shadow of the Great Game*, 343.
10. Ibid., 346.
11. Malhotra, Iqbal, and Maroof, Raza, *Kashmir's Untold Story: Declassified*, Bloomsbury, New Delhi, 2019, p. 50.
12. Sarila, *Shadow of the Great Game*, p. 337.
13. Ibid.
14. Malhotra Raza, *Kashmir's Untold Story*, p. 50.
15. Ibid.
16. Ibid.
17. Sarila, *Shadow of the Great Game*, pp. 343–344.
18. Letter from Nehru to Sheikh Abdullah, dated 4 November, 1947, in Nehru, Jawaharlal, *Selected Works of Jawaharlal Nehru*, Vol. 4, B.R. Publishing Corporation, Delhi, p. 319.
19. Sen, L.P., *Slender Was the Thread: Kashmir Confrontation 1947–48*, Orient Longman, New Delhi, 1994, p. 8.
20. Ibid.
21. Dasgupta, *War and Diplomacy*, p. 21.
22. Ibid., 22.
23. Ibid., 22–23.

24. Ibid., 24–25.
25. Ibid., 25.
26. Malhotra and Raza, *Kashmir's Untold Story*, p. 53.
27. Letter from Patel to Maharaja of Kashmir, dated 3 July, 1947. Patel, Vallabhbhai, *Sardar Patel's Correspondence, Volume I*, Durga Das (ed.), Navjivan Publishing House, Ahmedabad, 1971, pp. 32–33.
28. Letter from Jawaharlal to Vallabhbhai Patel, dated 27 September 1947: Patel, Vallabhbhai, *Sardar Patel's Correspondence, Volume I*, Durga Das (ed.), Navjivan Publishing House, Ahmedabad, 1971, 45–46.
29. Dasgupta., *War and Diplomacy*, p. 39.
30. Raghavan, Srinath, *War and Peace in Modern India*, Orient Blackswan, New Delhi, 2010, pp. 105–106.
31. Dasgupta, *War and Diplomacy*, p. 39.
32. Ibid.
33. Sen, *Slender Was the Thread*, p. 20.
34. Ibid., 21.
35. Malhotra and Raza, *Kashmir's Untold Story*, p. 58.
36. Sen, *Slender Was the Thread*, p. 3.
37. Letter from R.L. Batra, deputy prime minister of Jammu and Kashmir, to Patel, dated 3 October 1947. Patel, *Sardar Patel's Correspondence*, p. 48.
38. Letter from Patel to Baldev Singh, dated 7 October 1947. Patel, *Sardar Patel's Correspondence*, p. 57.
39. Dasgupta, *War and Diplomacy*, p. 40.
40. Letter from Patel to Mahajan, dated 21 October 1947, quoted in Dasgupta, *War and Diplomacy*, p. 62.
41. Letter from Jawaharlal to Mahajan, dated 21 October 1947, in Nehru, *Selected Works*, p. 274.
42. Diary entry dated 28 October 1947, quoted in Campbell-Johnson, Alan, *Mission with Mountbatten*, Robert Hale, London, 1951.
43. Sen, *Slender Was the Thread*, pp. 19, 37.
44. Diary entry for 28 October 1947, quoted in Johnson, *Mission with Mountbatten*.
45. Sen, *Slender Was the Thread*, p. 37.
46. Ibid., 37–38.
47. Dasgupta, *War and Diplomacy in Kashmir*, p. 44.
48. Ibid., 45.
49. Ibid.
50. Sarila, *Shadow of the Great Game*, p. 354.
51. Dasgupta, *War and Diplomacy in Kashmir*, 46.
52. Ibid.
53. Ibid., 47–48.
54. Ibid.
55. Ibid., 49.
56. Ibid.

57. Sen, *Slender Was the Thread*, p. 45.
58. Ibid., 78–100, 195–199.
59. Ibid., 76, 82.
60. Dasgupta, *War and Diplomacy in Kashmir*, p. 50.
61. Sarila, *Shadow of the Great Game*, p. 359.
62. Dasgupta, *War and Diplomacy in Kashmir*, p. 51.
63. Hodson, Henry Vincent, *The Great Divide: Britain-India-Pakistan*, Oxford University Press, Delhi, 2000, p. 507.
64. Ibid.
65. Dasgupta, *War and Diplomacy in Kashmir*, pp. 51–52.
66. Ibid., 52.
67. Cable from Jawaharlal to Attlee, 25 October, 1947, in *Nehru, Selected Works*, Vol. 4, pp. 274–275.
68. Ibid.
69. Cable from Attlee to Jawaharlal, File No. L/P & S/13/1845b, India House Office Records, London.
70. Letter from Jawaharlal to Liaquat Ali Khan, dated 28 October 1947, in Nehru, *Selected Works*, Vol. 4, pp. 288–289.
71. Malhotra and Raza, *Kashmir's Untold Story*, p. 61.
72. Ibid.
73. Sarila, *Shadow of the Great Game* p. 350.
74. Ibid., 355.
75. Ibid., 358.
76. Sarila, *Shadow of the Great Game*, p. 360.
77. Sen, *Slender Was the Thread*, pp. 113–114.
78. Sarila, *Shadow of the Great Game*, p. 360.
79. Khanduri, C.B., *Field Marshal Cariappa: His Life and Times*, Lancer, New Delhi, 1995, pp. 165–166.
80. Sarila, *Shadow of the Great Game*, p. 361.
81. Ibid.
82. Sen, then a Brigadier, has given a graphic eye-witness account of the situation in his book, *Slender was the Thread*, pp. 108–148.
83. Dasgupta, *War and Diplomacy in Kashmir 1947–1948*, p. 114.
84. Ibid., 116.
85. Ibid., 117.
86. Ibid., 118.
87. Ibid.
88. Letter from Jawaharlal to Ayyangar, dated 3 February 1948, in Nehru, *Selected Works*, Volume 5, pp. 205–207.
89. Letter from Jawaharlal to Krishna Menon, dated 16 February 1948, and also a letter from Jawaharlal to Vijaya Lakshmi Pandit on the same date, in Nehru, *Selected Works*, Volume 5, pp. 218–224.
90. Letter from Jawaharlal to Attlee, dated 8 February 1948. Nehru, *Selected Works*, Volume 5, p. 211.

91. Letter from Mountbatten to Attlee, dated 8 February 1948, in File No. L/WS/1/1140, India Office Records, London.
92. Dasgupta, *War and Diplomacy in Kashmir*, pp. 121–122.
93. Ibid., 162.
94. Ibid., 165.
95. Ibid., 167.
96. Ibid., 168.
97. Ibid.
98. Ibid., 170.
99. Ibid.
100. Holt, Thaddeus, *The Deceivers: Allied Military Deception in the Second World War*, Skyhorse Publishing, New York, 2007, p. 339.
101. Dasgupta, *War and Diplomacy in Kashmir*, p. 171.
102. Ibid.
103. Ibid.
104. Ibid., 182.
105. Ibid., 183.
106. Telegram No. 1461, dated 29 November 1948 from Grafftey-Smith to CRO, File No. L/WS/1/1144, India Office Records, London.
107. Ibid.
108. Ibid.
109. Ibid.
110. Dasgupta, *War and Diplomacy in Kashmir*, p. 194.
111. Mathai, M.O., *Reminiscences of the Nehru Age*, Vikas Publishing House, Delhi, 2015, p. 55.
112. Dasgupta, *War and Diplomacy in Kashmir*, p. 195.
113. Report from Nye to CRO, dated 29 December 1948, File No. L/WS/1/1145, India Office Records, London.
114. Sen, *Slender Was the Thread*, pp. 139–140.
115. Mullik, B.N., *My Years with Nehru: Kashmir*, Deep Publication, Agra, 1972, pp. 33–34.
116. Ibid., 16.
117. Malhotra and Raza, *Kashmir's Untold Story*, p. 90
118. Ankit, Rakesh, 'Kashmir, 1945–66: From Empire to the Cold War,' 2017, University of Southampton, PhD thesis, eprints.soton.ac.uk.Ibid.
119. Ibid.
120. Malhotra and Raza, *Kashmir's Untold Story*, p. 98.
121. Mullick, *My Years with Nehru*, pp. 18–19.
122. Ibid., 19.
123. Ibid., 18.
124. Ibid.
125. Malhotra and Raza, *Kashmir's Untold Story*, p. 103.
126. Mullick, *My Years with Nehru*, p. 26.

127. Rohmetra, R., Tribute to Syama Prasad Mukherjee, *Daily Excelsior*, 23 June 2013, dailyexcelsior.com.
128. Sharma, Urmila, and S.K. Sharma, *Indian Political Thought*, Atlantic Publishers, New Delhi, 2006, p. 381.
129. Kumar, Arvind, 'Mudaliar, Mookerjee, not Nehru, built India's scientific institutions,' *Sunday Guardian*, 20 April, 2019, https://tinyurl.com/25dmy9pf. Accessed on 14 October 2024. Malhotra and Raza, *Kashmir's Untold Story*, p. 105.
130. Ibid., 105–106.
131. Mullick, *My Years with Nehru*, p. 29.
132. Ibid.
133. Ibid., 40.
134. Singh, Raghavendra, 'S.P. Mookerjee's Death Left Some Unanswered Questions,' *The Indian Express*, 20 June, 2019, https://tinyurl.com/4ty3mcn4. Accessed on 14 October 2024.
135. Mullick, *My Years with Nehru*, pp. 42–43.
136. Ibid., 44.
137. Ibid.
138. Ibid.
139. Ibid., 44–45.
140. Ibid.
141. Mathai, M.O., *Reminiscences*, pp. 201–202. Also, Tunzelmann, *Indian Summer*, p. 356.
142. Mullick, *My Years with Nehru*, p. 68.
143. Ibid., 48–49.
144. Ibid., 51.
145. Ibid., 53.
146. Ibid., 65.
147. Ibid., 68.
148. Ibid., 87.
149. Ibid., 89.
150. Ibid.
151 Ibid., 97.
152. Ibid., 98.
153. Ibid., 105.

Chapter 12: The Orphan of Politics: Tibet

1. Powers, John, *History as Propaganda: Tibetan Exiles versus the People's Republic of China*, Oxford University Press, London, 2004, pp. 168–169.
2. 'Songsten Gampo,' *Wikipedia*, https://tinyurl.com/yxywt3br. Accessed on 19 July 2020.
3. Ibid.
4. Ibid.

5. Hiroyuki, Suzuki, 'Tibetan Dialects Spoken in Shar kog and Khod po khog,' *East and West*, Vol. 54, No. 1, 2009, pp. 273–283.
6. Leifer, Walter, *Himalaya—Mountain of Destiny: A Study in Geopolitics*, Oxford Book Company, Calcutta, 1962, p. 29.
7. Ibid.
8. Ibid.
9. Bell, Charles, *Tibet Past and Present*, Motilal Banarsidass, Calcutta, 1992, pp. 271–273.
10. Leifer, *Himalaya*, p. 32.
11. Ibid., 33.
12. Ibid.
13. Ibid., 34.
14. Ibid.
15. Ibid., 36.
16. Ibid.
17. Knaus, John Kenneth, *Orphans of the Cold War: America and the Tibetan Struggle for Survival*, Public Affairs, New Delhi, 1999, p. 4. Knaus was a CIA case officer who helped train and direct Tibetan guerrillas against the Chinesein the late 1950s and in the 1960s. Afterwards, he became an Associate at Harvard University's Fairbank Center for East Asian Research.
18. Dutt, Subimal, *With Nehru in Foreign Office*, Minerva Associates Publication, Calcutta:, 1977, p. 77.
19. Ibid.
20. Ibid.
21. Alexandrowicz-Alexander, C.H., 'The Legal Position of Tibet,' *The American Journal of International Law*, Vol. 48, No. 2, 1954, pp. 265–74.
22. Dutt, *With Nehru in Foreign Office*, p. 74.
23. Nehru, Jawaharlal, *The Discovery of India*, Penguin Books, Gurgaon, 2010, p. 219.
24. Mehta, Jagat S., *Tryst Betrayed: Reflections on Diplomacy and Development*, Penguin, New Delhi, 2010, p. 109.
25. Ibid.
26. Knaus, *Orphans of the Cold War*, p. 5.
27. Ibid., 12.
28. Ibid.
29. Nehru, Jawaharlal, 'Inter-Asian Relations,' *India Quarterly*, Vol. 4, October-December, 1946, pp. 323–327, https://tinyurl.com/bd5kzxvk.
30. Knaus, *Orphans of the Cold War*, p. 23.
31. Ibid.
32. Ibid., 26.
33. Ibid., 49.
34. Ibid., 51.
35. Ibid., 63.
36. Ibid., 66.

37. Ibid., 65.
38. Ibid., 71–72.
39. Ibid., 72.
40. Ibid.
41. Dutt, *With Nehru in Foreign Office*, p. 76.
42. Ibid., 75.
43. Knaus, *Orphans of the Cold War*, p. 73.
44. Ibid., 74.
45. Ibid., 75.
46. Dutt, *With Nehru in Foreign Office*, p. 83.
47. Ibid.
48. Ibid.
49. Bstan-'dzin-rgya-mtsho, *Freedom in Exile*. Abacus, London, 1998, p. 113.
50. Dutt, *With Nehru in Foreign Office*, p. 90.
51. Ibid.
52. Knaus, *Orphans of the Cold War*, pp. 59–60.
53. Ibid., 172.
54. Ibid., 172–173.
55. Bstan-'dzin-rgya-mtsho, *Freedom in Exile*, p. 161.
56. Ibid., 139.
57. Dutt, *With Nehru in Foreign Office*, p. 154.
58. Ibid.
59. Ibid., 156.
60. Ibid., 157.
61. Ibid.
62. Ibid.
63. Ibid.
64. Ibid., 150.
65. Riedel, Bruce, *JFK's Forgotten Crisis: Tibet, the CIA, and the Sino-Indian War*, HarperCollins Publishers India, Noida, 2016, p. 32.
66. Ibid., 33.

Chapter 13: The Chinese Episode

1. Verma, Shiv Kunal, *The War That Wasn't: The Definitive Account of the Clash between India and China*, Aleph Book Company, New Delhi, 2016, p. 86.
2. Ibid.
3. Ibid., 87.
4. Riedel, Bruce, *JFK's Forgotten Crisis: Tibet, the CIA, and the Sino-Indian War*, HarperCollins Publishers India, Noida, 2016, p. 58.
5. Verma, *The War That Wasn't*, p. 25.
6. Palit, D.K., *War in High Himalayas: The Indian Army in Crisis, 1962*, Lancer International, New Delhi, 1991, p. 74.

7. Ibid., 100.
8. Ibid.
9. The Himmatsingji Committee was formed under Major General Himmatsingji, deputy minister of defence, as chairman, and included Lt. Gen. Kulwant Singh, K. Zakaria, head of the Historical Division of the Ministry of External Affairs, S.N. Haksar, joint secretary, Ministry of External Affairs, Group Captain M.S. Chaturvedi from the Indian Air Force, and Waryam Singh, deputy director of the Intelligence Bureau. This Committee, officially known as the North and North East Border Defence Committee, sent its report in two parts, which are still classified. Among other things, the Committee recommended the reorganization of the administrative divisions of NEFA, the opening of new districts and an increase in the staff manning the new posts, the extension of these administrative centres further towards the McMahon Line and the formation of a Frontier Service cadre for service in the frontier areas.
10. Palit, *War in High Himalayas*, p. 100.
11. Ibid., 90.
12. Ibid., 91.
13. Verma, *The War That Wasn't*, pp. 21–22.
14. Ibid., 26.
15. Ibid.
16. Ibid.
17. Ibid., 27.
18. Ibid., 34.
19. Ibid.
20. Palit, *War in High Himalayas*, p. 91.
21. Ibid., p. 86.
22. Ibid., pp. 91–92.
23. Ibid., p. 92.
24. Ibid.
25. Ibid.
26. Ibid.
27. Ibid., p. 106.
28. Ibid., p. 162.
29. Ibid., pp. 177–178.
30. Ibid., p. p. 181.
31. Dalvi, J.P., *Himalayan Blunder: The Curtain-raiser to the Sino-Indian War of 1962*, Natraj Publishers, Dehradun, 2010, p. 134.
32. Ibid., p. 138.
33. Ibid.
34. Ibid., p. 166.
35. Palit, *War in High Himalayas*, p. 192.
36. Ibid., 196.
37. Ibid., 204. DMO Palit maintained a close liaison with the IB chief, B.N.

Mullik and came to know this from him.
38. Dalvi, *Himalayan Blunder*, pp. 184–185
39. Palit, *War in High Himalayas*, pp. 301–302
40. Ibid., 342.

Chapter 14: The Making of a Dynast

1. Dutt, Subimal, *With Nehru in Foreign Office*, Minerva Associates Publication, Calcutta, 1977, p. 41
2. Ibid., 37.
3. Ibid.
4. Pandit, Vijaya Lakshmi, *The Scope of Happiness: A Personal Memoir*, Speaking Tiger Publishing, New Delhi, 2018, p. 286.
5. Ibid., 374.
6. Mathai, M.O., *Reminiscences of the Nehru Age*, Vikas Publishing House, Delhi, 2015, p. 142.
7. Pandit, *Scope of Happiness*, p. 69.
8. Frank, Katherine, *Indira: The Life of Indira Nehru Gandhi*, HarperCollins Publishers, London, 2001, pp. 122–124.
9. Padmaja's elder sister, Leelamani, told this to Durga Das more than once. See Das, Durga, *India: from Curzon to Nehru and After*, Collins, London, 1969, p. 384.
10. Pandit, *Scope of Happiness*, p. 69.
11. Sahgal, Nayantara, *Jawaharlal Nehru: Civilizing A Savage World*, Penguin, New Delhi, 2010, p. 16.
12. Andrew, Christopher, and Vasili Mitrokhin, *The World Was Going Our Way: The KGB and the Battle for the Third World*, Basic Books, New York, 2005, p. 316.
13. Ibid.
14. Ibid.
15. Rajgopal, P.V., ed., *I was Nehru's shadow: From the Diaries of K.F. Rustamji*, Wisdom Tree, New Delhi, 2014, p. 46.
16. Pandit, *Scope of Happiness*, p. 134.
17. Mathai, *Reminiscences of the Nehru Age*, p. 2.
18. Ibid., 12–13. Mathai claimed to have persuaded Hutheesing to decline the offer to save Nehru from the allegation of nepotism.
19. 'Rise of Voices,' *Time*, 6 July 1959.
20. Ali, Aruna Asaf, *Private Face of a Public Person: A Study of Jawaharlal Nehru*, Radiant Publishers, New Delhi, 1989, p. 18.
21. Chattopadhyay, Tapan, *The INA's Secret Service in Southeast Asia: Its Background, Infrastructure, Resources and Activities During World War II*, Readers Service, Kolkata, 2011, pp. 107–108. Also, Sareen, T.R., *Japan and the Indian National Army*, Mounto Publishing House, New Delhi, 1996, p. 126.

22. Ibid., 78–79.
23. Lohia, Ram Manohar, *Guilty Men of India's Partition*, Rupa Publishers, New Delhi, 2008, p. 33.
24. Ibid.
25. Rajgopal, *I was Nehru's Shadow*, p. 59.
26. Lohia, *Guilty Men of India's Partition*, p. 19.
27. Ali, *Private Face of a Public Person*, p. 71.
28. Ibid.
29. Price, Ruth, *The Lives of Agnes Smedley*, Oxford University Press, Oxford, 2005, p. 406.
30. Ibid., 414.
31. Ibid.
32. Rajgopal, *I was Nehru's Shadow*, p. 39.
33. Singh, K. Natwar, *One Life is Not Enough*, Rupa Publications, New Delhi, 2014, p. 71.
34. Mehta, *The Tryst Betrayed*, p. 50.
35. Ibid., 54–55.
36. Ibid., 55.
37. Dutt, *With Nehru in the Foreign Office*, p. 29.
38. Ibid., 30.
39. Andrew and Mitrokhin, *The World Was Going Our Way*, p. 314.
40. Ibid., 315.
41. Moraes, Frank, *Witness to an Era*, Vikas Publishing House, New Delhi, 1973, p. 180.
42. Frank, *Indira*, p. 205. Mathai has also mentioned this in his *Reminiscences of the Nehru Age*.
43. Ibid.
44. Ibid., 206.
45. Ibid., 242.
46. Balachandran, Vappala, *A Life in Shadow: The Secret Story of ACN Nambiar*, Roli Books, New Delhi, 2016. p. 252.
47. Mathai, *Reminiscences of the Nehru Age*, pp. 16–17.
48. Balachandran, *Life in Shadow*, p. 249.
49. Ali, *Private Face of a Public Person*, pp. 42–43.
50. Ibid., 43.
51. Gopal, *Selected Works of Jawaharlal Nehru, Vol. I*, Oxford University Press, New Delhi, 2015. p. 267.
52. Ali, *Private Face of a Public Person*, pp. 50–51.
53. Das, Durga, *India: From Curzon to Nehru and After*, Collins, London, 1969, p. 369.
54. Ibid., 369–370.
55. Gandhi, Sonia, ed., *Two Alone, Two Together: Letters between Indira Gandhi and Jawaharlal Nehru, 1940–1964*, Hodder, London, 1992, p. 614.
56. Indira Gandhi to Padmaja Naidu, Nehru Museum Library, Delhi.

57. Nehru, Jawaharlal, *A Bunch of Old Letters*, Asia Publishing House, New Delhi, 1960, p. 1.
58. Das, *India*, p. 370.
59. Ibid., 370–371.
60. Frank, *Indira*, p. 249.
61. Biju Patnaik travelled with the IB chief, B.N. Mullick, to Pahalgam to discuss the plan with Nehru. Mullick disagreed with the plan. See Mullick, *My Years with Nehru*, 107–108.
62. Das, *India*, p. 372.
63. Desai, Morarji, *The Story of My Life, Volume II,* Macmillan India, Delhi, 1974, p. 204.

EPILOGUE

1. Seton, Marie, *Panditji: A Portrait of Jawaharlal Nehru*, Rupa Publications, Delhi, 1967, p. 404.
2. Malhotra, Inder, *Indira Gandhi*, Hodder, London, 1989, p. 78.
3. Ibid.
4. Frank, Katherine, *Indira: The Life of Indira Nehru Gandhi*, HarperCollins, London, 2001, p. 278.
5. Ibid., 279.
6. Malhotra, *Indira Gandhi*, p. 83.
7. Ibid., 84.
8. Sahgal, Nayantara, *Indira Gandhi: Her Road to* Power, Frederick Ungar, New York, 1982, p. 5.

INDEX

Abdullah, Begum, 174, 205
Abdullah, Sheikh, 176–178, 180, 182, 183, 190, 191, 196–206
Abyssinian memorandum, 102, 103
Ali, Aruna Asaf, 240
All Bengal Students Conference, 71
All India Home Rule League, 29
All India Muslim League, 38
All-India Progressive Writers Association (AIPWA), 105
All India Trade Union Congress (AITUC), 72–74
All India Youth Congress, 74
All Parties Conference, 65, 66, 71, 75, 95, 124, 125
Allahabad Seva Samiti, 31
Ambedkar, B.R., 216
Amery, Leopold, 140
Andrews, C.F., 37, 40, 73, 102
Aney, M.S., 124
Ansari, Dr Mukhtar Ahmed, 52, 98
Article 370 in J&K, introduction of, 198, 200
Attlee, Clement, 66, 136, 144, 155
Auchinleck, Field Marshal Sir Claude, 163
Ayyangar, N.G., 190, 191, 198
Azad, Maulana Abul Kalam,, 53

Bahuguna, H.N., 12
Bakula, Kushok, 199
Baldwin, Roger, 87, 90
Baptista, Joseph 'Kaka', 72
Bardoli Satyagraha, 69

Bedi, P.L., 197
Belgaum Pact, 58, 59
Bengal Pact, 56
Berlin India Committee (BIC), 80
Besant, Annie, 18, 29, 31, 38, 40, 45, 64, 120
Birkenhead challenge, 65
Birla, G.D., 113–115, 141, 220
Bose, Dr Sunil Chandra, 111
Bose, Sarat Chandra, 75, 105, 165
Bose, Subhas Chandra, x, 47, 60, 63, 64, 66–70, 74–77, 82, 89, 94, 95, 97–99, 104, 107, 108, 110, 111, 113, 118, 131, 134, 136, 138, 143, 146, 148, 153, 239
BPCC, purges in, 118
Bradley, Ben, 99, 102
Brussels Congress, 83–86, 88, 212
Bucher, Lt Gen. Roy, 177, 188, 189, 193–196
Buddhist Association of Ladakh, 199
Bulganin, Nikolai, 107

Cabinet Mission plan, 146
Calcutta Disturbances Commission of Enquiry, 160
Cariappa, Gen. K.M., 188, 194–196
Cawthorn, Maj. Gen. W.J., 194
Chagla, M.C., 125
Champaran satyagraha, 41
Chandra, Baba Ram, 33–35
Chattopadhyay, Sarat Chandra, 75, 105

Chattopadhyaya, Virendranath, aka
  Chatto, x, 62, 80
Chauri Chaura incident, 121
Chiang Kai-shek, General, 87, 146,
  147, 152, 213, 214
Chiang Kai-shek, Madame, 87, 240
China Aid Committee, 110
Chittagong revolutionaries, 75
Chou Enlai, 245
Churchill, Sir Winston, 135, 139
Comintern, 52, 62, 67, 72, 75,
  81–83, 85, 87, 88, 90, 93, 99, 106
Commonwealth Relations Office
  (CRO), 187, 190, 194, 195
Communist Party of Great Britain
  (CPGB), 63, 74, 86, 99
Communist Party of India (CPI), 63,
  105, 107, 163
Congress Democratic Party, 77, 96
Congress Socialist Party, 105, 106,
  116
Cow Protection Society (1882), 38
Cripps Mission, 142, 146, 148
Cripps, Sir Strafford, 101, 145, 155
Cunningham, Sir George, 137, 186
Curzon, Lord, 38, 211

Dalai Lama, 209–214, 217–222
Das, Chittaranjan, ix, 30–32, 34,
  44–46, 49–52, 54, 55, 58, 59, 70,
  119, 120, 122
Dasgupta, Promode, 107
Delhi Accord (1952), 200
Delhi Manifesto, 89, 94, 95
Delhi Proposals (1927), 123, 125
Democratic National Conference,
  204
Desai, Morarji, 246, 248–251
Dutt, Clemens Palme, 74
Dutt, Rajani Palme, 99

Einstein, Albert, 86, 88
Emery, Leopold, 144

Fazl-i-Husain, 126
Fleming, Col. Peter, 194
Forward Policy, 225, 226, 232
Fourteen Points, 126, 127

Gandhi, Feroze, 248
Gandhi, Indira, 12, 241, 249, 253
Gandhi-Irwin Pact, 97, 98
Gandhi, M.K., ix, 1, 30, 37, 46, 60
Gandhi Wing, 70
Gaya Congress (1922), 50
Ghosh, Prafulla Chandra, 160
Gibarti, Louis, 85, 88
Gilani, Pir Maqbool, 202, 205, 206
Gilgit Agency, 174, 196, 199
Giri, V.V., 73
Gokhale, Gopal Krishna, 29, 37, 39,
  42, 58
Gorky, Maxim, 86
Goswami, Tulsi Charan, 53
Government of India Act (1919),
  56, 66
Gracey, Gen. Douglas, 181
Grafftey-Smith, Sir Lawrence, 187,
  189, 195, 196
Gupta, Shiv Prasad, 91

Hardinge, Lord, 39
Haripura Congress (1938), 108, 110
Henderson, Loy W., 214
Himmatsingji Committee, 226
Hindu Mahasabha, 124, 125, 129,
  165, 200
Huq, Fazlul, 112–114, 130, 139
Hutheesing, Gunottam, 238
Hutheesing, Krishna, 238

Independence for India League (IIL),
  67, 89, 94, 239
Independent, party newspaper, 43
Indian Majlis, 25
Indian National Army (INA), 153,
  155, 179, 233, 239
Indian Nationalist Party, 80

Instrument of Accession, 170, 175, 181, 184, 187, 198
Inter-Services Agency (ISI), 194, 197, 198
Iqbal, Sir Muhammad, 128, 129
Irwin, Viceroy, 77, 95, 97, 127
Ismay Plan (Plan Balkan), 165, 167
Iyengar, Srinivasa, 60, 76, 96

Jallianwala Bagh incident, 44
Jayakar, M.R., 53, 54, 62, 120, 122, 125
Jinnah, Muhammad Ali, x, 30, 46, 95, 119
Jinnah, Rattanbai (Ruttie) Petit, 120
Jinnah's Fourteen Points, 126
Johnson, Col. Louis, 147, 149
Johnston, J.W., 73
Joshi, N.M., 73

Kak, Ram Chandra, 173, 174, 176
Kalelkar, D.B. (Kaka), 44
Kamaraj Plan, 206, 248, 249
Kashmir Communist Party, 204
Kashmir Political Conference, 198
Kaur, Rajkumari Amrit, 108
KGB, interest of, 238, 242
Khaliquzzaman, Chaudhry, 45, 129, 130, 135
Khan, Abdul Ghaffar, 168, 187
Khan, Hakim Ajmal, 49, 50
Khan, Liaquat Ali, 128, 130, 160, 161, 166, 173, 178, 185, 186, 189, 194, 195
Khan, Sir Sikandar Hayat, 130
Khan, Sir Syed Ahmad, 38
Kheda movement, 68
Kher, B.G., 130
Khilafat movement, 34, 120
Khrushchev, Nikita, 107
Kidwai, Rafi Ahmed, 202, 203
Kisan Congress, 35
Kripalani, J.B., 44, 64, 74, 100, 105, 116, 169, 248

Krishak Praja Party (KPP), 112, 113

Lall, Diwan Chaman, 72
Lansbury, George, 86, 88
League Against Imperialism (LAI), 62, 67, 72–74, 83–91, 94, 101, 102
Linlithgow, Viceroy, 109, 133
Lockhart, Gen. Rob, 175–182
Lohia, Ram Manohar, 5, 104, 156, 165, 168, 239, 248
Longju incident, 227
Lucknow Congress (1916), 37, 39

Madhok, Balraj, 200
Mahajan, Mehr Chand, 177, 180, 196, 197
Malaviya, Madan Mohan, 29, 38, 39, 45, 49, 53, 62, 120, 129
Mathai, M.O., 242, 243, 245
Mazumdar, Ambica Charan, 37
Medical Mission to China, 110, 111
Menon, V.K. Krishna, 241
Menon, V.P., 162, 167, 168, 170, 175, 183, 184
Messervy, Gen. Frank, 179
Misra, Gauri Shankar, 34, 35, 36
Mohammad, Bakshi Ghulam, 198, 201–206
Mookerjee, Syama Prasad, 200, 201
Mountbatten, Lord Louis, 161
Muddiman Committee, 122
Munzenberg, Wilhelm 'Willi', 83, 85, 88, 89, 90
Mullik, B.N., 197, 198, 201, 203, 206, 225, 226, 243
Munshi Premchand, 105
Muslim Conference, 126, 197
Muslim League National Guard, 179

Nagpur Congress (1920), 35, 120
Naidu, Padmaja, 237, 243
Naidu, Sarojini, 41, 61, 62, 85, 104, 105, 123, 130, 247
Nambiar, A.C.N., 63, 84, 85, 86, 91,

100, 102, 108, 109, 241, 243
Nanda, Gulzarilal, 251, 252
Narayan, Jayaprakash, 104, 116, 168, 206
National Conference, 178, 198, 200, 202, 203, 204
Nationalist Party, 80, 122
Nazi officials, meeting with, 109
Nehru, Kamala, 111
Nehru, Motilal, ix, 1–18, 20–24, 26–28, 30–32, 34, 35, 37, 38, 41–46, 48, 49, 50, 51, 53–56, 58–62, 66, 68, 70, 71, 74–78, 80, 91, 95, 120, 122–125, 127
Nehru Report, 67, 68, 70, 124–126, 128
Nehru, Swarup Rani, 8, 10, 13, 32, 42, 43
Noel-Baker, Philip, 187, 190–192, 194, 195
North-East Frontier Agency (NEFA), 224–227, 229, 231, 232, 233
Nye, Sir Archibald, 194

OMS, Soviet intelligence, 83, 85, 109
Operation Gulmarg, 176, 178, 179, 187

Pandit, Vijaya Lakshmi, 4, 30, 43, 86, 163, 237, 243, 252
Pant, Govind Ballabh, 115, 116, 169, 205, 247
Paranjpye, Dr R.P., 123
Patel, Vallabhbhai, x, xi, 44, 48, 50, 52, 60, 68, 69, 74, 75, 77, 78, 97, 98, 100, 104, 108, 142, 153, 155, 160–164, 166, 168–171, 173, 175–178, 180, 182–185, 193, 194, 197
Patnaik, Biju, 248, 249, 250
Prasad, Dr Rajendra, 44, 48, 50, 53, 98, 100, 104, 108, 117, 118, 129, 131, 135
Pratapgarh peasant movement, x

Quit India Movement, 151
Quit Kashmir movement, 177
Qureshi, Shuaib, 64

Rai, Lala Lajpat, 45, 62, 72, 120
Rai, Lt Col. Ranjit, 184, 255
Rajagopalachari, C., 44, 46, 48, 50, 53, 60, 74, 77, 104, 148, 151, 239
Ramgarh, 117, 138
Reading, Viceroy, 49
Responsive Cooperation Party, 122
Rigzin, Chhewang, 199
Round Table Conference, 49, 56, 95–97, 128
Rowlatt Bill, 43
Roy, Dr Bidhan Chandra, 107, 111
Roy, Evelyn Trent, 83
Roy, M.N., 51, 52, 63, 81, 88, 91, 92

Saha, Dr Meghnad, 110
Saha, Gopinath, hanging of, 51
Saklatvala, Shapurji, 91, 102
Santiniketan ashram, 40, 243
Sapru, Tej Bahadur, 17, 29, 38, 44, 66, 94, 123–125
Saraswati, Swami Sahajanand, 50, 105
Sarkar, Nalini Ranjan, 113, 114
Sastri, Srinivasa, 42, 44
Satyagraha Sabha, 43
Scheduled caste system, origin of, 112
Sen, Brig. (later Lt Gen.) L.P., 188
Sengupta, J.M., 74
Servants of India Society, 29, 42, 58
Shafi, Muhammad, 124
Shastri, Lal Bahadur, 12, 245, 247–252
Simon Commission, 65, 66, 71, 95, 128
Singh, Karan, 200, 202, 203
Singh, Maharaja Hari, x, 173, 178, 182, 183
Sitaramayya, Pattabhi, 53, 108, 115

Skeen Committee, 58
Smedley, Agnes, 80, 83, 84, 85, 92, 110, 111, 240
Songtsen Gampo, 207, 208
Spratt, Philip, 63
Suhrawardy, Huseyn Shahid, 84, 114, 130, 159, 160, 165
Sun Yat-sen, Madame, 85, 86
Swaraj Bhavan, 254

Tagore, Rabindranath, 18, 105, 243
Tegart, Charles Augustus, 25
Thimayya, Gen. K.S., 225, 227–231, 241
Thondup, Gyalo, 213, 214, 218
Thorat Plan, 229, 230
Tibet, Anglo-Chinese contract regarding, 211
Tibet, beginning of Buddhism, 211
Tibet, issue of postage stamp (1912), 212

Tibet, treaty with China (822), 208
Tibetan resistance, CIA help to, 220
Tilak, Bal Gangadhar, ix, 29, 30, 45, 119, 120
Tolstoy, Captain Ilya, 213
Tolstoy, Leo, 47
Treaty of Nanking (1842), 210
Tripuri Congress (1939), 108
two-nation theory, 38

Unionist Party, 164

Wavell's Breakdown Plan, 161
Wavell, Viceroy, 150, 154, 158, 160–162, 165
Willingdon, Viceroy, 97, 98, 120
Workers and Peasants Party, 90

Yagnik, Indulal, 69, 105

Zetland, Marquess of, 109

www.ingramcontent.com/pod-product-compliance
Lightning Source LLC
Chambersburg PA
CBHW031422150426
43191CB00006B/358